DATE DUE

The Failure of the Prussian Reform Movement, 1807-1819

Publication of this book has been made possible by a grant from the Hull Memorial Publication Fund of Cornell University.

The Failure of the Prussian Reform Movement, 1807-1819

WALTER M. SIMON

ichael

Department of History, Cornell University

Cornell University Press ITHACA, NEW YORK

PRINTED IN THE UNITED STATES OF AMERICA BY THE

VAIL-BALLOU PRESS, INC., BINGHAMTON, NEW YORK

To *H. C. F. B.*

Preface

IF THIS were a German book as well as a book about Germany, it would probably be equipped with a forbidding subtitle explaining away the title. Since it is not, this function is relegated to the Preface. I do not, of course, mean to imply that the reform movement of the years 1807–1819 in Prussia was a total failure. It accomplished many important things, some of which are mentioned in these pages. But it was, I believe, on balance a failure, because it fell far short—disastrously short, it may be— of the objectives that its moving spirits had set themselves and because its successes were on the whole minor compared to its frustrations.

While I have tried to make clear, as the narrative proceeds, where success ends and failure begins, I have concentrated on the negative side of the ledger, because it is there that work needs to be done. Professor Guy Stanton Ford noted over thirty years ago in his *Stein and the Era of Reform in Prussia* that the opposition to the reforms had not been explored, and this deficiency has not been made good in the meantime, either in Germany or elsewhere,[1] while the achievements of the reform movement and the careers of many of its leading spirits have had more than their due share of attention by historians. The reader who wishes a balanced picture of the reform movement will therefore not

[1] The short final chapter in Reinhold Aris, *History of Political Thought in Germany, 1789–1815* (London, 1936), is hardly adequate even as an introduction.

find it here; it is my hope, rather, that the proper perspective will be attained when this account is taken in conjunction with existing histories of the reform movement. Reasons of space alone would have prohibited any attempt to strike the balance within this volume.

At least a bow must, however, be made here in the direction of one phase of the reform movement which is virtually ignored in the text, perhaps the sole major phase in which the goals aimed at were substantially achieved, namely, the educational reforms under the aegis of Humboldt in 1809–1810. These could have been of tremendous significance if their effects had been combined with those of the other elements in the comprehensive program of reform; even without such cross-fertilization, the importance of the advances in schools and universities was far from negligible. But these and other signs of progress—for instance, the religious unification of 1817 or the Customs Law of 1818—can be but barely mentioned and must be taken for granted if space is to be found for adequate discussion of the three principal facets of the reform movement: the agrarian, the constitutional, and the military.

Some guidance to the arrangement of the book may be helpful. The method employed is predominantly chronological. Part One is introductory: the first brief chapter considers the failure of the reform movement in the perspective of German history in the nineteenth century; the following chapter provides the setting for the main body of the book by describing the agrarian, social, and constitutional scene in Prussia before the reforms—feudalism on the land, royal absolutism in government—and the measures taken by Baron Stein, the first and greatest of the reformers, to change that scene during his ministry of 1807–1808. Part Two is concerned with the fate of agrarian and constitutional reform under the chancellorship of Baron Hardenberg between 1810 and 1818, with a chapter covering the intervening years 1808–1810. In Part Three the chronological scheme is abandoned in favor of the topical method for a consecutive account of the varying fortunes of the military reformers beginning with Stein's ministry and continuing to the end of 1818. The topical approach seemed possible and desirable here because of a unique continuity in personnel. Finally, the first chapter in Part Four relates the ultimate downfall of the reform movement in the year 1819, with special attention to constitutional problems. The conclusion summarizes and further analyzes the causes of the failure.

I have tried hard to maintain the correct historical attitude of impartiality and to do justice to the sincerity and intelligence of all parties concerned; but no useful purpose would be served if I attempted to disguise the fact that my reaction to the failure of reform is one of regret, though not always for the same reasons that move some of the German historians of the period. I hope that I have avoided the worst pitfalls of what Professor Butterfield would call "Whig history."

Much of the material of the book was first used in a doctoral dissertation, written under the direction of Professor Hajo Holborn at Yale University, under the title "The Survival of Authoritarian Prussia in the Age of Reform, 1807–1819." To Professor Holborn I wish to express my deep appreciation for the ways, too numerous to mention, in which he has directly and indirectly helped to make this volume possible. Needless to say, I am alone responsible for any errors. Without the support, moral and otherwise, of my wife, I should not have persevered in this undertaking.

W. M. S.

Ithaca, New York
December 1954

Contents

PART ONE

Introductory

CHAPTER I

The Survival of German Authoritarianism in the Nineteenth Century

THE centenary of the revolutions of 1848 was greeted with more headshaking than celebrations. In all countries of Europe, and in America as well, the occasion provoked a spate of explanations for the failure of those movements. Most costly, perhaps, was the failure of 1848 in Germany; so, at least, might think many a German living in the aftermath of catastrophe a hundred years later. In 1848 Frankfurt had been the focus of hope for a constitutional and united Germany; in 1948 Frankfurt was the seat of a foreign military government in one section of a Germany again divided.

The late dean of German historians, Friedrich Meinecke, born little more than a decade after the Year of Revolutions, was deeply conscious in 1948 of the moral and material decline that he had witnessed. The key to it, in his opinion, was Germany's refusal in the nineteenth century to abandon the *Obrigkeitsstaat* ("authoritarian state") for a *Gemeinschaftsstaat* ("commonwealth"). Meinecke discerned three "critical alternatives in the history of Germany" when Germany had the opportunity of becoming a commonwealth, characterized by "an active and effective participation of all strata of society in the life of the state"; instead, it chose each time to remain faithful to the twin principles of authoritarianism and militarism. Eighteen forty-

3

eight itself was one of these turning points; the others came in 1819, when the Prussian reform movement died, and in 1866, when one of the aims of 1848, liberalism, was sacrificed to another, nationalism.[1]

It was in terms similar to Meinecke's that the Prussian reform movement of the early nineteenth century was itself conceived. Meinecke's definition of a "commonwealth" admirably describes the aspirations of Baron Stein, the principal progenitor of the movement. His measures were expressly designed to replace the narrow-minded, bureaucratic, indolent *ancien régime* with a system in which an educated populace participated in the government of its own affairs. This was the foundation of his entire reform program. It demanded mobilization not only of the material, but even more of the moral, resources of the nation. It demanded fostering of a spirit of civic co-operation and responsibility. "If the nation is to be ennobled," Stein wrote in 1807, at the beginning of the reform period, "the oppressed sections of the population must be endowed with freedom, independence, and property." [2]

Had this motto prevailed, it is not unduly optimistic to believe that Prussia and Germany might well have taken a different course in 1848. Indeed, in view of the crucial importance of Prussia's internal structure both in 1848 and in 1866, there is good ground for asserting that of Meinecke's three crises, the one culminating in 1819, the subject of the present investigation, was the most decisive. In 1819 Prussia, reverting to the political, social, and military forms of the *ancien régime,* turned her back on the political heritage of western Europe: on the Enlighten-

[1] Friedrich Meinecke, *1848: Eine Säkularbetrachtung* (Berlin, 1948), especially pp. 8–9, 27–29. I have made use of the translation printed under the title "The Year 1848 in German History: Reflections on a Centenary" in the *Review of Politics,* X (1948), 475–492. Meinecke had arrived at a somewhat similar formulation much earlier; cf. his *Leben des Generalfeldmarschalls Hermann von Boyen* (Stuttgart, 1896–99), II, 389–392.

[2] The best single source for Stein's reform ideas is his "Nassauer Denkschrift," written during the spring of 1807; Freiherr vom Stein, *Briefwechsel, Denkschriften und Aufzeichnungen* (ed. Erich Botzenhart; Berlin, n.d.), II, 210–231 (hereafter Botzenhart, ed., *Stein*); see also below, pp. 29–30. The translation is the author's (as throughout unless otherwise indicated).

ment, on English constitutionalism, and on the French Revolution. In this year was confirmed the political cleavage between Germany and the West which was to prove disastrous not only for Germany but for all of Europe.

The death of the reform movement, with the greatest part of its promise unfulfilled, was proclaimed by the dismissal, in the last days of 1819, of Wilhelm von Humboldt and Hermann von Boyen, the last two of Stein's followers still in office. But though this event offers a convenient symbol, in reality the extinction of the reform movement was neither adventitious nor sudden. From the very beginning Stein and his colleagues had been plagued by obstacles of various kinds which had foiled some of their plans entirely and left others only partially executed. The purpose of the following chapters is to analyze these obstacles, to identify their origins, and to explain why the reform movement lacked the strength to overcome them; or, in other words, to discover why Prussia clung to a political and social system which made it certain that when Germany was finally unified, German cultural values were submerged by unreconstructed Prussian militarism and authoritarianism.[3]

[3] Cf. Meinecke, *1848,* p. 28.

CHAPTER II

The Prussian *Ancien Régime*

and the Reforms of Stein

THE Prussian reform movement was made possible by the Prussian collapse in the wars against Napoleon. The catastrophe of Jena and Auerstädt in 1806 dispelled overnight the inhibitions that had confined earlier attempts at reform to sporadic and local success. On those battlefields lay displayed, for all to see, the inherent weaknesses and anachronisms that riddled the Prussian state. Precisely because the two great eighteenth-century kings had made the army the foundation and the focal point of the state, Jena and Auerstädt meant the collapse not only of the army itself, but of the whole civil superstructure of society. Equally, it was not merely the army but the entire nation that had to be rebuilt.

Therefore Baron Stein, whose ultimate goal was the liberation of Prussia (and through Prussia of Germany) from the French conqueror, knew that this object could never be attained by introducing military reforms alone. These, indeed, were vital, and Stein appointed General Scharnhorst to direct them; [1] but he himself devoted his energies to reconstructing the civil organization of the state. His formula for the salvation of Prussia penetrated into all departments of public life: it was no less than the restoration and mobilization of the nation's resources.

[1] As noted in the Preface, military reforms beginning in Stein's ministry are treated in Part III as a topical unit separate from the general chronological development.

Stein conceived reform as a coherent whole. He devoted his attention to such diverse areas as education, internal and external trade, and religious toleration. But the most essential changes which Stein sought to introduce lay in the spheres of agrarian, constitutional, and military affairs, and it is with these aspects of reform that the following pages are primarily concerned.

The fundamental feature of the *ancien régime* that stood in the way of "participation of all strata of society in the life of the state" was the dependent status of the great mass of the rural population; and this circumstance explains why Stein, intent upon throwing off the yoke of Napoleon, had to turn first to a reform of the Prussian agrarian system. The dependence of the agricultural population was twofold: personal and economic. The peasants were *erbuntertänig,* that is to say they were legally bound to the land on which they lived and hence to its owner, and they were transferred with the land if it changed hands. Roughly speaking, they were serfs (though lawyers distinguished between *Leibeigenschaft,* which was true serfdom, and *Erbuntertänigkeit*): they were unfree men in that among other things they could not move elsewhere, could not marry without their lord's consent, and could will their tenancy, if it was inheritable at all, only to a relative approved by the lord. Furthermore, their minor children were required to perform domestic duties in the lord's household. Politically, the serfs were in practice the subjects not of the king but of their lord.

In addition to this personal and political dependence, the Prussian peasants were burdened with economic obligations. These arose not out of their personal status as serfs but rather out of the conditions under which they occupied their land. Very few farmers held their acreage in freehold, and these were not serfs; the rest possessed various kinds of leasehold, ranging from hereditary tenure of the land itself under a regular contract to a precarious right of usufruct alone, governed only by local custom. But regardless of the degree of security with which they were settled on their farms, all of these leaseholders (and, anomalously, even some of the freeholders) were obliged under the terms of their tenure, as it were in lieu of rent, to perform certain services and to pay certain tributes, usually in kind, to their lord. Like the tenures themselves, these obligations varied. Some were relatively light, while others were intolerable: some peasants were compelled to work on the lord's land for six days a week, with only Sundays and moonlight nights to cultivate their rented fields. Generally speaking, the insecure and poverty-stricken peasants seem to have far outnumbered the secure and prosperous ones.

There was, it is true, some compensation for the peasant, particularly the system of *Bauernschutz* (protection of the peasant), which prohibited the lord from practicing *Bauernlegen,* i.e., evicting his tenants and reabsorbing their acreage into his own manorial land. The lord was also required to make essential repairs on the peasant's dwelling, to sustain him and his family if the harvest failed, and to advance his taxes if he defaulted on them; but in these matters the state exercised virtually no direct supervision. In fact, short of the prohibition on *Bauernlegen,* which was enforced by the state, the lord held unlimited sway on his feudal domains. This power, of course, overlapped from the agricultural to the political sphere. All local government in rural areas was carried out by the landed nobility, extending to complete control over religion, police, and the administration of justice. Since this political power, in accordance with its feudal origins, derived from the ownership of land, members of classes other than the nobility were normally prohibited from acquiring land held by a noble. Finally, in addition to the perpetual political sovereignty which they exercised as a class over the remainder of the rural population, the nobles' special position in the state was manifested in their freedom from taxation. This also was a survival from feudal days, when their ancestors had been vassals of a feudal overlord and had done service for him by bearing arms rather than by paying taxes. The bulk of the tax burden was thus placed on those who were least able to bear it, the peasants.

The central government of Prussia was based not so much on feudalism as on decadent absolutism; but it was certainly as far removed as were the administration of agriculture and local government from Stein's ideal of enlightened popular participation in matters of public concern. Frederick the Great had perfected *Kabinettsregierung,* government from the royal study (*Kabinett*). Such a system was perhaps tolerable when it was presided over by a genius who had the will and the capacity to interest himself in all governmental problems; but even Frederick in the closing years of his reign had found the increasing complexity of public administration too much for him, and his successors on the throne had not even attempted to master it. Thus, in practice, national policy was made by the counselors and secretaries in the king's personal service, not by the ministers who were officially charged with carrying on the government. The ministers' effectiveness was further reduced by the division of responsibility into provinces rather than into departments. For example, no one minister had a coherent picture of the nation's finances, although he might be familiar with all the problems of Silesia, ranging from the taxability of monasteries to the condition of the roads. Furthermore, the ministers had no official collective responsibility, or even regular channels for exchange of information. It need hardly be mentioned that the *ancien régime* possessed no legislature and no machinery for ascertaining the desires and opinions of the people; although in some provinces of the kingdom there survived consultative Diets or Estates of the Realm (*Stände*), composed exclusively of nobles and deputies of incorporated cities, which no longer met except to pay homage to a new king.[2]

The reigning monarch throughout the reform period was Frederick II's great-nephew, Frederick William III. Sober, pious, industrious, a weak man whom his exalted position sometimes

[2] There are many excellent sources for more ample information concerning the features of the *ancien régime* mentioned here. Among the best are Friedrich Meinecke, *Das Zeitalter der deutschen Erhebung 1795–1815* (Bielefeld and Leipzig, 1906), chap. ii; and, in English, Guy Stanton Ford, *Stein and the Era of Reform in Prussia, 1807–1815* (Princeton, London, and Oxford, 1922). For the extremely involved agrarian situation, which I have greatly oversimplified, see Georg Friedrich Knapp, *Die Bauern-Befreiung und der Ursprung der Landarbeiter in den älteren Theilen Preussens* (Leipzig, 1887), I, 1–80; cf. also, in English, J. H. Clapham, *The Economic Development of France and Germany 1815–1914* (4th ed., Cambridge, 1948), pp. 33–41. See also below, pp. 90–91.

frightened into obstinacy, this king was called upon to bear
burdens too great for his capacity. With an instinctive sympathy
for the oppressed classes among his subjects, he never understood the causes or the remedies for their misery. The hesitant
and piecemeal reforms accomplished during the first years of his
reign reflected his temper much more accurately than did the
bold designs of Baron Stein. Frederick William III was acutely
uncomfortable in the presence of superior intelligence and
stronger character, especially when, like Stein, their possessors
did not trouble to conceal them. None of his contemporaries
could say much more for him than that he was well intentioned;
let two of them, hostile to him from different points of view,
speak for themselves:

He had been untouched by modern economic theories, but he had
a genuine desire to free the lower classes from their burdens, by
which he understood, however, only improvement of their material
circumstances, not their spiritual development. . . . His powers of
analysis were at times, in periods of tranquillity, nothing short of
acute, but only if it was a question of discovering the weaknesses of a
thing or of a person; in this respect he possessed a truly remarkable
facility. . . . But directly the matter to be adjudged required serious
decisions which might lead to complications, his powers of discern-
ment became confused, and on those occasions he became anxious
whenever possible to avoid responsibility.[3]

That was the judgment of Hermann von Boyen, an ardent reformer. From another direction comes the voice of the *Junker,*
Ludwig von der Marwitz:

He was by nature averse to action but enough of an absolute monarch to have grasped the principle, and to have insisted on it whenever necessary, that: "I am king, and that which I command shall be
done; nobody else has any voice in it!" For his character was composed of two elements which complemented and determined each
other: love of peace and quiet and fear of all business, balanced by
obstinacy and despotism.[4]

[3] Friedrich Nippold, ed., *Erinnerungen aus dem Leben des General-
Feldmarschalls Hermann von Boyen* (Leipzig, 1889–90), II, 18–19 (hereafter
Boyen, *Erinnerungen*).

[4] Friedrich Meusel, ed., *Friedrich August Ludwig von der Marwitz: Ein*

Where Boyen and the reformers wished to replace royal absolutism with constitutionalism, Marwitz and others in the
Prussian aristocracy wished to replace it with what had gone before, political feudalism. It was a question of some importance
whether these two opposing factions would isolate the monarchy
or whether the monarchy would seek an alliance with one in
order to defeat the other. Frederick William III personally disliked pomp; he broke precedent by inviting members of the
bourgeoisie to court functions; it might be said that he had an
essentially bourgeois mind. Yet history linked him and his throne
to the welfare of the nobility, not of the bourgeoisie. His royal
power, like that of all the other German princes of the *ancien
régime,* stemmed from the same feudal origins to which the
nobility owed their position. Inroads into the hereditary privileges of the nobility might suggest the feasibility of inroads into
the hereditary power of the monarchy. There was little conso-
lation in the fact that it was an Imperial Knight who proposed
to invade the domain of the aristocracy in the name of the
monarchy.

For there can be no question that Stein's reform program
was certain to antagonize large sections of the Prussian nobility.
Their privileges were intimately involved in the existing agrarian
and military, even the political, structure of the state. They
therefore had a vested interest in the *status quo* and were bound
to exercise their considerable influence in efforts to ensure its

---

märkischer Edelmann im Zeitalter der Befreiungskriege (Berlin, 1908–13),
I, 525–526 (hereafter Meusel, ed., *Marwitz*).

There is no satisfactory biography of the king. The closest approxima-
tions are the essays of Karl Griewank, ed., *Briefwechsel der Königin Luise
mit ihrem Gemahl Friedrich Wilhelm III. 1793–1810* (Leipzig, n.d. [1929]),
pp. 17–26, and Eugene Newton Anderson, *Nationalism and the Cultural
Crisis in Prussia, 1806–1815* (New York, 1939), pp. 257–297. For an excellent
example of the king's reluctance to make even the most routine decisions,
see Hans Schneider, "Die Entstehung des preussischen Staatsrats 1806–1817:
Ein Beitrag zur Verfassungsreform Preussens nach dem Zusammenbruch,"
Zeitschrift für die gesamte Staatswissenschaft, 102 (1942), 519–520. The documents printed in Georg Küntzel and Martin Hass, eds., *Die politischen Testamente der Hohenzollern nebst ergänzenden Aktenstücken* (2 vols., Berlin,
1911), though of some interest, do not go beyond the year 1798.

preservation. Generally speaking, the Prussian aristocracy were politically conservative. Those of them who were soldiers wished to preserve the *ancien régime* because it provided them with exclusive access to high military honors; those of them who were courtiers, because absolute monarchy, especially when the king was weak, offered much scope for palace intrigue and unofficial power; all of them, because the existing system guaranteed them cheap farm labor and power in local government.

But many of the nobles, like Marwitz, wished not merely to preserve the privileges which they enjoyed under absolute monarchy but, as indicated above, to increase them. They were not so much conservative as reactionary. They yearned for the days of pre-absolutist *Libertät,* when the electors were only the highest among the feudal hierarchy and when no obedience was due them except that prescribed by the feudal relationship. These reactionary nobles were wont to emphasize the historical uniqueness of their particular province and to minimize the power of the central government, for it had been in their individual provinces that the electors of Brandenburg, even while imposing their absolutism at the center, had guaranteed to the nobles freedom from taxation and from national interference in local government. These nobles urged reactivation of the moribund provincial Estates.[5]

This picture of the Prussian nobility as an obdurate and selfish class needs, of course, much qualification. In the first place, almost all of the great reformers were themselves of aristocratic birth, and among them Humboldt, Boyen, and Schön were native Prussians. In the second place, it was not only in defense of their own privileges but also in defense of honest political convictions and a sound political theory that many of the nobles resisted change, as we shall see hereafter. In the third

[5] These distinctions among the conservatives have often been made; see especially Bruno Gebhardt, *Wilhelm von Humboldt als Staatsmann* (Stuttgart, 1896–99), II, 362–363; Gerhard Ramlow, *Ludwig von der Marwitz und die Anfänge konservativer Politik und Staatsanschauung in Preussen* (Berlin, 1930), pp. 40–44; cf. also Sigmund Neumann, *Die Stufen des preussischen Konservatismus: Ein Beitrag zum Staats- und Gesellschaftsbild Deutschlands im 19. Jahrhundert* (Berlin, 1930), pp. 49–51, 72–73.

place, it was not only the upper class that opposed the reforms. For example, many bourgeois civil servants felt themselves no less threatened than the nobles. As its administrative arm, they had a vested interest in absolutism. Government under an absolute monarch was very agreeable: it required routine ability rather than imagination; above all, it was eminently simple. A decision, once made, need never be reviewed; there was no interference, no need for negotiation or compromise. And a civil servant enjoyed great prestige in the *ancien régime.* It was in this latter respect that the civil servants felt particularly aggrieved by Stein. Not only did he disturb their established routine with administrative changes but he also insisted, after Napoleon's armies had overrun most of Prussia, on moving the capital to territory still unoccupied in order to preserve some show of independence. Life in Memel, in the remotest corner of East Prussia, offered civil servants few of the attractions of Berlin.[6]

The bourgeoisie in general, moreover, did not hesitate to place obstacles in the way of reform when their interests were at stake. Historically it is customary to regard the bourgeoisie as the bearers, and not the opponents, of political and social progress in modern Europe. This relationship did not hold true in Prussia. There the bourgeoisie, having never been the partners of absolute monarchy, had never acquired the confidence to express opinions about public affairs; and compared to the middle class in Britain, France, or the Netherlands, the bourgeoisie in Prussia, because of the backwardness of the country's economic development, were in any event numerically negligible. There was, in fact, nothing in Prussia that could be called "public opinion," nor were there even leaders who attempted to shape one (of which more hereafter). It was his awareness of this circumstance that caused Stein to place so much emphasis on educating the people to participation in government. The reform of the schools and universities was intended to lay the

[6] For the attitude of the civil service, see Boyen, *Erinnerungen,* I, 300–301. After the government's return to Berlin, many civil servants who had remained behind and who had thereby lost seniority to those who had followed the king to Memel joined the ranks of the opposition (*ibid.,* II, 6).

basis for useful practical experience in public life; but in the absence of any thoroughgoing social reform, which alone would have made such practical experience possible, the educational innovations may merely have contributed to the notorious isolation of German intellectuals from politics in the nineteenth century.

More worrisome to Stein than even the powerful native opposition was the presence in Prussia of the French army of occupation. After the military collapse of Prussia Napoleon occupied all of the country save one province. Although the French troops were gradually withdrawn and the court and the government eventually returned to Berlin, French garrisons were maintained at strategic places. Moreover, Napoleon exacted indemnities amounting to more than the total annual income of the truncated Prussian state, with the threat of reoccupation if the payments were not made. This indemnity indirectly helped Stein's cause, since it made imperative drastic reform in the system of taxation, which in turn was to have favorable consequences for agrarian and constitutional reform. Even in the military sphere Napoleon involuntarily promoted reform: under the Treaty of Tilsit, specific limitations had been placed on the size of the Prussian army, and this restriction suggested to the reformers a way of overcoming the military caste system while at the same time improving the army's efficiency. But in the short run Napoleon handicapped Stein by forcing him to spend many months of his year in office in Berlin trying to negotiate with the French a reduction in the indemnity. In his absence the cause of reform lagged, and his enemies plotted against him. Moreover, the question of Franco-Prussian relations split the reformers and therefore weakened them. Stein himself, after the failure of the Berlin negotiations, planned a secret mobilization of Prussia for an early war of liberation, whereas many others sympathetic to reform continued to oppose such a risky policy and instead counseled patience and moderation toward the conquerors.[7]

[7] Most prominent in this group were Hardenberg and his protégé Altenstein: see Gerhard Ritter, *Stein: Eine politische Biographie* (Stuttgart and Berlin, 1931), II, 82, and cf. below, pp. 33–34.

This dilemma illustrates the way in which the injection of questions of nationalism complicated all the problems of the reform period. Most writers simply absorb the Prussian reform movement into the early nineteenth-century pattern of alliance between liberalism and nationalism. They base their view on the one hand on the reformer Stein's sponsorship of Prussian national revolt against Napoleon, and on the other hand on the fact that many of the Prussian conservatives collaborated with or even gained personal advantage from the French occupation, and therefore did their best to suppress any movement toward liberation. But such an appraisal oversimplifies the issue. In Germany there was always a latent conflict between loyalty to the territorial states, which already existed and reached far back into the past, and loyalty to the nation-state, which was still a mere dream. This conflict was further sharpened for German liberals by the espousal of liberal political doctrines by some but not by others of the territorial states. The same dilemma in reverse confronted the conservatives, who were drawn to the old historic political entities but were reluctant to support them when they went liberal. An additional complication prevailed more particularly in Prussia. Here the traditional structure of society and government was embodied more emphatically in the individual provinces that composed the kingdom than in the kingdom as a whole. All of these circumstances produced in Prussia an extremely involved set of allegiances, on the part of both conservatives and liberals, to three different objects of loyalty: nation, state, and province.

Still another factor which rendered the relationship of nationalism to the Prussian reform movement even more complex was the partial derivation of the liberal creed from the French Revolution. In the sense that the liberals (especially Hardenberg) could plausibly be accused of wishing to import French ideas into Prussia, the conservatives could pose as defenders of indigenous values. All conservative spokesmen in Prussia pilloried the principles of the French Revolution—Gentz, Adam Müller, Friedrich Ancillon; usually they echoed Burke. The liberals were portrayed as Jacobins, regicides, and revolutionaries; proposals for reform were often described in terms evocative of the Reign of Terror.[8] English ideas were likewise condemned; thus a leading conservative, Count York, on Stein:

Unfortunately for us, the man has been in England and has borrowed his political philosophy from there; and now the centuries-old institutions of Great Britain, a rich country whose foundations are sea power, trade, and industry, are to be grafted on to our poor agrarian Prussia.

He continued in similar vein about "professors who give ill-digested lectures on Adam Smith." [9]

Baron Stein was, indeed, a man of cosmopolitan background. He also brought to the innumerable problems confronting him when he took office in October 1807 high intelligence, great patriotism, and valuable political experience. As a Knight of the Empire he was himself too intimately involved in Germany's past to be a radical; but as a Rhinelander he was too much influenced by western ideas and culture and felt too little affinity for the stolid and narrow-minded Prussian aristocracy to acquiesce in the Prussian *ancien régime*. Education and travel confirmed his natural inclinations in favor of the English pattern of political evolution, although he was not untouched by French rationalism and the French Revolution. He was conscious that though changes in the Prussian state were imperative, there were also many traditions and institutions to be respected. He sought to graft western political theory and experience on to the German historical heritage. Finally, Prussia represented for him not an end, but a means. Prussia must be regenerated, he felt, not for her own sake, but so that she might become an effective leader in the regeneration, and eventually in the liberation, of Germany.

Attracted by the fame of the great Frederick, Stein had entered into Prussian service in the last years of the latter's reign and soon acquired a reputation as a conscientious and imaginative administrator. He had risen rapidly through various posts in

---

[8] See, for example, the thought processes of Friedrich Otto von Diericke, *Ein Wort über den preussischen Adel* (Berlin, 1817), pp. 49, 103.

[9] Quoted in Joh. Gust. Droysen, *Das Leben des Generals Grafen York von Wartenburg* (4th ed., Leipzig, 1863), I, 131–132; cf. *ibid.*, I, 126–128, and Franz Schnabel, *Freiherr vom Stein* (Leipzig and Berlin, 1931), pp. 80–82.

provincial government to the head of the Prussian government in Westphalia, and finally, in 1804, he had been called to Berlin as a minister. In the course of the next two years he sponsored several significant economic reforms; but he was conscious that any thoroughgoing program of reform such as, in his judgment, the country needed for its struggle with Napoleon was impossible so long as power, without corresponding responsibility, rested with the king's secretaries. Accordingly he urged the king to form a responsible and effective council of ministers. The king refused; Stein, the proud Imperial Knight, declined to accept a ministerial position in a reorganized government unless his recommendations were fully adopted; and finally, in January 1807, the king dismissed Stein for disrespect and insubordination, in an order recalling all the willfulness of royal absolutism in its prime.

In these circumstances Stein's appointment, only nine months later, as the king's first minister is a measure of the king's and of the country's desperation. Frederick William III swallowed his pride in order to harness Stein's energy to the welfare of his state. Stein, although ill, at once accepted unconditionally and arrived in Memel in the first days of October.[10]

While this event signalizes the beginning of the Prussian reform period, this is not to say that there had been no reforms before. Apart from Stein's own activities during his first ministry, several other figures took leading parts in the introduction of changes in various provinces. The greater part of these "reforms before the reform" concerned themselves with aspects of the agrarian feudal system. The most impressive record was made in the province of New East Prussia, land which had fallen to Prussia as a result of the third partition of Poland in 1795. Here the conquered Polish nobility had not the power of resistance of the Prussian nobility in other parts of the kingdom, and re-

[10] Ritter's *Stein* is the standard biography. There is a brilliant summary of a crowded life in Schnabel's *Stein* and there are excellent brief character sketches in the latter's *Deutsche Geschichte im neunzehnten Jahrhundert* (new ed., Freiburg, 1948–52), I, 319–344, and Hans Rothfels, "Stein und der deutsche Staatsgedanke," in his *Ostraum, Preussentum und Reichsgedanke* (Leipzig, 1935), pp. 33–48. For the remaining literature, see the bibliography.

form could be imposed from above without disturbance. Still, the experience gained in carrying out reform in this province proved valuable when later similar measures were projected on a larger scale. Among the changes instituted were abolition of serfdom, more effective legal protection of peasants against the lords, and amalgamation of farms too small to be economically viable into larger ones.

More influential even than these reforms in the Polish territories was the abolition of serfdom on all crown lands throughout Prussia. Here the king could act in a private capacity as landowner and not in his public capacity as sovereign. This was, of course, a step of great significance for the development of agriculture and for the very considerable number of peasants whom it emancipated. But again, it was a reform undertaken under particularly auspicious circumstances, for there could be no question of the king's right to do as he pleased on his own domains. This measure, therefore, was no indication that its principles could be extended to areas where powerful resistance could be offered by forces opposing reform. The contrast between the easy path of the innovators in New East Prussia and on the crown lands and the difficulties they encountered elsewhere when emancipation of peasants was suggested before 1807 is, in fact, remarkable.[11]

But under the impact of the collapse of the army before Napoleon and of the Treaty of Tilsit, according to which Prussia ceded to France all her lands west of the Elbe, lost all

[11] For a general view of the "reforms before the reform," see Otto Hintze, "Preussische Reformbestrebungen vor 1806," in his *Historische und politische Aufsätze* (Berlin, n.d.), III, 29–59; and Max Lehmann, *Freiherr vom Stein* (Leipzig, 1902–5), II, 57–63. For New East Prussia, see Gerhard Ritter, "Die preussischen Staatsmänner der Reformzeit und die Polenfrage," in Albert Brackmann, ed., *Deutschland und Polen: Beiträge zu ihren geschichtlichen Beziehungen* (Munich and Berlin, 1933), pp. 207–219; Kurt von Raumer, "Friedrich Leopold von Schrötter und der Aufbau Neu-Ostpreussens," *Historische Zeitschrift*, 163 (1941), 282–304. (German interest in Poland increased greatly under Hitler.) For the crown land reform, see Knapp, *Bauern-Befreiung*, I, 91–114. (Strictly speaking, serfdom had not disappeared completely on the crown lands by 1807; local anomalies remained, but they are not important for our purposes.) Cf. also Ford, *Stein and the Era of Reform in Prussia*, p. 207; Meinecke, *Zeitalter der deutschen Erhebung*, p. 34.

territories taken from Poland since 1772, and accepted the Continental System, more energetic steps were taken in the direction of reform. Even before Stein's recall, most of the groundwork had been laid for abolishing serfdom throughout the kingdom. The initiative in this matter was taken, appropriately enough, by the two men who had directed the reforms in New East Prussia, Friedrich von Schroetter and Theodor von Schön. Persuaded by their arguments, the king ordered each of them to study the question in detail and to draft a decree. In his order Frederick William wrote: "The abolition of serfdom has consistently been my goal since the beginning of my reign. I desired to attain it gradually; but the disasters that have befallen the country now justify, and indeed require, speedier action." [12]

The king, Schroetter, and Schön were all three motivated in their desire to emancipate the serfs primarily by strictly economic rather than by humanitarian, political, or social reasons.[13] Followers of Adam Smith, Schroetter and Schön held that increased economic productivity, so essential to the country in its parlous state, could best be achieved by removing all restrictions from free exploitation of the land. Serfdom was in their view to be ended mainly because it was inefficient. They saw as an obvious corollary to the abolition of serfdom the abolition of the system of *Bauernschutz,* because it also was an artificial element in what should be a free and natural economy, because it was justified only as a *quid pro quo* for serfdom, and, finally, because no unnecessary hindrance should be placed in the way of those from whom most of the increased productivity was expected—the lords of the large estates.

Although agreed in principle on the idea that *Bauernschutz*

[12] Cabinet Order of August 23, 1807, in [Magnus Friedrich von Bassewitz,] *Die Kurmark Brandenburg . . . während der Zeit vom 22. Oktober 1806 bis zu Ende des Jahres 1808* (Leipzig, 1851–52), I, 634, n.

[13] Significantly, when Schroetter first prompted the move toward emancipation, he did so because, as minister responsible for the sole province remaining under the king's rule, he was hard pressed to pay the French occupation costs, and he thought that more taxes could be collected only if the rural economy were improved (see Knapp, *Bauern-Befreiung,* II, 147; Hans Haussherr, *Erfüllung und Befreiung: Der Kampf um die Durchführung des Tilsiter Friedens 1807/1808* [Hamburg, 1935], p. 58).

was intimately linked with serfdom and that abolition of one should involve abolition of the other, Schroetter and Schön nevertheless proposed to deal with the matter differently. Schroetter, with strict logic, wanted *Bauernschutz* abolished all at once, while Schön, more temperately, proposed to abolish it by stages, thus cushioning the peasants to some extent. Schön feared that unrestricted freedom of transaction in land would result in a wholesale acquisition of peasant land by the owners of the large estates. Admitting that from the point of view of scientific agriculture very small peasant holdings were unproductive, Schön proposed that instead of being absorbed into the estates of the nobility such small holdings should be combined into larger peasant farms.

It seems probable that, left to himself, the king would have chosen Schroetter's draft in preference to Schön's,[14] but the final form of the Emancipation Edict was actually determined by Stein, within a week of his arrival in Memel. Stein preferred Schön's draft, but not for Schön's reasons. Where the latter had acted chiefly on economic motives, the new minister brought moral and political considerations to bear. He insisted that the principle of free ownership of land must be modified to restrict selfish exploitation of the poor peasants by the rich and educated nobles. Schön's idea of creating economically independent peasant holdings likewise appealed to Stein for his own reasons: he believed in a strong peasant class and in the beneficial moral effects of owning property.[15]

Although in principle Stein favored retention of *Bauernschutz* in some form, in fact he merely postponed the problem with a compromise formula sanctioning absorption of peasant holdings if permission were first obtained from the provincial government; but the provincial governments were given no criteria by which to judge cases as they were brought before

[14] See the Cabinet Order cited in n. 12 above.

[15] For the early history of the Emancipation Edict, see Ritter, *Stein,* I, 328–338; Knapp, *Bauern-Befreiung,* I, 130–136, II, 169–170; Georg Winter, "Zur Entstehungsgeschichte des Oktoberedikts und der Verordnung vom 14. Februar 1808," *Forschungen zur brandenburgischen und preussischen Geschichte,* XL (1927), 1–33.

them. In fact, the famous Emancipation Edict of October 9, 1807, left numerous other specific questions unanswered. Two things it stated clearly: all peasants were declared free men as of November 11, 1810, and all land was made available to members of all classes, breaking down the previous class barriers. But in other respects the text of the edict was ambiguous and misleading—perhaps because it had been drawn up too hastily or because too many people had had a hand in it, most probably because the authors were not completely clear in their own minds what exactly they wanted. The most disturbing ambiguities arose out of a failure to distinguish clearly between those aspects of agrarian feudalism which, owing to the abolition of serfdom as the personal status of the peasants, were to be discontinued and those aspects which, being based upon tenure of land, were to remain in force. Nobody knew whether a lord was still obliged to assist his newly liberated peasants in cases of emergency or to pay their defaulted taxes; or, conversely, whether the lord still had the right to punish an emancipated peasant for unsatisfactory performance of services on his land.[16]

Much depended on the solution of these problems. If they were resolved in a sense favorable to the owners of large estates, it was a tenable view that the edict benefited the latter more than the peasants. The lords continued undisturbed in the exercise of their prerogatives in local government; they remained exempt from the land tax; they still disposed of cheap and plentiful peasant labor. If now they could secure permission to absorb peasant land and relief from their other obligations toward the peasants, their political position would be unaffected and their economic position would be stronger than ever. The fact was that the emancipation of the serfs, though an indispensable prerequisite to any further reform of conditions on the

---

[16] On the ambiguities of the October Edict, see Ritter, *Stein*, I, 344–345. The text is printed in Wilhelm Altmann, ed., *Ausgewählte Urkunden zur brandenburgisch-preussischen Verfassungs- und Verwaltungsgeschichte* (Berlin, 1897), II, 1–3; it is also available in G. H. Pertz, *Das Leben des Ministers Freiherrn vom Stein* (Berlin, 1850–55), II, 23–27. The most troublesome phrase (para. 12) reads: "All obligations to which as free men the peasants are subject by virtue of land tenure or of a special contract are to continue in force."

land, was by itself of more formal than practical significance if the peasants were not given some measure of economic independence as well. Such a step would involve confiscation of all or some of the land which peasants held in unfree tenure and its distribution to the peasant population in freehold, without labor obligations in lieu of rent. As one of Stein's friends rhetorically asked: "What difference does it make in the daily life of the subject if the formula is proclaimed: After today there shall be no more serfdom?" [17] Equally, the edict's destruction of class barriers in the ownership of land could, in practice, prove of more harm than benefit to the peasants, so long as they were not given the means to maintain themselves independently but were, on the contrary, obliged to continue working for their landlord just as if they were still his serfs.[18]

The nobility, of course, were quick to see the possibilities offered by interpretations of the edict favorable to themselves. The majority of them, no doubt, would instinctively have resisted emancipation altogether, but increasing numbers of them recognized that serfdom was an inefficient system of labor and that in any case outright opposition was in the circumstances a futile stand. They devoted themselves, therefore, to exploiting emancipation to their own advantage.

They had begun their efforts even before the edict was promulgated. Getting wind of Schroetter's and Schön's work on an emancipation law, a group of East Prussian nobles [19] had written to the king that emancipation must be made as palatable as possible to the landowners by permitting completely unrestricted transactions in land, "so that each landowner may at his convenience appropriate, enlarge, diminish, or put to other use his peasant acreage, which in any case belonged originally to him." They also requested that the decree be kept secret until its official publication to prevent "untimely disturbances," that

---

[17] Vincke, quoted in E. von Bodelschwingh, *Leben des Ober-Präsidenten Freiherrn von Vincke* (Berlin, 1853), I, 452–453.

[18] On the defects of the October Edict, cf. Ford, *Stein and the Era of Reform in Prussia*, pp. 203–205.

[19] Originally the Edict had been intended to apply only to East Prussia, the only province then directly under the king's control; but Stein on his arrival ordered extension of the law to the whole kingdom.

mass migration of farm labor to the cities be prohibited, that domestic service continue for five years, and that the lords be relieved of all obligations toward their peasants. The king had referred the matter back to Schroetter, recommending that he heed the nobles' requests whenever compatible with the aims of the reform. Schroetter's draft had gone far in meeting the objections; and, as we have seen, it was not until the arrival of Stein that some of the more extreme results of Schroetter's devotion to economic liberalism were eliminated from the decree.[20]

The agitation of the landed nobles naturally intensified after the edict was published with Stein's emendations. They insisted that far from being in the future restricted in their dealings with their former serfs they ought on the contrary to be entitled as of right to some indemnity for emancipation. "The nobles were disappointed and indignant. They accused Stein of using the state as a guinea pig for newfangled foreign theories . . . and complained that the edict showed no understanding for the social significance of entailed land [gebundenen Bodenbesitzes]."[21]

After its promulgation, the edict encountered particularly violent resistance in Silesia. The landowners of this province had become the most ruthless in the kingdom in the treatment of their tenants. Here feudalism had degenerated into a parody of itself. Frequently land was no longer held by hereditary right but had passed from one aristocratic family to another, the price in many cases being exorbitant. The serfs, being bound to the land, had passed with it from owner to owner. But as land values had risen each successive owner was more intent than his predecessor on exploiting the serfs to the maximum extent in order to compensate himself for the high price he had paid

[20] For this early opposition to tangible benefits for the peasants, see Knapp, Bauern-Befreiung, II, 158–161; Lehmann, Stein, II, 274–275; Ritter, Stein, I, 333. Knapp and Lehmann, evidently referring to the same document, differ as to some details. For Stein's attitude toward the nobles, see e.g., Botzenhart, ed., Stein, II, 296.

[21] Schnabel, Deutsche Geschichte, I, 356. Cf. also Walter Görlitz, Stein: Staatsmann und Reformator (Frankfurt am Main, 1949), pp. 203–204, especially for the famous hyperbole of Baron Reck: "Better three battles of Auerstedt than one October Edict."

for the land. The Silesian peasant was therefore oppressed by the double burden of decadent feudalism and nascent capitalism.

The Silesian opposition took various forms. At first some nobles requested postponement of the edict's application to Silesia until it could be properly explained to the peasants. But when Stein refused, the nobles took no special pains to undertake any such explanation; on the contrary, with the help of many of the provincial officials, including the governor, they attempted to conceal the edict from the peasants altogether. As a result, of course, the illiterate peasants got garbled versions of it from various sources, and many of them received the impression that they were no longer obliged to render any service to the lords. Out of all this confusion arose, in the summer of 1808, a small peasants' rebellion, which the lords were not above invoking the help of French occupation troops to quell.

Toward the Silesian troubles Stein's attitude was firm but conciliatory. He authorized the punishment of landowners who disobeyed the law or who used French help to further their aims; but he also persevered in seeking the nobles' co-operation and in urging the provincial government to work for a correct understanding of the edict.[22]

But even before the Silesian resistance had reached its climax Stein himself had been forced to recognize that the Emancipation Edict was on the one hand ambiguous and on the other hand an illogical half-measure, from the point of view of improving the peasants' lot. Further legislation was clearly needed. Accordingly, Stein issued a supplementary decree on February 14, 1808, which applied, however, only to the province of Prussia.[23]

[22] For the Silesian opposition, its background, and its consequences, see Lehmann, *Stein*, II, 346–355; Schnabel, *Stein*, pp. 76–77; Johannes Ziekursch, *Hundert Jahre schlesischer Agrargeschichte* (Breslau, 1915), pp. 279–280, 290–291; Botzenhart, ed., *Stein*, II, 308, 329. For some additional names and details, see Görlitz, *Stein*, pp. 204–205.

[23] The province of Prussia consisted of the administrative districts (*Regierungsbezirke*) of East Prussia, West Prussia, and Lithuania. It is not strictly accurate to speak at this time of the *province* of *East* Prussia (as I do elsewhere), but the phrase has become customary due to later developments. Furthermore, reference to "Prussia" alone is usually best reserved to apply to the whole kingdom.

Its chief purpose was to clarify the provisions of the Emancipation Edict covering the right of landowners to absorb peasant holdings under the new free status of land. The edict had stated that such a procedure required the permission in each case of the provincial government involved. The provincial governments were meanwhile at a loss as to the conditions under which such permission was to be granted.

The preparation of the Prussian decree largely repeated the pattern set by the preparation of the Emancipation Edict itself. Again, disagreement between the radically liberal ideas of Schroetter and the more moderately liberal ones of Schön was resolved by Stein in favor of the latter. Accordingly, the decree provided that permission for absorption of land rented to peasants was to be granted only in cases where the peasant's tenure was either not hereditary, or of recent standing, or both; and the condition was imposed that an amount of peasant land equal to that acquired by the lord be leased out in large units on hereditary tenure free from labor obligations. This latter provision represented a victory for Schön's idea of creating an independent peasant class. Still, even in Schön's version the nobles were given considerable scope for absorbing small peasant holdings; the system of *Bauernschutz*, which had protected the peasant class against territorial encroachments by the nobility, had been considerably weakened.[24]

Nevertheless, the landowners were in general very hostile to the decree. The principle of free trade in land contained in the Emancipation Edict had reconciled many of them to the abolition of serfdom, and now they felt, or professed to feel, that the balance had been upset to their disadvantage. The Prussian provincial Diet demanded restitution of compulsory domestic

[24] On the decree of Feb. 14, 1808, see Knapp, *Bauern-Befreiung*, I, 137–146, II, 206–207; Ritter, *Stein*, I, 338–341; Ford, *Stein and the Era of Reform in Prussia*, p. 206. For the text of the decree, *Sammlung der für die königlichen preussischen Staaten erschienenen Gesetze und Verordnungen von 1806 bis zum 27sten Oktober 1810* (Berlin, 1822), pp. 189–193. Even after this decree, the status of the lords' other obligations toward the peasants remained in doubt until the Hardenberg legislation of 1811 (cf. Ritter, *Stein*, I, 344).

service for five years by way of compensation,[25] but Stein refused. More persistent opposition was offered by a body newly created by the Diet, the Committee of the East Prussian–Lithuanian Estates, an association dominated, of course, by nobles. This group wrote to Stein setting out their objections under several heads. In the first place, they regarded the decree as unconstitutional, since the land in question belonged to the lords: if they wanted to lease it out to peasants in exchange for labor, that was their business, and if they wished to end this arrangement, that was their business too. In short, the government had no right, in their view, to tell them what they might or might not do with their land. In the second place, the right to absorb peasant land was a just and necessary compensation for the abolition of serfdom and should not in turn be paid for by alienating other land; in any case, the scheme for creating independent peasant holdings equal in size to the land absorbed was unrealistic, since there were not enough farmers capable of running them. Even if there were, the scheme was artificial, since such holdings were not essential to efficient agriculture. As an alternative, the group suggested that landowners be permitted to appropriate half of their peasant land in return for maintaining the families resident on the other half either as tenants on nonhereditary leases or as day laborers. In conclusion, they said of the decree: "The peasant would receive something to which he has no right and which would often be useless and burdensome to him, while the lord would lose what has rightfully belonged to him and to his family."

Stein rejected these remonstrances. He replied that neither the indefinite enlargement of estates held by the nobility nor the proliferation of small farms was desirable for efficient agriculture. The nobles persisted in their demands, and this time Stein, out of patience, issued a warning to them not to utter opinions "which so obviously conflict with the prevalent spirit and with the economic conditions of the people." [26]

In one other agrarian matter Stein remained firm despite

[25] The Diet was in session to consider other matters; cf. below, p. 31.

[26] On the opposition to the February decree, see Schnabel, *Stein*, p. 76; Lehmann, *Stein*, II, 332–337; Knapp, *Bauern-Befreiung*, II, 207–209.

strong opposition. This concerned abolition of the *Mühlen-zwang*, the milling monopoly.[27] In preparation by Schroetter since Stein's arrival, a decree embodying this reform was submitted to the East Prussian Diet in February 1808, where it met with an unfavorable reception. Stein nevertheless persisted, and the decree was published on March 29. The millowners pleaded total ruin and promised to build more mills wherever needed. If the reform were not repealed, they demanded compensation. Schroetter made the reply characteristic of the economic liberal, that millers who made good flour would not suffer from lifting of the monopoly; Stein, for his part, merely referred to the public weal, and the reform stood.[28]

There still remained other aspects of the agrarian scene, some more important than the milling monopoly, which Stein wished to reform, only to be prevented by circumstances beyond his control; namely, by the French conquerors. The best example of such a reform which went by default was the abolition of "patrimonial justice," the nobles' judicial power over the residents of their estates and one of the vital elements in their control of local government. The matter was set in motion by a Cabinet Order inspired by Stein to Karl von Schroetter, provisional minister of justice and the brother of Friedrich, instructing him to draft a law establishing a unified legal system, which would imply absorption of patrimonial and other special tribunals into the state judicial organization. The minister was not much taken with the idea and dwelt on the necessity of placating the nobles, a sentiment in which he was strongly supported by the latter. Schroetter took no action until Stein, in Berlin negotiating with the French, lost sight of the question.

But the nobles themselves raised the matter again, and rather unwisely. The Committee of the East Prussian–Lithuanian Estates complained to the governor of the province, Hans von

[27] This monopoly consisted in a prohibition on grain being milled (even by hand) except at the licensed mills.

[28] Lehmann, *Stein*, II, 310–315. For text of the decree, see: *Gesetz-Sammlung* for 1806–1810, pp. 217–222. It may or may not be of any significance that much of the opposition in this matter came from millowners who were not nobles.

Auerswald, of the increasing costs of maintaining their judicial system. Auerswald reacted by recommending to Stein the abolition of patrimonial justice. Stein, through the pen of Schön, now pressed Schroetter anew, but the latter still hesitated. He objected that abolition would mean real hardship to some nobles and that the minister of justice, of all people, should not set a precedent of depriving people of their traditional rights. He suggested persuading the nobles to give up the privilege voluntarily. But this recommendation was not fortunately timed, for the Committee of the Estates almost simultaneously submitted another memorandum favoring retention of patrimonial justice. They pleaded altruism: it was actually an annoying and an expensive duty rather than a privilege, since usually they waived a fee. Furthermore, they were often able to settle disputes without litigation. If the institution were abolished, people would have to go to town to litigate. There would result loss of time and money, drunkenness, and neglect of agriculture.

Stein, however, was not swayed by the arguments either of the nobles or of Schroetter on their behalf. He sarcastically assured the former that abolition would not hinder them in furthering the public interest by amicably arbitrating disputes. But once again the French took a hand, and this time decisively. Before the decree abolishing patrimonial justice could be published, the king was forced by Napoleon to dismiss Stein. The matter was not further pursued by his successors.[29]

It is, of course, impossible to project with certainty the course which reform of feudal conditions on the land would have taken if Stein had remained in office. Still, the evidence is strong that Stein deserves credit, despite able and important assistance from others, for the reforms completed during his ministry. He not only resisted, with determination and sometimes with good humor, mounting pressure from outside the government and found ways of insulating the king against it; he was also faced

[29] On patrimonial justice, see Lehmann, Stein, II, 358–367, 594–596; Ritter, Stein, I, 345–348; Ernst von Meier, Die Reform der Verwaltungs-Organisation unter Stein und Hardenberg (Leipzig, 1881), pp. 403–409. A similar pattern may be seen in the question of the nobles' police powers: see ibid.; Ritter, Stein, I, 410–412.

with informed and tenaciously held rival proposals and with grudging co-operation from some officials. Comparison with the turn of events under the weak succeeding ministry lends color to the view that, by intangible means, Stein's strong convictions and his strong personality were an essential ingredient for the success of his reforms.[30]

Such questions as abolition of patrimonial justice were, obviously, matters which overlapped from the agrarian into the political realm. They were agrarian because the *status quo* was based on the lords' position as owners of the land on which the peasants worked, but they were political to the extent that they were elements in a system of local government.[31] Seen from this point of view, Stein's failure to curb the nobles' virtual monopoly of local government in the rural areas stands in remarkable contrast to the success which attended his efforts at introducing the concept of self-government, as opposed to patriarchal government, in the cities,[32] again suggesting the importance of the landed nobles' opposition.

Stein himself, characteristically, saw the whole problem of constitutional reform, rural and urban, local, provincial, and national, as essentially indivisible. His views are concisely collected in his famous "Nassauer Denkschrift" of 1807. Here the introduction of self-government in both town and country is regarded as preparatory to eventual amalgamation of a town

[30] G. F. Knapp, the leading authority on the agrarian reforms, maintained (*Bauern-Befreiung*, I, 146) that even Stein, under the influence of Schön, yielded overmuch to the nobles. The attack on this position by Georg Winter ("Zur Entstehungsgeschichte des Oktoberedikts," pp. 31–33) seems well taken. Winter emphasizes Stein's and Schön's desire to accomplish the reforms as smoothly as possible. Knapp was right, however, in holding that Schön was no enemy of the landed nobles in principle: cf. Eduard Wilhelm Mayer, *Das Retablissement Ost- und Westpreussens unter der Mitwirkung und Leitung Theodors von Schön* (Jena, 1916), p. 77.

[31] Cf. Ritter, *Stein*, I, 414–415, 418–420.

[32] This reform can be no more than noted here, where we are concerned especially with those aspects of the reformers' program that failed of adoption. The matter is fully dealt with in the Stein biographies and in Theodor Winkler, *Johann Gottfried Frey und die Entstehung der preussischen Selbstverwaltung* (Stuttgart and Berlin, 1936). Ironically, the cities did not necessarily want self-government; cf. Winkler, *op. cit.*, pp. 143–144, 147.

with its surrounding countryside under a single elected administrator. Moving to the larger provincial unit, Stein deplored both bureaucratic and aristocratic government: the former because a "hireling" could never acquire the familiarity and sympathy with provincial problems necessary to solve them satisfactorily, the latter because it likewise left large areas of talent and devotion untapped. He proposed, accordingly, to revive, or in provinces where they had never existed to establish, the provincial assemblies (Diets), but in altered form so as to admit persons other than nobles, specifically, "all men of considerable means." Members were to be elected by the various communities, rural and urban. Apart from the practical advantages which he expected from such a system, Stein stressed above all

the reawakening of a spirit of community and civic pride, the employment of dormant or misapplied energies and of unused knowledge, harmony between the views and desires of the nation and those of the administrative authorities of the state, the revival of patriotism and of the desire for national honor and independence

that his program would bring about.[33]

A representative system of provincial government depended on a certain amount of political education and experience in the local communities and therefore on reforms in local government. But in the other direction, Stein envisaged the provincial representative assemblies, in turn, partly as training schools for politics whose graduates would then be equipped to participate intelligently in high affairs of state. He wrote to Hardenberg:

It is essential to accustom the nation to manage its own affairs and to grow out of this immaturity where an ever-officious government seeks to keep people. The transition from the old state of affairs to a new order must not be too sudden, and men must be gradually accustomed to act on their own initiative before they are convened in large assemblies and entrusted with great issues to discuss.[34]

[33] Botzenhart, ed., *Stein,* II, 210–231. Cf. also Stein to Reden, June 7, 1807, *ibid.,* II, 208–209.

[34] Stein to Hardenberg, Dec. 8, 1807, *ibid.,* II, 313; cf. Stein to A. von Humboldt, Jan. 27, 1808, *ibid.,* II, 362; Ritter, *Stein,* I, 293–294, 421–422.

For the time being, however, representative assemblies were to be restricted to the provinces and their internal affairs; and Stein proceeded forthwith to apply the principle to East Prussia, the only province at that time directly under the king's control. An assembly was convened to meet on February 2, 1808, consisting not only of nobles, but also of a modest number of *Köllmer,* or free peasants, [35] and in addition some hereditary tenants on crown lands. The immediate occasion of this assembly was to secure approval and credit backing for the sale of some of the crown lands, the proceeds to go toward paying the French war indemnity; and one reason, no doubt, for the presence of the yeomen farmers was to obtain additional credit. In these respects this assembly is a striking instance of the impact of the French occupation on Prussian domestic affairs. On the other hand, one must conclude from Stein's theoretical position that he had long-range purposes in mind as well. Certainly the effect was to set a precedent both for active participation of provincial representative assemblies in provincial government and for limited extension of membership in such assemblies to classes other than the nobility. The free peasants, having assumed the same financial obligations as the noble landowners, were entitled to the same rights, which included a voice in future disposition of the province's financial problems. [36]

After the assembly had completed its work (from Stein's point of view very satisfactorily), [37] a decree was published creating the Committee of the Estates as the authorized representative body for all landowners of the province.

[35] The *Köllmer* were a distinctively East Prussian phenomenon, owing their existence as peasant freeholders unencumbered by feudal duties to historical developments peculiar to East Prussia (cf. Ford, *Stein and the Era of Reform in Prussia,* p. 169). They were not a numerous class.

[36] For the background of this assembly, see Ritter, *Stein,* I, 423–426; Paul Hassel, *Geschichte der preussischen Politik 1807 bis 1815* (Leipzig, 1881), I, 138–139. Details are to be found in Max Hein, *Geschichte der ostpreussischen Landschaft von 1788 bis 1888* (Königsberg, 1938), pp. 39–45. For Stein's intentions, see further the Cabinet Order of Jan. 31, 1808, in Lehmann, *Stein,* II, 207.

[37] Besides assenting to the government's proposals concerning the sale of crown lands, the assembly had also passed the first Prussian income tax (see below, pp. 46–47).

But since [the decree continued] such a committee consisting of only a few members cannot perform the functions of assemblies of Estates [*ständischer Versammlungen*] with respect either to the maintenance of a communal spirit, of nationalism, and of a concern for the welfare of all the people, or to the creation of an organ which can bring the desires and needs of his subjects to the king's attention, it is my wish that a Diet meet annually in Königsberg for the discussion of matters concerning the Estates.[38]

Thus Stein projected in concrete form a regular provincial assembly in East Prussia. Auerswald, the governor of the province, drafted a constitution for this Diet in which he followed closely the principles of Stein's "Nassauer Denkschrift." He provided for a unicameral assembly, composed of rural deputies selected by local assemblies and urban deputies selected by city dwellers, with relatively wide franchise. But this draft proved abortive; the available evidence offers no reasons.[39]

At the top of the pyramid of Stein's projects for constitutional reform in Prussia rested, of course, his plans for reorganizing the national government. Besides looking forward to an eventual representative assembly on a national scale, Stein also pressed for immediate changes within the administration. We have already seen that his insistence on ministerial responsibility brought about his dismissal at the end of his first ministry. Such a reform involved, above all, drastic reduction in the powers of the king's personal aides and secretaries. Stein succeeded in attaining this end at the beginning of his second ministry, when Frederick William III agreed to remove his favorite and only remaining counselor, Karl Friedrich Beyme —another proof of the king's willingness to sacrifice his personal convenience to the state's welfare. Stein's second principal objection to the old system of government had been the distribution of ministerial tasks by provinces instead of by functions, and this objection was removed by dismissing the ministers in charge of all the provinces occupied by Napoleon—that is to say, all but East Prussia. When the provinces later returned to

[38] Cabinet Order to Auerswald of Feb. 27, 1808, Botzenhart, ed., *Stein*, II, 382–383.

[39] But cf. the conjectures of Ritter, *Stein*, I, 425–426.

Prussian rule, provincial ministers were not reappointed, but instead, under a plan approved by the king on the day of Stein's dismissal and decreed into law the following month, five functional ministries were created.[40]

Stein had further envisaged, under the head of constitutional reform, a council of state as a supreme executive body, as well as the eventual national assembly. He was not in office long enough to progress beyond the preliminaries in these matters.[41] Even so, it became sufficiently apparent that the idea of a national assembly was distasteful to some reformers, as well as to adherents of absolutism, because of considerations of foreign policy. A national assembly was regarded by such men as Scharnhorst, Gneisenau, and Boyen, with the sympathy of Stein, as a potential medium for arousing the people to rebellion against the French conqueror; for them this idea constituted an additional reason for creating such an assembly. But by the same token it constituted for those opposed to such a bold foreign policy a reason for rejecting a Prussian assembly for the immediate future. Thus, for example, Hardenberg in a memorandum to the king:

While the participation of the nation in affairs of state, in its defense, etc., is on its merits and in view of present circumstances highly desirable, such matters must be handled with the greatest caution to ensure that popular participation remain compatible with a monarchical constitution and to prevent it from degenerating into something revolutionary. In view of the ever-increasing . . . danger that Napoleon may intend to annihilate Prussia, manipulation and utilization of the spirit of national solidarity is, to be sure, of the utmost importance; yet it must, above all, be done prudently and cautiously so that it may not defeat its own purpose by spoiling everything.

[40] "Publikandum betr. die veränderte Verfassung der obersten Staatsbehörden," Dec. 16, 1808, printed in Altmann, *Ausgewählte Urkunden*, II, 35–45 (para. 2).

[41] The council of state was accepted in principle in the decree of Dec. 16, but then became the subject of dispute; see below, pp. 44–45. Some very interesting documents were produced in connection with the national assembly: see especially Ritter, *Stein*, I, 428–441; Botzenhart, ed., *Stein*, II, 508–511, 564–566.

For it was essential to attract the attention of the French as little as possible to events in Prussia: "And what would be better calculated to cause a dangerous stir than an imprudent and premature agitation of the people?" [42]

Hardenberg's views prevailed, and thus Stein's grandest conception accompanied its author into exile. Nothing, after all, was closer to the heart of Stein's philosophy than a national assembly through which a united, confident, and enlightened people could express itself. Although, therefore, Stein had succeeded in removing much of what was most characteristic of the government of the *ancien régime,* he accomplished only a portion of his program, and he certainly fell far short of replacing absolute with constitutional government.[43]

The act which at one stroke deprived Stein of any chance of bringing his reform projects to fruition was Napoleon's order for his dismissal. French agents had discovered Stein's plotting against the conquerors. The king had no choice but to obey; on November 24, 1808, Stein was discharged, and shortly afterwards he went into exile in Austria. Stein's departure was greeted with much rejoicing on the part of his enemies.[44] "One madman has been crushed," said Count York. "The rest of the crew of vipers will dissolve in their own

[42] Hardenberg's memorandum of Nov. 12, 1808, in Hassel, *Geschichte der preussischen Politik,* I, 568–575. Cf. Ritter, *Stein,* I, 426–427, 441; II, 75–76; Paul Haake, "König Friedrich Wilhelm III., Hardenberg und die preussische Verfassungsfrage," *Forschungen zur brandenburgischen und preussischen Geschichte* (hereafter Haake, "Verfassungsfrage," followed by volume and page numbers referring to the *Forschungen*), XXVI, 528.

[43] Before we leave the subject of constitutional reform under Stein, one other project requires mention: participation in both provincial and central government of representatives of the Estates. The scheme was tried in East Prussia with unedifying results. The representatives quarrelled with the officials, and before long the Estates came to the conclusion that the representatives' salaries were not worth paying and recalled them. Details can be found in Ernst Walter Zeeden, *Hardenberg und der Gedanke einer Volksvertretung in Preussen 1807–1812* (Berlin, 1940), pp. 51–62.

[44] There is evidence that some of them even helped to bring about his overthrow. See Ritter, *Stein,* II, 81; Alfred Stern, *Abhandlungen und Aktenstücke zur Geschichte der preussischen Reformzeit 1807–1815* (Leipzig, 1885), pp. 3, 14–15; Görlitz, *Stein,* pp. 274–277, and for the part played by the queen, pp. 258–259.

venom." [45] Marwitz later looked back on Stein's ministry and commented:

He inaugurated . . . the revolutionizing of our fatherland: the war of the propertyless against property, of industry against agriculture, of fluidity against stability, of crass materialism against divinely ordained institutions, of (so-called) utility against law, of the present against the past and the future, of the individual against the family, of the speculators and money-changers against the land and the trades, of desk-bred theories against conditions rooted in the country's history, of book learning and self-styled talents against virtue, honor, and character.[46]

But in fact Stein's influence could be felt long after he himself had gone. Even more important, perhaps, than any specific reforms he had accomplished was the new mood of activity and co-operation which he introduced into the dead and stuffy atmosphere of the *ancien régime*. On the other hand, Stein was well aware that in his year of office he had brought Prussia only a part of the way on the path of reform which was to lead to national regeneration. In recognition of this fact, Stein left for the benefit of his successors (and, incidentally, of inquisitive posterity) a remarkable document which has become known as his "Political Testament." [47] In it he committed to the trust of future Prussian statesmen those projects which he himself would have undertaken had he been granted more time. He recommended abolition of enforced labor based on unfree tenure of land—"These services imply a certain dependence and arbitrary treatment of the servant which are detrimental to the development of the national spirit" [48]—and of the nobility's monopoly on political power in rural government, especially with respect to the administration of justice.

[45] Droysen, *York*, I, 135.

[46] Meusel, ed., *Marwitz*, I, 492–493.

[47] It is now well known that this document was actually drawn up, not by Stein, but by Theodor von Schön (cf. Lehmann, *Stein*, II, 606 and citations *ibid.*); but Stein signed it and it was certainly of his inspiration if not of his pen. The document is printed in Botzenhart, ed., *Stein*, II, 583–585.

[48] He likewise urged abolition of the system of domestic service, which had somewhat different historical origins from other forms of servile labor and therefore a slightly different status.

He urged the extension of self-government into provincial and national affairs, crowned by the establishment of a Prussian parliament (*eine allgemeine Nationalrepräsentation*) which would

give the nation's highest rulers a means of ascertaining the wishes of the people and of infusing vitality into official actions. . . . On the execution or shelving of such a plan depends the weal or woe of our country, for in this way alone can the national spirit be positively awakened and vitalized.

But a prerequisite for the successful operation of this comprehensive scheme for popular participation in government was a reform of the Prussian nobility in order to end their isolation from the other classes and to make them suitable leaders of public opinion: "By the establishment of a connection between the nobility and the other classes, the nation will be forged into a coherent whole."

It was unnecessary for Stein to mention, in this "Political Testament," the problems of military reform, since Scharnhorst, his chosen deputy in military affairs, was to stay at his post even after Stein's departure and could be expected to pursue the aims which they had together formulated. These included replacement of the canton system of recruitment, under which only peasants were required to serve in the army, by a system of universal military service without favor or exemption; followed by the creation of a reserve army or *Landwehr* which in peacetime was part of the civilian population and which would therefore provide a link between the civilian and military aspects of public life and would serve to eliminate the strident and brutal militarism so characteristic of the old army unleavened by civilian influences.

It was not to be expected, of course, that completion of Stein's reform program could be attempted without meeting powerful opposition. There is no certainty that Stein himself, if he had remained in office, could have accomplished all of his aims; the only certainty is that few of them were accomplished by those who followed him and that his ministry marked the high point of the reform movement.[49] Stein's "Political Testament" fell into the hands of inadequate executors. It was not so much that they were not sincere reformers; rather, their program surpassed their performance. The failure was one of character more than of intellect.

[49] It is fair to add, however, that Stein himself would never have undertaken certain of the reforms completed by his successors: for instance, Hardenberg's abolition of the guild system in 1810 and his emancipation of the Jews in 1812. Stein was anti-Semitic. See Ritter, *Stein,* I, 445; Kurt von Rohrscheidt, *Vom Zunftzwange zur Gewerbefreiheit* (Berlin, 1898), pp. 197–199; Stern, *Abhandlungen und Aktenstücke,* pp. 228–262.

PART TWO

Hardenberg

CHAPTER III

Interlude:

The Altenstein-Dohna Ministry

THE story of the reform movement after Stein's dismissal is substantially the story of Hardenberg. For nine of the eleven remaining years of the reform period he was chancellor of Prussia, a position created especially for him and carrying with it more power than any minister, including Stein, had ever had; and even during the intervening two years Hardenberg was active behind the scenes. Frederick William III would have liked to appoint him as Stein's direct successor, but Napoleon would not permit it. Instead Hardenberg remained an unofficial adviser and secured the nomination of his protégé Baron Altenstein to the finance ministry in the place of Stein's candidate, Schön; and Altenstein often spoke with his master's voice. He shared the leadership of the government from November 1808 to June 1810 with Count Alexander Dohna, a member of a prominent East Prussian aristocratic family, who as minister of the interior assumed the principal responsibility for domestic reforms.

So far as agrarian affairs were concerned, Dohna had the interests of the peasants at heart and subscribed with conviction to the principle of emancipation: "Experience has always and everywhere shown that an economy can be run better with free than with unfree men." [1] But not long after the arrival

[1] In a letter (dated March 1, 1809) to Baron Richthofen, in Rohrscheidt, *Vom Zunftzwange zur Gewerbefreiheit*, p. 246; cf. Hans Haussherr, *Die Stunde Hardenbergs* (Hamburg, 1943), pp. 168–169.

of the new ministry the East Prussian nobles, perhaps scenting a better opportunity for advancing their cause, once again raised the issue of *Bauernlegen* of which Stein had already disposed by the decree of February 1808. They wrote to Dohna (February 22, 1809) demanding the unlimited right to combine peasant farms or to absorb them into their own manorial land without the obligation of leasing out freehold land imposed by that decree. Tenants not liable to service, they said, were of no use to them. Dohna twice rejected their demands, and finally the entire body of deputies of the East Prussian Diet wrote (May 8) to the king soliciting his support against Dohna. The king referred the matter to the two leading ministers, and both maintained that the weakness of the peasants required a transitional period of protected peasant ownership before laissez-faire could be given free rein and that nothing proved this necessity so much as the nobles' insistent denial.

The East Prussian–Lithuanian Committee of Estates now tried Altenstein. Repeating their demands, they pointed out in their supporting arguments that most peasants were able to cultivate only small sections of their land, the rest of which thus lay idle,[2] and that therefore the absorption of peasant land by the lords would be beneficial to both parties if the peasants were either left with a manageable piece of property or else hired as farm laborers. This time Altenstein was impressed. Though still holding that the government ought to build and maintain a sound peasant class, a cause which was not furthered by the creation of large numbers of day laborers, he also admitted (January 8, 1810) that in the short run the restrictions imposed by the decree of 1808 were economically very onerous to the landowners. He suggested that they might have free disposition of half of their peasant land.

A third member of the government now became involved in the affair. Beyme, the minister of justice, wrote a scathing memorandum (March 9, 1810) reminiscent of Stein, which reflected on Altenstein as much as it did on the nobles:

---

[2] They did not mention that this was so because the peasants had to spend so much of their time working on the lord's land.

The Committee of the Estates seems to regard people as unimportant; it is interested only in the best possible cultivation of the land. . . . The noble landowners would rather raise prices by selling their grain abroad than feed it to the laborers at home. They cannot be blamed for this, but the state has the duty of caring for all of its citizens.[3]

In the end, the East Prussian nobility did not succeed in persuading the government to amend the decree of February 1808. But as the other provinces returned to the king's rule from French occupation, it became necessary to provide for them instructions for carrying out the Emancipation Edict so far as it concerned free trade in land. The question was whether the safeguards for the peasants retained in East Prussia would be extended to those in the other provinces. Dohna was in favor of doing so, and he succeeded in duplicating the East Prussian decree virtually without opposition in Silesia. The province of Brandenburg, however, proved more difficult. Here he was confronted on the one hand by a provincial governor (Sack) who, with the asserted support of public opinion, urged the abolition of all obligations to service coupled with prohibition on absorption of peasant land except in instances where the peasant could not maintain himself, and on the other hand by provincial nobles who were bent on shaping the Emancipation Edict more favorably to themselves. Their demands were similar to those submitted earlier by the East Prussian Estates. Dohna still stuck doggedly to the terms of the East Prussian decree, and finally with few alterations achieved its extension to Brandenburg, as well as to Pomerania.[4]

[3] For the preceding three paragraphs, see Knapp, *Bauern-Befreiung*, II, 210–213.

[4] For this paragraph, see *ibid.*, II, 216–219; Magnus Friedrich von Bassewitz, *Die Kurmark Brandenburg . . . während der Jahre 1809 und 1810* (Leipzig, 1860), pp. 674–675; Otto Schönbeck, "Der kurmärkische Landtag vom Frühjahr 1809," *Forschungen zur brandenburgischen und preussischen Geschichte*, XX (1907), 57–61. Schönbeck attributes to Sack unfriendly sentiments toward the peasants (pp. 46–49), which seems inconsistent with the documents. See the decree for Silesia, March 27, 1809, in *Gesetz-Sammlung* for 1806–1810, pp. 552–555; the decree for Brandenburg and Pomerania, Jan. 9, 1810, *ibid.*, pp. 626–629.

The inference to be drawn from the fate of agrarian reform under Dohna's aegis is that he was stubborn enough to insist on the extension of measures already in existence but not resourceful enough to devise new ones. As soon as a more energetic atmosphere was created in high government circles by the advent of Hardenberg, Dohna showed himself willing and able to work more actively for reform.

Dohna's limited capacities were more obviously demonstrated by his attitude toward the two chief issues of constitutional reform bequeathed to him by Stein. These were the establishment of a council of state and the formation in the other provinces of modernized provincial assemblies of the type created in East Prussia by Stein. Here again Dohna's intentions were good, but they were often at variance with his indecisive temperament.[5]

Stein had envisaged a council of state (*Staatsrat*) as a supreme executive body to deliberate upon matters transcending the sphere of any one minister and to consist of princes of the royal house, the ministers, the leading undersecretaries, the king's cabinet secretary, and a number of specially appointed councilors of whom the majority were to be retired ministers. In part this was a scheme whereby Stein himself, as a councilor, could retain some influence in high affairs of state despite his enforced dismissal as a minister. But Stein's larger purpose was to achieve further decentralization in the government by reducing the power of the ministers and correspondingly increasing the influence of the high civil service, represented by the undersecretaries.[6] Nobody, naturally, was more in favor of this plan than the undersecretaries; and it was Wilhelm von Humboldt, who was undersecretary for education in the ministry of

[5] His own contemporaries confirm this verdict. See Sack to Stein, May 4, 1809; Kunth to Stein, Sept. 23, 1809; Merckel to Stein, Dec. 12, 1809, Botzenhart, ed., *Stein*, III, 120–121, 176, 208; also Friedrich von Raumer, *Lebenserinnerungen und Briefwechsel* (Leipzig 1861), pp. 111–112. Schön's tribute to Dohna's strength of character (*Aus den Papieren des Ministers und Burggrafen von Marienburg Theodor von Schön* [Halle, 1875–83], VI, 55; hereafter Schön, *Papiere*), refers to special circumstances and a later period.

[6] Memorandum of Stein to the king, Oct. 28, 1808, Botzenhart, ed., *Stein*, II, 556–557; cf. Ritter, *Stein*, I, 372–374.

the interior, who assumed leadership in the campaign for a council of state.

His principal foe was Altenstein. Hardenberg's disciple shared his master's absolutist leanings and was unwilling to shed part of the power that had just become his. Altenstein had persuaded the king, immediately after his appointment, to suspend Stein's decree of November 24, 1808, in which a council of state had definitely been projected. In its place was issued the order of December 16, in which it was merely stated (para. 1) that details about the organization of a council of state would be announced at some time in the future. This postponement "was the kind of decision that Frederick William III most liked making." The other ministers, including Dohna, acquiesced.[7]

But Dohna, under the diligent pressure of Humboldt, soon began to give the council of state wavering support, without being able to persuade his colleagues. Finally, after over a year of wrangling, the ministers agreed on a report to the king (March 17, 1810) in which they described Stein's project as likely to lead to a diminution in royal authority and as especially unsuited to critical times when strong and quick decisions were needed. They suggested instead regular meetings of the ministers alone to discuss those matters intended by Stein to come before the council. Dohna tried unsuccessfully to obtain the admission to these meetings of Humboldt and Niebuhr, another undersecretary, on the ground of their personal ability; but this proposal satisfied neither the other ministers nor Humboldt himself, who stood on principle. The king accepted the ministers' report, and shortly afterwards Dohna referred to Stein's idea of a council of state as a "still-born monstrosity." Humboldt delivered himself of this comment on the ministry:

Dohna is completely undependable. His only program is to let things continue as they are until they are disturbed by accident or disintegrate of their own futility. Altenstein is in favor of neither a council of state nor a plurality of ministers. His aim is to concentrate

[7] Rudolf Lobethal, *Verwaltung und Finanzpolitik in Preussen während der Jahre 1808–1810* (Berlin, 1914), pp. 13–16.

power in his own ministry. . . . But Altenstein is nevertheless the only minister who is active and enterprising.[8]

The story had a dual epilogue, interesting if only because it was so characteristic of the two personalities involved. The proud and perhaps somewhat self-righteous Humboldt resigned rather than continue in a subordinate position. He subscribed to the tenet of neohumanism that the human personality must be given unlimited scope for development. The pliable and well-meaning Dohna indulged in self-recrimination as soon as Hardenberg took office, and he now insisted on the urgent need for the very institution which he had called a "monstrosity" only a month before.[9] Thus the sequence of events followed the same pattern as in agrarian reform. Dohna, too irresolute to press consistently for reform on his own initiative, belatedly acquired the courage of his convictions when the final decision lay elsewhere.

A similarly bleak picture must be drawn of the situation during the Altenstein-Dohna ministry in the matter of representative assemblies, the other main item of constitutional reform bequeathed by Stein to his successors. As the various provinces were returned to Prussia by the French, their assemblies were convened to deal with the same financial problems with which Stein had confronted the East Prussian assembly of February 1808: namely, the necessity for funds to pay the French indemnity, especially for credit in advance of the sale of crown lands, which could be placed on the market only gradually if the price of land were not to drop sharply. The East Prussian assembly, despite a few recalcitrants, had

[8] For this paragraph, see *ibid.*, pp. 22–31, 39–40; Gebhardt, *Humboldt*, I, 345–347; S. A. Kaehler, *Wilhelm von Humboldt und der Staat: Ein Beitrag zur Geschichte deutscher Lebensgestaltung um 1800* (Munich and Berlin, 1927), p. 522; Humboldt to Schön, Oct. 31, 1809, Wilhelm von Humboldt, *Gesammelte Schriften* (ed. Albert Leitzmann and others; Berlin, 1903–36), XVI, 233. Further details confirming Dohna's indecision are in Schneider, "Entstehung des preussischen Staatsrats," pp. 492–496.

[9] Dohna's report to the king, July 6, 1810, Adalbert Bezzenberger, ed., *Aktenstücke des Provinzial-Archivs in Königsberg aus den Jahren 1786–1820 etc.* (Königsberg, 1898), p. 4. Cf. Lobethal, *Verwaltung und Finanzpolitik*, pp. 47–48; Haussherr, *Die Stunde Hardenbergs*, pp. 192–193.

been amenable to Stein's demands and had not only approved the sale of crown lands but had also instituted a provincial income tax to be levied on all classes of the population. This was the first income tax in the kingdom of Prussia from which the nobles were not exempt. But the assembly had at least as much political as financial significance. From Stein's point of view, the members' co-operative attitude was a good omen for the development of representative institutions.

But the Altenstein-Dohna government did not handle the matter with the same resolution as had Stein. Whereas Stein had taken advantage of the occasion to modify the membership of the assembly in East Prussia by the inclusion of free peasants, the new government in 1809 called the Estates in Brandenburg and Pomerania without reducing their traditional domination by the aristocracy (although Dohna seems to have contemplated such a step).[10] The immediate result was that in the other provinces the government met with a much less co-operative attitude toward the current financial problems than Stein had encountered in East Prussia; but in the long run a more important outcome of the government's action consisted in the failure of these provincial Diets to advance the cause of representative government. It became clear that in many ways it was better to have no representative bodies at all than merely to resuscitate the old ones. It was demonstrated that such traditional bodies were not fit instruments for the promotion of parliamentary concepts, but on the contrary they tended only to revive the feudalism of which they were remnants. Decadent feudalism was decidedly no improvement over absolutism.

The meeting of the Brandenburg Estates may serve as an example of the experiences of the Altenstein-Dohna government with the nobility outside East Prussia. Johann August Sack, the governor of the province and a follower of Stein's, reported to the king that the mood of the people was excellent, especially among the middle classes in Berlin, and from them he expected cheerful assumption of the burdens of defeat.

[10] On the membership question, see Zeeden, *Hardenberg*, pp. 66–67; and Haussherr, *Die Stunde Hardenbergs*, pp. 107–108.

"Unfortunately the same mood does not prevail among some sections of the upper classes, who egotistically look less to the common good than to their own advantage." [11] But the provincial Diet was composed mainly of members of these classes, and they confirmed Sack's diagnosis. To be sure, they passed an income tax, but they cast it in a form radically different from the East Prussian precedent. Peasants were to be taxed at a higher rate than lords; the nobles were allowed to make their own tax assessment and to supervise the administration of the tax.[12]

Sack's troubles were not over with the passage of the tax measure. When he set about trying to collect the tax, the noble members of the supervising committee refused to attend conferences, and documents containing fantastic demands for discrimination in favor of the nobles arrived in Berlin. But it was the appointment of Hardenberg as chancellor, rather than these obstructions, that scotched the Brandenburg income tax. In his private capacity as a Brandenburg landowner, Hardenberg had opposed the tax on two grounds during the meeting of the Estates: it forced revelation of an individual's income, and, because it was a provincial tax, it undermined the growth of a unified state. Now, as chancellor, he was in a position summarily to suspend the tax. Sack, of course, was

[11] Sack's report, Feb. 14, 1809, Herman Granier, ed., *Berichte aus der Berliner Franzosenzeit 1807–1809* (Leipzig, 1913), p. 358. Cf. the exemplary behavior of the Brandenburg nobles in the preceding years described in [Bassewitz,] *Kurmark Brandenburg 1806–1808*, II, 139.

[12] Details on the Brandenburg income tax are in Otto Schönbeck, "Kurmärkische Landtag," pp. 64–65, 75–82, 94–101; and *id.*, "Die Einkommensteuer unter den Nachfolgern Steins," *Forschungen zur brandenburgischen und preussischen Geschichte*, XXV (1913), 152. Against Sack's analysis, however, must be held on the one hand the resistance of urban representatives in the assembly to a special tax to be imposed on the guilds (*Gewerbesteuer*), unsuccessful because the cities did not have sufficient votes, and on the other hand the sizable minority among the nobility who opposed their colleagues' selfish demands, e.g., Marwitz, who described his fellow deputies as "miserable specimens" (Walther Kayser, *Marwitz: Ein Schicksalsbericht aus dem Zeitalter der unvollendeten preussisch-deutschen Erhebung* [Hamburg, 1936], pp. 205–206).

outraged and blamed the result entirely on the scheming of the nobles, while Stein declared that the latter "deserved to be chastised with scorpions." [13]

Sack had repeatedly pointed out to the central government that the only way to pry the nobility from their traditional privileges was to broaden the basis of membership in the provincial assemblies, as Stein had done in East Prussia. But Dohna, although he agreed in principle, refused to challenge the nobility on this central issue while he had the power to do so; after Hardenberg had taken office Dohna characteristically became bold and advised him that the resistance of the Brandenburg aristocracy could be overcome only with a new system of representation.[14]

Hardenberg's appointment as chancellor in June 1810 was a result of the financial difficulties of the Altenstein-Dohna government. Altenstein, as minister of finance, by the spring of 1810 had confessed failure in raising the funds with which to pay the French indemnity and recommended as a last resort the cession of the province of Silesia to Napoleon against release from the indemnity. The king was much disturbed. He bethought himself of Hardenberg, still in enforced retirement; secret messengers were sent, secret conferences were held, and at the end Hardenberg undertook to find means of paying the indemnity if he were permitted to return to office. Frederick William III prevailed upon Napoleon to allow him

---

[13] For the later fate of the Brandenburg income tax, see Schönbeck, "Einkommensteuer," pp. 158–172. For Hardenberg, see Haussherr, *Die Stunde Hardenbergs,* pp. 83–85, 255, and his letters cited in Karl Mamroth, *Geschichte der preussischen Staats-Besteuerung 1806–1816* (Leipzig, 1890), pp. 137–143. Sack to Stein, Aug. 31 and Sept. 11, 1810, and Stein to Reden, Aug. 9, 1810, Botzenhart, ed., *Stein,* III, 305–307, 296.

Similar conclusions concerning the value of semifeudal Estates were suggested by the experiences of the Altenstein-Dohna government in trying to introduce an income tax in Pomerania and Silesia: see Schönbeck, "Einkommensteuer," pp. 154–158; Zeeden, *Hardenberg,* pp. 73–78. On Silesia, see also Rolf Grabower, *Preussens Steuern vor und nach den Befreiungskriegen* (Berlin, 1932), pp. 243–246.

[14] Zeeden, *Hardenberg,* pp. 71–72; p. 82, n. 7.

to bring Hardenberg back into the government and forthwith made the latter a virtual dictator.[15]

Hardenberg's advent was greeted by most friends of reform with gratification and relief. To be sure, Schön and Niebuhr refused to work for the chancellor because they opposed his financial schemes (and probably also because they resented the intrigues that had attended his return), but they acted contrary to the urgent advice of Stein, and to most people it was abundantly clear that little could be expected in the way of reform so long as its direction rested in Dohna's uncertain hands. The disposition was to regard the Altenstein-Dohna ministry as an unfortunate but unimportant interlude: under Hardenberg's energetic leadership the cause of reform would once more prosper. Even Schön, for all his personal antagonism to the chancellor, would have been no better pleased with a prolongation of the Altenstein-Dohna government. Looking back later on their ministry, he wrote:

There was no attempt to stifle the enthusiasm that had been kindled in the people since October 9, 1807; but there was, on the other hand, a reluctance to abandon the good old days. The domination of ideas, or even of thought, in the government was ended, all the plans of Stein's day were put aside, and everything went rapidly backwards.[16]

[15] The circumstances of Hardenberg's recall are told in great detail in Haussherr, *Die Stunde Hardenbergs,* Part II, chap. iii.

[16] On the attitude of Stein, Schön, and Niebuhr toward Hardenberg, see Schön's memoranda of Nov. 30, 1810, and April 11, 1811, in Mamroth, *Geschichte der preussischen Staats-Besteuerung,* pp. 437, 466; Niebuhr to Stein, Nov. 10, 1810, Botzenhart, ed., *Stein,* III, 469–470; Ritter, *Stein,* II, 113–117; Haussherr *Die Stunde Hardenbergs,* Part II, chap. iv. Cf. also the opposition of Hippel (generally regarded as a reformer), Wilhelm Steffens, *Hardenberg und die ständische Opposition 1810/1811* (Leipzig, 1909), pp. 32–33. For Schön's comment on the Altenstein-Dohna ministry, see Schön, *Papiere,* I, 59–60.

CHAPTER IV

Hardenberg and Stein

BARON HARDENBERG, like Stein, was not a native Prussian but had entered Prussian service long before the reform period.[1] His first post was in Ansbach-Bayreuth, a territory newly acquired by the Prussian crown, which he administered from 1792 to 1806. Here Hardenberg had created an efficient, autocratic governmental machinery free from the feudal encumbrances present elsewhere in the kingdom.[2] It is a significant symptom of the fundamental difference between the two men that while Stein, in Westphalia, strove in his reforms to improve upon the existing organs of government, notably the provincial Estates, Hardenberg, in Ansbach-Bayreuth, remodeled the administration to his own taste without going out of his way to maintain points of contact with historically formed patterns.

Probably more than any other Prussian statesman of the period, Hardenberg was a product of eighteenth-century rationalism and of the French Revolution to the extent that it reflected the Enlightenment. He was contemptuous of feud-

[1] There is no good comprehensive biography of Hardenberg. Note, however, the brilliant character sketch in Meinecke, *Zeitalter der deutschen Erhebung*, pp. 52–54, with accompanying portraits; for an introduction to his ideas, see Zeeden, *Hardenberg*, pp. 29–37. For the monographic literature, see the bibliography.

[2] This early phase of Hardenberg's career has been well treated by Fritz Hartung, *Hardenberg und die preussische Verwaltung in Ansbach-Bayreuth von 1792 bis 1806* (Tübingen, 1906).

alism as an inefficient and irrational system of landholding and
farming based on tradition and prejudice. He subscribed to
the absolutism of the Enlightenment: absolutism was the
simplest and most rational manner of governing. The moral
objectives of policy so prominent in Stein were heavily out-
weighed with Hardenberg by practical considerations; his
chief concerns were power and efficiency. Therefore he thought
much more in terms of the state than in terms of people: the
state, to develop and to assert its power, must be unhampered
in its dispositions by sentimental or personal considerations,
and the purpose of reform should be to consolidate the power
of the state by clearing away obstacles to efficient administration. Hardenberg was "the last representative of that same
enlightened absolutism which he was supposed to overcome." [3]

Early in 1807, at the end of Stein's first ministry, Hardenberg became the leading minister of Prussia and at once set
about introducing into the central government the same autocratic methods which he had practiced in Ansbach-Bayreuth.
He succeeded where Stein had failed in prevailing upon the
king to end *Kabinettsregierung*, abhorrent to him as an anachronistic and irregular system of government that limited the
power of the ministers. But he was able to undertake no further
reorganization before Napoleon in July, after the Treaty of
Tilsit, compelled Frederick William III to dismiss him. It
suited Napoleon to keep the king docile; Hardenberg's energy
and purposefulness were inconvenient.

From his enforced retirement Hardenberg, on the king's
request, drew up a lengthy document in which he set forth his
views on the problems of Prussian government. This so-called
"Rigaer Denkschrift" of September 12, 1807, is the counterpart of Stein's "Nassauer Denkschrift" of a few months earlier,
and it offers many instructive points of comparison between
the two reformers. [4]

Hardenberg's basic purpose was "to destroy everywhere

[3] Schnabel, *Deutsche Geschichte*, I, 459.
[4] Hardenberg's memorandum is printed in full in Leopold von Ranke,
ed., *Denkwürdigkeiten des Staatskanzlers Fürsten von Hardenberg* (Leipzig, 1877), IV, Appendix.

powerless and anachronistic institutions and . . . to create
new forces for the march of progress toward perfection." He
proposed to launch

a revolution in the good sense of the word, which will lead directly
to the great goal of increasing the dignity of human life, by the
exercise of wisdom in the government and not through the pressure
of violence either from within or from without . . . Democratic
principles in a monarchical government: this seems to me the mix-
ture appropriate to the present *Zeitgeist*.

Radical reforms were needed, but not through radical methods:
"Their execution should not be entrusted to large com-
posite assemblies, and only a few government officials should
be asked for their opinion. . . . A small number of well-
informed and discerning individuals should direct the reforms."

Fundamental to a successful reform program, in Hardenberg's view, was the development of a feeling of national co-
hesion. Barriers between provinces should be eliminated and
provincial differences reduced "in order to give the whole
country a single national character": "The whole state shall
in future be called *Prussia.*" A positive measure to achieve
national solidarity would be the election of national representatives from all provinces, who would serve to direct the
attention of their constituents away from provincial toward
national problems. The representatives would not constitute
a danger to monarchy or to effective government if they were
attached to various administrative departments, instead of
meeting in a separate assembly of their own. Political equality
would be promoted by their election from among all classes
of the population, and this political equality would be matched
by a degree of social and economic equality, without indulg-
ing in the excesses of the French Revolution. Hardenberg was
an economic no less than a political pupil of the Enlightenment: "It follows from the fundamental principle of restricting
natural freedom only so much as circumstances require, that
the capacities of citizens of all classes must be developed and
put to the fullest possible use"; he actually used the phrase

"laissez faire." "Every position in the state without exception" should be open to all classes of the population according to merit. Hardenberg advocated free trade, free transactions in land, uniform taxation in town and country, and abolition of the guild system and of monopolies such as the milling monopoly. Tax exemption for the nobility must be abolished. Peasants must be permitted to acquire land, and their feudal obligations to the lords must be terminable against compensation (Hardenberg did not elaborate on these points), but—and here Hardenberg's authoritarianism becomes apparent—"it will be necessary in the peasant's own interest to limit severely his right to object to any decision." Similarly, patrimonial justice should be abolished in criminal cases;

but the landowner must retain the means of compelling his peasants, laborers, and servants, swiftly and without cost, to fulfill their obligations; and though these people must not be denied a hearing, neither must the landlord be made dependent in these matters on the arbitrary decisions of a judge who may be far away.

This reservation could be paraphrased: "The lord is to retain control over the administration of justice in all cases where he has a personal interest."

Despite many similarities between this program and Stein's —similarities which led Stein himself, then and for many years afterwards, to regard Hardenberg as a comrade and ally—the fundamental political philosophies of the two men were obviously very different. Hardenberg proposed to do away much more completely with the feudal and medieval tradition in Prussian society, but he was inclined to preserve those accretions which were due to the rise of absolutism, most pronounced since the seventeenth century. Stein, less intent upon building a rational state along absolutist lines, had a profound appreciation of the importance of preserving, if possible, institutions that were part of the historical heritage of the people, even when they were anachronistic (although, of course, he did not hesitate to destroy those that he considered actively harmful). Stein was also less doctrinaire in economic matters than Hardenberg; in fact, he was much less devoted to theories of all kinds, preferring to judge individual issues without fitting them into a preconceived pattern. He had a lively sympathy for the impact of political decisions on the people and a sincere desire to educate them gradually toward participation in those decisions instead of imposing them from above, as Hardenberg clearly indicated he wished to do. Stein realized that good government, even in a country as backward as Prussia, was something more than efficient administration.

The difference between the two men extended to the personal as well as the political plane. Where Stein was inclined to be puritanical and austere, Hardenberg was an epicurean. Foreign affairs were always more congenial to him than domestic, and a secret treaty, which involved intrigue against foreign diplomats in elegant surroundings, took priority over dull projects like tax reform, which required hard work behind a desk. He was, in fact, inclined to carry the techniques of diplomacy over into his handling of domestic affairs. When he encountered opposition he often attempted to evade it rather than overcome it. Stein, on the other hand, although he was slower to take actions likely to arouse opposition, proved more ruthless in pressing home his decision once he had made up his mind. On one occasion Stein himself advised Hardenberg to be firmer in his treatment of recalcitrant nobles.[5]

Hardenberg's maneuvers, furthermore, were not usually successful, the opposition being neither deceived nor mollified by his gracious manner. Marwitz, for example, one of the leaders among the nobility, hated Hardenberg far more that he hated Stein. Privately he was inclined to agree with both reformers that many members of the Prussian aristocracy were unfit to be leaders of society; but while Stein and Marwitz concluded from this circumstance that the nobility ought to be improved, Hardenberg seemed to argue that they ought to be abolished. From Marwitz' point of view Hardenberg combined all the worst features of French Revolutionary radicalism with all the worst features of *ancien-régime* absolutism. Just because Stein's ideas were less "modern" than the chancellor's, they conflicted

[5] He recommended the example of Richelieu (memorandum of Sept. 12/13, 1810, Botzenhart, ed., *Stein*, III, 329).

less sharply with the reactionary tendency among the nobles.

This circumstance has enabled some historians to maintain plausibly (although, I think, wrongly) that Stein had more in common with Marwitz than he did with Hardenberg.[6] But very few among their contemporaries would have agreed with this interpretation, certainly not Stein or Hardenberg themselves. The general expectation was that, with due allowance for personal differences, Hardenberg would complete Stein's reform program. How this expectation came to be disappointed is the burden of the following chapters.

[6] This interpretation became popular under the National Socialist regime, which was very interested in the reform period and accomplished a complete reclassification of all its major figures: "We are interested nowadays [i.e., after the Nazi rise to power] . . . no longer in the supposed 'liberalism' or 'conservatism' of the aspirations of those times; our standard of judgment, rather, is the basic idea of a reform of the state in a popular [*völkischen*] direction, and we distinguish between the men and the forces of the period according to whether they were friends or foes of this new popular conception of the state. . . . The old contrast between 'reformers' and 'opponents of reform' is obsolete. . . . We see on the one hand the idea of a popular reform of the state embodied in the figures of Scharnhorst, Stein, Marwitz, Jahn, Fichte, Arndt, and Kleist; and we see on the other hand the chancellor Hardenberg as the opponent and destroyer of popular reform: we see the . . . bureaucratic and capitalistic *System Hardenberg,* which contains within itself the most diverse forces, liberal and reactionary, ranging from the economic individualism of Schön and the cultural individualism of Humboldt to the police-state despotism of Metternich" (Walther Kayser, "Marwitz und die unvollendete preussisch-deutsche Erhebung," *National-sozialistische Monatshefte,* VII [1936], 114–115). To test the validity of this classification for the men concerned, cf. e.g., Marwitz' estimate of Scharnhorst, below, pp. 152–153. Cf. also Haussherr, *Die Stunde Hardenbergs,* an extremely hostile study. The author stresses Hardenberg's friendship with Jews, although he regretfully admits that he did not marry one, as an earlier Nazi writer had asserted.

CHAPTER V

The Constitutional Crisis

of 1811

FINANCIAL questions were closely interwoven with constitutional issues throughout the reform period. Financial need had enabled Stein to call the East Prussian assembly and to shape it into a form calculated to advance the cause of government through representative assemblies; financial need had brought down the Altenstein-Dohna government and substituted for the royal absolutism of the *ancien régime* the ministerial absolutism of Hardenberg; now financial need was to involve Hardenberg himself in a major constitutional crisis.

The Financial Decrees of October 27 and 28, 1810

As soon as he came to power, Hardenberg appointed a commission to study the Prussian tax problem. In its report (July 4, 1810) the commission recommended taxing of land belonging to nobles (hitherto exempt), the abolition of guilds and destruction of the remaining barriers to freedom of trade and enterprise, and the imposition of various indirect taxes in both town and country. An income tax, of course, was out of the question with Hardenberg. The commission was fully alive to the political implications of its report, which included "the destruction of many personal and material privileges." But all the proposed measures depended on each other

like links in a single chain: as soon as one link is removed, the whole plan becomes illogical and defective. . . . We are convinced that without such ruthless measures the work of reform would remain superficial and fragmentary; and on the other hand we consider it not only unjust but impossible to curtail the privileges of the various classes unequally.[1]

In his own plan, based on the commission's report, Hardenberg also recognized, in fact seized upon, the constitutional changes that a thoroughgoing reform of the Prussian finances implied. The consolidation of all the various provincial and local debts to the French into one national debt not only was a necessary financial measure but would also serve to centralize the country's administration: Hardenberg was determined "not to perpetuate provincialism, but rather to introduce nationalism."[2]

Hardenberg was not prepared for the furor that the financial legislation with which he implemented his program provoked in the ranks of the nobility. The most controversial of the innovations introduced by the laws of October 27 and 28, 1810, was the imposition of a tax on all land, including that of the nobility.[3] The law justified in the following words the end

[1] Report in Mamroth, *Geschichte der preussichen Staats-Besteuerung*, pp. 194–197.

[2] Hardenberg's "Finanzplan nach den neueren Erwägungen," August 1810, Botzenhart, ed., *Stein*, III, 708–717. Its financial principles did not differ substantially from those of the commission, although it differed in detail. Hardenberg proposed a so-called "class tax," which was really a disguised form of the income tax which he despised (such a tax was introduced for a short time in 1811) (cf. Mamroth, *Geschichte der preussischen Staats-Besteuerung*, pp. 599–612); he also proposed a forced loan on half of the new land tax, remitting future payments of that half of the tax. Hardenberg further connected agrarian reform with his financial measures; his action in this matter will be discussed in the following chapter. Stein expressed general approval of the plan, with reservations (Stein's memorandum of Sept. 12/13, 1810, Botzenhart, ed., *Stein*, III, 319–331).

[3] This was contained in the "Edikt über die Finanzen des Staats und die neuen Einrichtungen wegen der Abgaben usw.," printed in the *Gesetz-Sammlung für die königlich-preussische Staaten* for 1810–1811, pp. 24–31. The financial legislation of these two days also included: "Edikt über die neuen Consumtions- und Luxus-Steuern"; "Edikt wegen Aufhebung des Vorspanns"; "Edikt wegen der Mühlen-Gerechtigkeit und Aufhebung des Mühlen-Zwangs, des Bier- und Branntwein-Zwangs in der ganzen Monarchie"; "Edikt über die Aufhebung der Natural-Fourage- und Brod-

of one of the chief traditional privileges of the Prussian nobility:

The burden of the new taxes shall be lightened as much as possible by means of a thoroughgoing reform of the whole system of collecting revenue, which will subject everybody in the kingdom to the new obligations according to the same principles. . . . All exemptions shall be abolished which are incompatible with both natural justice and the principles inspiring the administration of neighboring countries.

The enunciation of this equalitarian theory was sufficient by itself to arouse the ire of some sections of the nobility. It suggested unmistakably that Hardenberg's legislation was inspired by political as well as by financial motives. The law tacitly assumed the right of the government unilaterally to revoke ancient privileges which had been regarded as part of the fundamental law of the country. But if anybody still doubted the constitutional implications of Hardenberg's fiscal reform, he must have been convinced by the inconspicuous inclusion in the decree of the highly important statement that the king intended "to give the nation properly constituted representative bodies both in the provinces and for the whole country, of whose advice we shall be happy to make use." Here it was implicitly stated that the government had the power to institute changes in the political structure of the country without consulting the population, or any part of the population. But the nobles had already demonstrated in 1809, during the discussions over provincial taxation, that they would oppose any attempt to alter the composition of the provincial Diets except with the consent of those Diets themselves.[4] In fact, the fiscal laws of October 1810 produced on a nationwide scale much the same results as the fiscal proposals of 1809 had pro-

Lieferung" (Oct. 30), *ibid.*, pp. 33–39, 77, 95–97, 78. An excellent summary of these laws and of their significance may be found in Conrad Bornhak, "Die preussische Finanzreform von 1810," *Forschungen zur brandenburgischen und preussischen Geschichte,* III (1890), 555–608, especially pp. 590–593. Cf. Haussherr, *Die Stunde Hardenbergs,* pp. 258–268, for a hostile interpretation.

[4] Cf. Zeeden, *Hardenberg,* pp. 71–72.

duced in the provinces: opposition in defense not only of the economic but also of the political *status quo*.

The immediate resistance to the October decrees was of the utmost vehemence.[5] A typical note was struck by the Committee of the East Prussian–Lithuanian Estates:

The new legislation, from which we expected our health and salvation, has increased our misfortune and brought us closer to ruin. The first pillar of the state, the sanctity of law, has been shattered with a stroke of the pen by the revocation of rights which our kings have vowed to uphold and which our laws have promised to protect.[6]

Some protests were even more extreme:

The principles of the new tax system imply the presumption that a landowner's property . . . is a piece of land belonging to nobody, which can be disposed of to gratify any bureaucrat's whim [*kameralistiche Laune*]. . . . The saying is true that it is better for one to die than for a whole people to perish; but the total destruction of such a respectable body of men as all the landowners of an agricultural state to achieve some unknown obscure purpose or to favor some section of the people or other—such an enormity is unprecedented [*das ist wenigstens noch unerhört*].[7]

The financial aspects of Hardenberg's legislation drew fire not only from the nobility but also from other sections of the population whose economic position was involved, especially from the urban middle class; but the leadership in the fight against the constitutional implications of the laws came from the ranks of the landed nobility alone. Soon the political struggle overshadowed the economic; and as a result the nucleus of resistance shifted from East Prussia, where the economy had been most thoroughly devastated by war but where the no-

[5] Steffens, *Hardenberg*, pp. 14–15. Cf. Reinhold Steig, *Heinrich von Kleist's Berliner Kämpfe* (Berlin and Stuttgart, 1901), p. 144: "The tone adopted exceeds the bounds of credulity."

[6] Memorandum to the king, Jan. 9, 1811, in Steffens, *Hardenberg*, p. 13.

[7] Landowners of Kreis Tapiau to the king and to Hardenberg, Dec. 17, 1810, *ibid.*, p. 27. The most extreme step was taken in another East Prussian district, whose Estates simply suspended collection of the land tax (*ibid.*, p. 16). But opposition was, of course, not universal: see e.g., Mamroth, *Geschichte der preussischen Staats-Besteuerung*, p. 533.

bility were politically more progressive, to Brandenburg, where the nobles retained the greatest measure of constitutional autonomy and guarded it most jealously.[8]

The two men who became the leaders of the opposition against Hardenberg at once seized upon the constitutional implications of the laws. Count Finckenstein wrote: "The manner of imposition of the tax is at once unpopular and illegal. It could have been both popular and legal if the Estates had been openly consulted beforehand and if all rights had been respected." [9] Marwitz roundly accused the government of using violence and affirmed that the tax exemption of the nobility's land was based "on numerous agreements [*Verträgen*] between the sovereign and the Estates." [10] Their position was that the nobility would have been willing to assume the new financial burdens voluntarily but did not propose to yield to governmental action which they considered dictatorial and invalid.

The aristocracy also clearly perceived another political implication of Hardenberg's laws: his intention to break down provincial barriers in order to unify the nation. But it was precisely through provincial autonomy that the nobility's political power, driven from the central government by the Great Elector and his successors, had been perpetuated; aristocratic special privileges were intimately bound up with provincial particularism. This was the reason the nobility were anxious to revive the provincial Estates and to preserve the unique features of the individual provinces. They opposed geographical uniformity for the same reasons that they opposed class uniformity. Thus, on the specific issue of taxation raised by Hardenberg's decrees, one spokesman of the aristocracy observed: "Equal taxation of all land in all provinces

[8] Cf. Friedrich Meusel, ed., "Eine Denkschrift des Grafen von Finckenstein 'Über die Freiheiten der Ritterschaft' (1811)," *Historische Zeitschrift,* 101 (1908), 337–338.

[9] Friedrich Meusel, ed., "Ein Aufsatz des Grafen von Finckenstein über Hardenbergs Finanzreform von 1810 etc.," *Forschungen zur brandenburgischen und preussischen Geschichte,* XIX (1906), 525–528.

[10] Meusel, ed., *Marwitz,* II¹, 172–176.

is idealistic nonsense." [11] But Hardenberg did not recognize that provincialism was itself a form of aristocratic privilege. He saw no incongruity in sharply rebuking expressions of particularism [12] and then yielding to the nobility by modifying some of the fiscal provisions of the October laws in their favor, barely a month after publication of the decrees.[13]

The widespread opposition aroused by those laws persuaded the chancellor of the desirability of establishing better public relations. In order to placate public opinion and to win support for his fiscal legislation, Hardenberg decided to call a national Assembly of Notables. But in so doing he involved the tax laws and his whole relationship with the nobility more inextricably than ever in the larger problem of the Prussian constitution.

The Assembly of Notables, 1811

It would be idle to pretend that the national assembly of the winter of 1810–1811 was, as such, a symptom of progress toward a constitutional monarchy in Prussia. The Assembly of Notables was a body designed by Hardenberg to resemble neither the provincial chambers favored by the nobility nor the truly representative parliament envisaged by Stein. Concerning both of these institutions Hardenberg's opinion was clear:

It is unnecessary to enumerate the defects of the existing so-called *ständischen* constitutions. To consult their upholders concerning a new representative institution would merely perpetuate foolishness. . . . The new institution . . . must emanate directly from the government alone, it must come as a welcome gift from above. . . . It can be only advisory, since otherwise . . . the monarchical form of government would be impaired. . . . The government alone must have the right to convene, to dismiss, and to propose legislation; great care must be exercised to forestall any crystallization of resis-

[11] Prittwitz, Nov. 24, 1810, in Steffens, *Hardenberg*, p. 185.

[12] E.g., Cabinet Order to landowners of Kreis Schaaken, January 1811, *ibid.*, p. 31; Hardenberg's message to four East Prussian deputies, March 6, 1811, in Zeeden, *Hardenberg*, p. 114.

[13] For details, see Mamroth, *Geschichte der preussischen Staats-Besteuerung*, pp. 447–450.

tance which might interfere, to the detriment of the country, with the government's actions.[14]

Hardenberg intended his creation to serve the interests neither of an entrenched aristocracy nor of incipient constitutionalism but only of autocracy. It was not supposed to be an independent body but only a sounding board and a propaganda device for calming the agitation throughout the country aroused by the October decrees. Hardenberg was frank in stating his purpose: "to explain the internal coherence of the measures taken and to eliminate all misunderstandings and requests for interpretation." [15] It was essential that such an assembly should be composed of reliable men, and they were therefore to be not elected but appointed. Hardenberg hoped to win over the Notables by the mere honor of being named such, or by the charm of his personality, or even, perhaps, by arguments. The Notables, convinced, would then return to their localities and spread the gospel.

But the chancellor defeated his own purpose. On the one hand, he prevented the assembly from being popular among the people by rigging it in favor of the nobility. "The assembly was branded from the beginning, on the basis of its composition, as the voice of the nobility; and . . . their feudal, agrarian, and particularist interests were definitely in the foreground." [16] On the other hand, the Assembly of Notables likewise met with a poor reception from many sections of the

[14] Hardenberg to Stein, September 1810, in Pertz, *Stein*, II, 518–520.

[15] Hardenberg to the provincial governments, Dec. 27, 1810, in Steffens, *Hardenberg*, pp. 18–19. His other stated purpose, of adjusting the laws to local conditions and requirements, was obviously in conflict with his policy of unification and may therefore be taken as propaganda. Haussherr, *Die Stunde Hardenbergs*, p. 241, suggests the possibility of Westphalian inspiration for the chancellor's conception of the functions of the assembly.

[16] Steffens, *Hardenberg*, p. 196. For details on the rigging of the assembly, see *ibid.*, pp. 19, 37–38, 52–53. Originally there were eighteen nobles out of a total membership of forty-seven; but Hardenberg yielded to the clamor of some nobles and appointed twelve more, while refusing to add to the number of the other classes. Others among the reformers recognized and rejected such pandering to aristocratic privilege: Humboldt, in Gebhardt, *Humboldt*, I, 363; Gneisenau to Stein, June 26, 1811, Botzenhart, ed., *Stein*, III, 412.

nobility. The Brandenburg nobles, taking the lead in the opposition against Hardenberg, denied the competence of the government to create by fiat a new constitutional organ and were not appeased by concessions to their class in the matter of membership. The properly constituted and legitimate representative bodies in Prussia, the nobles held, were the Estates of the provinces; they welcomed the reference to a future national assembly in the decree of October 27, 1810, as proof that "our monarch is persuaded of the beneficial effect of a representative [*ständischen*] constitution"; but they wanted assurances that "if the formation of a national representative assembly should involve changes in our provincial constitutions and in our prerogatives as Estates, such changes will take place only by way of an agreement with the Estates." [17] In other words, the nobility would acquiesce in a national assembly only if it were an enlarged version of the provincial Estates, duplicating all the traditional privileges preserved in the latter, and the Assembly of Notables did not fit this prescription. Marwitz complained significantly that the Notables had been convened on an individual instead of on a class basis. [18]

With such arguments the deputies of the Estates of the Kurmark (one of the divisions of the province of Brandenburg) extracted from Hardenberg permission to hold informal meetings of their own whose results would be submitted to him. [19] Thus there existed simultaneously in Berlin two separate representative bodies, one national and the other provincial, one appointed and the other elected. [20] The deputies, however, held that they alone were true representatives of their constituents; the Notables were merely an agency of the government, and any attempt on the government's part to obtrude them as a representative body was an imposture and an in-

---

[17] Memorandum of the deputies of the Kurmark Estates to Hardenberg, Jan. 22, 1811, Meusel, ed., *Marwitz*, II[1], 230. For the provincial aspect of opposition, see the memorandum of Finckenstein, December 1810, *ibid.*, II[1], 183; and cf. *ibid.*, II[1], 227–228.

[18] *Ibid.*, II[2], 97, n. 2.   [19] *Ibid.*, II[1], 213.

[20] I shall follow the example of Steffens, *Hardenberg*, p. 18, n. 1, in referring to "Notables" and "deputies."

vasion of the rights of the provincial Estates. "Whereas you [the Notables] have been called to give advice, our function is to protect rights, those of our constituents and among them your own." [21]

In this way the Assembly of Notables, which had been intended by Hardenberg as a means of subduing opposition, had instead become a bone of contention between the nobles who led that opposition and the chancellor. Nevertheless, the Notables can aspire to a modest place in the constitutional history of Prussia. They had the temerity to take their position as a national assembly seriously. They requested, in the modern parliamentary tradition of budget debates, technical financial evidence of the need for the new taxes imposed by the decrees of October 1810, instead of merely accepting the government's gloss on the laws. Hardenberg seemed quite unprepared for this Frankensteinlike turning of the creature on its creator. He by no means intended, he scolded them,

to make the right to levy taxes itself the subject of discussion by representatives. The kings of Prussia have never submitted the question of the amount of revenue required to provincial Estates or deputies. . . . Your presumptuous demand that the sovereign divest himself of his prerogatives, at this time when all patriots gather trustingly about the throne, is unconstitutional and arrogant in the extreme. [22]

Despite such rebuffs the Notables settled down to an objective consideration of the new tax laws. They arrived at very temperate conclusions, proposing various modifications in the laws but without any marked spirit of general hostility. Hardenberg received their reports and promised to consider them, adjourning the assembly until such time as amendments in the light of their suggestions could be formulated. In fact he did not reconvene them for many months, and then he merely had the revised legislation read to them without permitting any debate. Thereupon the Assembly of Notables was dissolved. [23]

[21] Kurmark deputies to Kurmark Notables, Jan. 21, 1811, *ibid.,* pp. 48–49.

[22] Quoted without date by Zeeden, *Hardenberg,* p. 122, n. 26.

[23] For details on the meetings and conclusions of the Assembly of Notables,

Clearly the complaint of one of Stein's faithful correspondents was justified, "that the present administration has abandoned the path you blazed . . . , that everything ostensibly designed to improve the constitution . . . has in reality only a financial purpose." [24] Hardenberg never intended the Assembly of Notables as a step in the direction of parliamentary government. He who had created the assembly took scarcely more notice of it than the Brandenburg nobles who disputed his right to create it. But despite the chancellor's negative attitude and despite shortcomings both in composition and in achievement, the Notables were not altogether without their effect on the future constitutional development of Prussia. They were the first consultative body ever to meet in that country on a national rather than a provincial basis; "and just because the Notables were not genuine representatives of the nation, the feeling of a need for a really representative assembly was kept alive," not least among the Notables themselves.[25] They had the satisfaction of being present at the birth of their successors; moreover, they had succeeded in considerably modifying Hardenberg's agrarian legislation.[26]

Yet it remains true that the Assembly of Notables occupied a distinctly secondary place during the few months of its existence. The real issues were being joined elsewhere. Arising originally, like the Notables, out of the fiscal laws of October 1810, the struggle between Hardenberg and the nobility had already, even before the assembly met, ceased to be merely financial and had taken on all the appearances of a constitutional crisis. This transformation was due in very large measure to Friedrich August Ludwig von der Marwitz, the most ardent defender of political feudalism among the Prussian nobility.

---

see Mamroth, *Geschichte der preussischen Staats-Besteuerung*, pp. 458–468; and Bornhak, "Preussische Finanzreform," p. 604.

[24] Schleiermacher to Stein, summer 1811, Botzenhart, ed., *Stein*, III, 423.

[25] Stern, *Abhandlungen und Aktenstücke*, p. 171.

[26] For details, see below, pp. 105 and 90.

Marwitz

Marwitz has always been singled out from among all the conservative Prussian noblemen of the early nineteenth century for special attention by historians, and a source collection centered in his person has been published.[27] This interest is justified for the reason that Marwitz, although he abhorred political theory and theorists,[28] himself developed and eloquently stated a set of political principles. While he accused Hardenberg of importing and perverting the ideas of Adam Smith to apply to a country where economic conditions were not suited to them, he combated him with the theories of another Briton, Edmund Burke.[29] Part of his opposition to the chancellor, no doubt, was caused by personal antagonism: Marwitz, scion of a long line of soldiers and petty rural nobles, instinctively disliked the urbane and sophisticated cosmopolitan, whom he described as shrewd and charming but careless and fickle.[30] But above all, Marwitz regarded Hardenberg as a real and dangerous revolutionary, who was subverting "the old constitution of the nation, which is still legally in force, though at present lying in obscurity." [31]

By this phrase Marwitz meant not so much the state of Frederick the Great as the Brandenburg of the days before

[27] Cited above, Chap. II, n. 4; see also the bibliography. It may be remarked in passing that Marwitz, since become the archetype of the Prussian Junker, hailed not from East Prussia, the legendary breeding ground of Junkers, but from the vicinity of Frankfurt on the Oder.

[28] "We must never admit that theory is of any value in affairs of state. Theory is for academic people. The state is a phenomenon in time and must therefore always be considered from a practical point of view. Politics must be based solely on history and experience." Marwitz in 1821, in Ernst Müsebeck, "Die märkische Ritterschaft und die preussische Verfassungsfrage von 1814 bis 1820," *Deutsche Rundschau,* 174 (1918), 166.

[29] For Marwitz' indictment of Hardenberg, see Meusel, ed., *Marwitz,* I, 532. Marwitz was not, of course, the man who developed Burke's theories in Germany to the fullest extent. In this connection one would turn to Adam Müller (see below, pp. 70–76) and to the Swiss Carl Ludwig von Haller and his monumental *Restauration der Staats-Wissenschaft* (Winterthur, 1816–1825).

[30] Meusel, ed., *Marwitz,* I, 529. [31] *Ibid.,* I, 532–533.

the Great Elector,[32] the days when the nobility shared political power with the electors in a semifeudal system. Marwitz and his colleagues laid great stress on the fact that the constitution effective during that time, far from having been legally abolished had been formally and repeatedly upheld, and as recently as 1798, at the accession of the reigning monarch.[33] Marwitz maintained in an address to the king, in genuine feudal style, that the Estates were the king's free vassals, not his blindly subservient subjects. Changes in the constitution could be made only by free agreement between king and Estates. The Estates were willing, Marwitz asserted, to assume new burdens and to sacrifice some of their constitutional rights, but only if they were consulted and if a new contract replaced the old. "Their property is nothing to them, but their free existence everything." [34]

Marwitz and his friends thus had in mind a dual aim: negatively, and in the short run, to confound Hardenberg by declaring his laws unconstitutional; positively, and in the long run, to achieve the restoration of "legitimate" government under a constitution which had been in abeyance for one hundred and fifty years before Hardenberg's advent. It was a constitution which denied equally the legality of absolute monarchy and the right of anyone except the traditional Estates of the Realm to restrain the monarch; parliamentarianism was as odious as absolutism:

[32] The contrary was suggested by Willy Andreas, "Marwitz und der Staat Friedrichs des Grossen," *Historische Zeitschrift*, 122 (1920), 44–82.

[33] In the "Assekurationsakte" of that year. For a brief review of these repeated guarantees, beginning with the "Rezess" of the Great Elector in 1653, see Heinrich Simon, *Das preussische Staatsrecht* (Breslau, 1844), II, 128–130. In practice, reduction of the nobility's political prerogatives had been balanced by a considerable improvement since the sixteenth century in their economic and social position on the land and by the opportunities reserved for them in the army. This pattern is clearest in the reign of the Great Elector himself: see F. L. Carsten, "The Great Elector and the Foundation of the Hohenzollern Despotism," *English Historical Review*, LXV (1950), 185–187, 197–199. The nobility, however, were not wont to emphasize these compensations.

[34] Marwitz to the king, Feb. 17, 1811, Meusel, ed., *Marwitz*, II¹, 289–290.

It can be neither just nor useful for every individual in the state to be represented [wrote Marwitz]. Not just, because the state must desire the good of the whole; whereas most individuals, though they are a part of the whole, yet have no idea wherein it consists, but strive, rather, always for their private advantage. . . . Not useful, because no good can ever come of the representation of the stupidity and indifference [Bewusstlosigkeit] characteristic of most people. It is, rather, the inner principle inspiring the life of each class that must be represented.[35]

The implication was, of course, that the nobility could and would represent the "life principle" of all the classes without representing their lack of intelligence. Yet Marwitz was acutely conscious of the failure of the nobility in recent decades to perform this function, and he knew that by no means all of his noble colleagues cared as much for matters of principle as he did.[36] The remedy, however, lay not in curtailing the aristocracy's privileges but rather in reviving in them a sense of the responsibilities of their historic position as the indispensable "intermediary class" in a monarchical state:

The true intermediary class between the king and the people is the landowners or Estates [Landesstände], distinguished by prerogatives. . . . A monarchy cannot maintain itself without an intermediary class thus distinguished. The essence of monarchy consists in one man commanding and many men obeying. But since the masses have a natural instinct not to obey, coercive regulations are necessary. . . . The masses can be restrained only by intermediaries . . . in whose own interest it is to prevent the masses from achieving unity.

The "distinguishing prerogatives" are necessary to secure respect for the intermediaries' authority; they must be consti-

[35] Marwitz' criticism of Stein's Political Testament, written Jan.–Feb. 1811, ibid., II¹, 244–245.

[36] "Let us not," Marwitz wrote, "be blind to the faults of our own class. Let us admit that if the provincial Estates had complete freedom of discussion, . . . they would grant no taxes at all. . . . They would display their shameful selfishness." At a time when the pressure of the French made it imperative to pay the indemnity, money must somehow be obtained and the Estates must grant what is asked; once the pressure was relieved, the nobility might establish their legal rights (Marwitz in a memorandum dated Dec. 8, 1810, ibid., II¹, 185–187).

tutionally guaranteed and must include participation in government and exemption from taxes.[37]

The Kleist Circle and Adam Müller

Marwitz was a practical man first and a theorist second. He was accustomed to express himself with unvarnished candor and almost deliberately eschewed the path of diplomacy, which he tended to identify with his adversary Hardenberg. But there was a group among the conservatives of a more abstract and also a more tactful bent, which through its most effective spokesman, Adam Müller, made common cause with Marwitz and his colleagues. This society, the *christlich-deutsche Tischgesellschaft,* was catholic in its membership but nonetheless cohesive in its goal, which might be defined as the maintenance of German individuality and German traditions. In the circumstances of the first decade of the nineteenth century, this object could be reached chiefly by two means: liberation from the French conquerors and defeat of the native innovators who threatened the heritage of the German past.

But the members of the society were intent upon preserving that heritage not so much for political as for emotional reasons. They had a deep respect for history and a romantic reverence for the past. The journal *Berliner Abendblätter,* through which its views reached a larger audience, was edited by the poet Heinrich von Kleist and had a markedly literary flavor. Kleist was a profoundly sincere patriot with a special attachment for the remote German past (his play *Die Hermannsschlacht* concerned, of course, the ancient Germanic hero Arminius), and on this account he resented radical departures from German tradition. Another important member of the society was the poet Achim von Arnim, one of the coauthors of the collection of German legends and folklore *Des*

[37] Marwitz' essay "Über die Notwendigkeit eines Mittelstandes in einer Monarchie," written in December 1810, *ibid.,* II¹, 194–200. Cf. the analogous reasoning of his attack on Stein's Emancipation Edict, *ibid.,* II¹, 240: "Serfdom was not a remnant of slavery. . . . It was, rather, a patriarchal bond linking the peasant to the noble, a bond which inculcated into the minds of the lowest class the idea of a higher law and nobler customs, and respect for a more civilized form of life."

Knaben Wunderhorn; the group also counted among its number such scholars as Fichte, Savigny, and Eichhorn. Generally speaking, these men were temperamentally opposed to any reform, although Achim von Arnim was an admirer of Stein who considered that Hardenberg was not carrying on the reform movement in Stein's spirit, while Fichte in his own way was as thoroughgoing an innovator as any and had a special affinity with such a humanist reformer as Humboldt.

Adam Müller, by profession a political theorist and the author of one of the classic German statements of conservatism,[38] was less straightforward than most of the other members in his motives for joining Kleist's circle. In 1809 he had applied to the Prussian government for employment as a political publicist. His plan was to edit an official journal explaining and defending the government's measures, and at the same time to publish, with secret official connivance, an "opposition" journal designed to take the wind out of the sails of the genuine opposition, especially of the extreme factions. The Altenstein-Dohna government liked the idea but seemed to have vague misgivings about it, with the characteristic result that in May 1810 Müller was finally put on the government payroll but without authority to start his editorial labors. After Hardenberg came to power in the following month, Müller again repeatedly offered his services, but Hardenberg declined to take him off the ice. Then when Kleist began to publish the *Berliner Abendblätter* in October, Müller abandoned his efforts to defend the government and decided instead to attack it; and he became a regular contributor to the *Abendblätter*. At the same time he blandly began to seek another official position, the chancellorship of the University of Frankfurt on the Oder. This application also was refused, Hardenberg's minister of the interior asserting that he did not know of any qualifications Müller had for appointment even as a lecturer (a patent injustice, in view of the *Elemente der Staatskunst*). But Müller was making enough of a nuisance of himself in Prussia for Hardenberg finally to get rid of him by appointing him his private representative in Vienna to explore the possi-

[38] *Die Elemente der Staatskunst* (Berlin, 1809).

bilities of a revolt against Napoleon. The chancellor was presumably not greatly distressed that Müller did not take his assignment very seriously and before long entered the Austrian diplomatic service.[39]

Opportunist though he was, it would be unfair to suppose that Müller's sudden entry into the ranks of the opposition against Hardenberg was dictated entirely or even primarily by pique. On the contrary, his earlier efforts to co-operate with the government were much less in character, for his political ideas were as sharply opposed to Hardenberg's as were those of Marwitz. Müller had arrived by a different route at much the same conclusions as Marwitz and his landowning brethren: the supreme importance of land and agriculture in the political as well as the economic structure of the country.

At the root of Müller's political theory was the organic concept of the state and society; if the state is recognized as an organism any radical measures to improve it are precluded. "It is the chief task of statesmanship always to keep the past generations alive for the present, never to lose sight of the immortality and the totality of political life." [40] The living symbol of the past is the nobility (just as the bourgeoisie represents the present); therefore "the nobility is the first and only necessary political institution in the state; *vis-à-vis* individual men and their ephemeral power, it represents the power and the freedom of the invisible and absent members of society." [41] But the nobility occupied this unique position by virtue of its historic connection with the land. Agriculture was the activity binding a nation's past with its future; it was the foundation of the patriarchal element in society; it was a "natural" activity contrasted with the "artificial" pursuits of commerce.[42]

[39] For these biographical data on Müller, see Jakob Baxa, *Adam Müller: Ein Lebensbild aus den Befreiungskriegen und der deutschen Restauration* (Jena, 1930), pp. 123–130, 140–142, 149–152, 164–165, 175–179. See also the sociological analysis of Müller and other conservatives in Karl Mannheim, *Essays on Sociology and Social Psychology* (London, 1953), pp. 119–133. In my opinion, Mannheim begs more questions than he answers, besides classifying Müller, wrongly I think but in good company, as a romantic.

[40] Müller, *Elemente der Staatskunst,* I, 256, 269–270.

[41] *Ibid.,* I, 264–266.

[42] Friedrich Lenz, *Agrarlehre und Agrarpolitik der deutschen Romantik*

It was therefore against those who would deprive agriculture of this historic function that Adam Müller was most violently opposed. Many of his articles in the *Berliner Abendblätter* consisted of attacks on Hardenberg thinly veiled as attacks against Adam Smith and his Prussian disciples Kraus and Thaer; [43] and to their economic individualism Müller opposed the economic corollary of the organic state, corporatism, with the nobility the most important corporation:

People nowadays conceive of the national wealth as nothing but the sum of all private fortunes; and from this absurd postulate they deduce the absurd conclusion that the several constituent parts of this sum, the separate private fortunes, could exist without being, in fact, parts of the sum, or in other words, could exist without a national wealth that encompasses and protects them all.[44]

Because of the nature of land, possession of it constitutes a trusteeship, and its owners have in it not only a physical but a moral property. When one speaks of protecting property rights, therefore, one must include both physical and moral property, and physical and moral property owners:

Moral persons, such as communities, corporations, and Estates, are not merely machines which can be discarded at will like useless things, when it seems to be to the advantage of physical persons. . . . These moral persons . . . are necessary intermediaries between the individual and the whole (i.e. the state or its symbol, the sovereign).[45]

It was, therefore, a natural consequence of his political thinking, as well as of his snubbing at the hands of Hardenberg,

(Berlin, 1912), pp. 80–87; cf. also *ibid.*, pp. 97–101, 161. The literature of political romanticism is, of course, vast; I would mention the exceptionally fine analysis of Schnabel, *Deutsche Geschichte,* I, 306–315, and the warning of the dangers of generalization in Paul Kluckhohn, *Persönlichkeit und Gemeinschaft: Studien zur Staatsauffassung der deutschen Romantik* (Halle, 1925), pp. 98–102.

[43] Baxa, *Adam Müller,* pp. 154–163; cf. Haussherr, *Die Stunde Hardenbergs,* pp. 280–281.

[44] Adam Müller, *Vermischte Schriften über Staat, Philosophie und Kunst* (Vienna, 1817), I, 76.

[45] Memorandum of Müller dated October 1810, Meusel, ed., *Marwitz,* II¹, 159–160. Note Müller's reference to the intermediary class as a probable source of Marwitz' essay on the subject (cf. above, p. 69).

that Adam Müller made overtures to Marwitz and his colleagues
among the Brandenburg nobles. They enlisted his literary
talents to draw up a comprehensive complaint against Hardenberg and specifically against his legislation of October 1810.
The document he produced, although itself of little practical
consequence, deserves its outstanding place in the opposition
literature of 1811 for its good sense, for its conciseness, and not
least for its disarming phraseology, with which Müller attempted to win over Hardenberg.

Müller began his memorandum with a review of Prussia's
situation when Hardenberg took office. She was under Napoleon's heel but had preserved her ancient institutions: "Prussian customs and laws could still continue in the old European
tradition; Prussia need not have sunk to the level of the newfangled states without form or foundation, which have only
an army, a police force, and a present, but no past and no
future." Müller flatteringly implied that Hardenberg was not
alone responsible for this deterioration, since part of the blame
lay with his predecessors. The chancellor had done well to
centralize power in his own hands and to promise a *ständisch*
representative constitution, but he was handicapped by a dual
set of laws, the old ones of Frederick the Great and the new
ones of Stein, though the latter were incomplete:

Herr von Stein, a great planner, though more able in planning than
in execution, had, besides, the misfortune of having no time for
execution and of having successors who spun intellectual webs of his
material, with great assiduity and good will, but without any practical vision. . . . The indolent, well-meaning administration that
preceded Your Excellency had not recognized the great verity that
to reorganize the Prussian state meant nothing else but to reorganize
the nobility and to reform the laws concerning land ownership. The
landowner was oppressed by all the perils of the day; . . . from one
direction economic ruin threatened him, and from the other direction his invisible birthright was being increasingly called into question by the *Zeitgeist*.

Turning now to the tax laws, the nobles agreed (through
the pen of Müller) that the king and the government had the
right to determine the amount of taxes necessary; but they

insisted on "the incontestable aristocratic privilege" of contributing taxes voluntarily on the basis of honorable and free negotiation between the king and themselves, "not as an enforced levy." Concerning the larger constitutional issues of the controversy, the nobles declared that they did not demand retention of the existing laws *in toto*, but rather retention and revival of "the traditional European spirit of our constitution, which consisted in the impossibility of dissolving contracts except by contracts, and in preference in cases of doubt for the *status quo*, on the basis of its successful survival through the centuries."

We are far from desiring a share of the legislative power which belongs without restrictions to our lord and king; we ask only that the great domestic affairs of the state be discussed and evaluated at annual meetings of a central consultative assembly based on Estates, partly elected from among the chief classes of the people, partly appointed by right of birth.

The nobles further asked for "the maintenance, revival, and wise modification of the provincial constitutions of this country. The various provinces differ too widely to permit of their treatment as a unit in financial and legislative matters." They conceded, however, that the provincial constitutions must allow room for an eventual development of national unity. Finally, the nobles expressed their belief that the state could be preserved only if "the old conditions of property holding and the traditional relationships of the various agricultural lands one to another" were kept inviolate. Under this heading they sought confirmation not only of the existing owners in their holdings but also of patrimonial justice, and apparently they even contemplated repeal of the emancipation of the serfs ("*Alle Dienst- und Unterthänigkeits-Verhältnisse*" were to continue).[46]

Despite Müller's persuasiveness on their behalf, when his

---

[46] Müller's memorandum, dated Feb. 11, 1811, is printed in full in Meusel, ed., *Marwitz*, II¹, 252–262, and with some imperfections in [Wilhelm Dorow, ed.,] *Denkschriften und Briefe zur Charakteristik der Welt und Litteratur* (Berlin, 1838–41), III, 220–234. For the circumstances of its composition and signing, see *ibid.*, III, 216–217.

completed draft was submitted to the nobles who had commissioned it, none among them would risk official displeasure
by putting their signatures to it except Marwitz; and it therefore went to Hardenberg in his name alone. As a result, the
memorandum had a far smaller practical effect than it deserved.
Nevertheless, the later phases of the crisis of 1811 produced
few arguments that had not been marshaled by Adam Müller;
the difference between his document and subsequent conservative attacks on Hardenberg lay more in the increased
sharpness of the latter than in the novelty of their ideas.[47] Indeed, as the rift between the chancellor and the nobility
widened, the constitutional crisis passed over from the sphere
of words increasingly into the sphere of action.

Hardenberg, the Nobles, and the Resolution of the Crisis

Since in 1811 the noble opposition, for reasons both geographical and historical, had its nucleus in Brandenburg,[48] and
since the Brandenburg nobility were increasingly led and symbolized by Marwitz, certain personal experiences of the latter
came to assume considerable public importance. It happened
that Marwitz administered on behalf of the Kurmark Estates
the provincial fund for relief of the poor (*Landarmenkasse*),
which had been entrusted to the Estates for centuries. Suddenly
Hardenberg ordered this fund to be surrendered to the government, and Marwitz refused. Thereupon, on February 13,
1811, in Marwitz' absence, the safe in which the money was
kept was forcibly opened by government agents and the funds

[47] See for instance the lengthy complaint written by Finckenstein, dated
May 18, 1811, on behalf of the nobles of Kreis Priegnitz, Meusel, ed.,
Marwitz, II¹, 339–351. All the arguments are familiar: unconstitutional
flouting of noble privileges, provincial particularism, need for an "intermediary class," etc.

[48] This is not to say that the other provinces did not contribute at all.
Cf. Steffens, *Hardenberg*, pp. 37–39, and see, e.g., the memorandum of the
Silesian nobles in R. Röpell, "Zur inneren Geschichte Preussens in den
Jahren 1811–12," *Uebersicht der Arbeiten und Veränderungen der schle-
sischen Gesellschaft für vaterländische Kultur im Jahre 1847* (Breslau, 1848),
pp. 341–348.

removed. On his return Marwitz immediately drafted a memorandum to the king which was signed by the Kurmark deputies
in Berlin, asserting that the Estates were willing to confer
on such matters as the transfer of the fund but that they strenu-
ously objected to highhanded and unilateral action by the government and to the use of force; and they requested an opportunity to negotiate "with some statesman or other" on this
incident and on any similar moves that might be contemplated
by the authorities.

The king's reply (drafted by one of Hardenberg's assistants,
Friedrich von Raumer) began by denying the plaintiffs' right
to style themselves "deputies of the Kurmark Estates" (despite
Hardenberg's specific permission for them to meet). As to the
change in administration of the relief fund, "that is, as to my
power as sovereign to order such a change, purely on the
grounds of my personal convictions and wishes, without the
agreement of any class among my subjects, I will allow no discussion whatsover." The document goes on to deny the contractual basis of the Estates' administration of the fund and
therefore their right to be consulted about its transfer.[49] Subsequently Marwitz went to see the minister of justice, Friedrich
von Kircheisen, in an effort to obtain judicial satisfaction of
his claim to the funds, but the minister placed the blame on
the Estates for putting the government in a position where it
had to force locks. The formal guarantees of the constitution
with respect to the fund had, he said, been superseded by events,
times had changed, and no court would uphold Marwitz' claim
any more. The latter's reaction is eloquently stated in his
description of Kircheisen as "the most contemptible wretch
I have ever seen." [50] Marwitz' mood was not improved when,
a few weeks later, again in his absence, a government official
appeared on his estate and persuaded the village mayor to
assume responsibility for collecting taxes on the estate in pur-
suance of the tax laws of October 1810. Marwitz took this in-

[49] For undiscoverable reasons, this letter was never actually sent off.

[50] For the episode of the *Landarmenkasse*, see Meusel, ed., *Marwitz*, II¹,
277–287.

cident as an insult to his position as owner of the estate and once again denounced the government's actions as highhanded and illegal.[51]

In the mood produced by these two incidents, Marwitz composed the most famous document of the noble revolt against Hardenberg in 1811, the so-called "Eingabe der Lebus-Beeskow-Storkowschen Stände." [52] The arguments are familiar: the laws of October 27 and 28, 1810, violated the constitutionally guaranteed contractual rights of the nobility, and they were the product of theorizing alien to Prussian conditions. Moreover, the promise of a representative assembly contained in that legislation was irrelevant, since representative institutions already existed in Prussia (the provincial Estates). The laws would equalize all classes and thereby eliminate the necessary "intermediary class." Land, instead of being the surest anchorage of the nation's stability, would become fluid. Soon it would all be in the hands of Jews, who would "become as landowners the principle representatives of the state, and so our venerable old Brandenburg-Prussia will become a newfangled Jew-state."

Then the signatory nobles, having reviewed all their fruitless past complaints and attempts to obtain an audience of the king, declared:

In view of these facts we have no choice but to yield to force. . . . But we wish to make it clear . . . that we yield only to force, that we have not divested ourselves of our legally acquired and firmly established prerogatives but on the contrary regard them as still in effect, until such time as Your Royal Majesty will see fit to negotiate new contracts with us concerning those of our privileges which may appear contrary to the public good and thereby to remove them *legally.*

The plaintiffs then turned their full wrath on Hardenburg and especially on one of his advisers, Raumer, like the chancellor not a native Prussian:

[51] *Ibid.,* II[1], 308–313.

[52] *Ibid.,* II[2], 3–22. Completed on March 22, 1811, the document was accepted by an assembly of the nobles of the districts mentioned in the title on May 9 and given to the king's secretary on June 10 (*ibid.,* II[2], 3, n. 1).

Instead of consulting *before the execution* of the laws with natives, who know and have their roots in the country and are hence devoted to it, the young foreigners who exercise influence on Your Royal Majesty's ministers have been permitted to experiment with their outlandish theories on *our* country. . . .

Hardenberg, to whom the king conveyed this document, wrote down his reactions in a series of marginal notes.[53] The chancellor was far from edified. Attacking the nobles' arguments, he maintained that the traditional Estates, which had not been consulted on important affairs of state for over a century, were obsolete and that new representative institutions were therefore necessary, that the perpetuation of provincial constitutional distinctions would strengthen provincial selfishness, and that noble landowners no longer had any right to special financial privileges but must take their place as citizens in common with the rest of the population. If the nobles wanted to form the "intermediary class," they would have to demonstrate their worth "by superior culture, by patriotism, and by noble deeds."

But Hardenberg did not content himself with an objective rebuttal of the nobles' reasoning. He felt their complaint as a personal assault on himself and on the government. An attack on a minister, he shrewdly pointed out, was at the same time an attack on the king from whom he derived his authority. He therefore urged the king to institute disciplinary measures against the originators of the offending document. A small number of noble landowners, the chancellor wrote, had attacked royal decrees and the principles on which they were built and had demanded a share in ruling the country. If this claim were admitted,

then practically everything that has been done by the glorious rulers of Prussia since the Great Elector would be invalid. They [the nobles] act as if they spoke as the representatives of the people, whereas in reality they are defending their own privileges to the detriment of the [rest of the] people.

The authority of the government, Hardenberg concluded, was at stake (even the French ambassador had commented on the

[53] Preserved in the margin in Meusel's edition, *ibid.*

seditious nature of the nobles' complaint), and half measures
were useless. He therefore recommended that Marwitz, the
author of the memorandum, and Finckenstein, whose signa-
ture appeared at the top of the list, be imprisoned and that those
of the other signers who were government officials be dismissed.[54] The second recommendation was suspended, but the
first was carried out; and for a month Marwitz and Finckenstein resided under firm though genteel guard in the fortress
of Spandau.[55] Marwitz was being punished as the symbol of
the noble opposition, but he was well aware by that time that
in fact he represented very few besides himself.[56] The basis
of his own stand against the government, he realized, was
juridical, that Hardenberg's acts were unconstitutional; while
his colleagues objected primarily on economic grounds, that
Hardenberg's acts involved them in financial loss. For him the
form of the legislation was crucial and the content secondary;
for them the order was reversed. He doubted whether, if the
fiscal decrees had not hurt them economically, most of his
fellow nobles would have been much concerned about their
legality.[57]

There were also those among the nobility who doubted the
wisdom of resistance to the government's program on any
grounds, whether principled or selfish. One leading Branden-

[54] Hardenberg to the king, June 23, 1811, Meusel, ed., *Marwitz*, II[1],
24–26.

[55] In the meantime, retribution less humiliating but more permanent had
been visited on the other principal organ of the opposition to Hardenberg's
government. On March 30, 1811, Kleist was obliged, on Hardenberg's personal orders, to cease publication of the *Berliner Abendblätter,* after only
six months of its existence. Shortly thereafter, Kleist, a melancholy soul,
committed suicide. On the whole episode of the *Berliner Abendblätter,* see
Steig, *Kleist's Berliner Kämpfe, passim,* and cf. Haussherr, *Die Stunde
Hardenbergs,* pp. 275–285.

[56] His colleagues made only halfhearted attempts to obtain Marwitz'
release from Spandau, which provoked him into a furious outburst against
them: Meusel, ed., *Marwitz*, II[1], 37–43; cf. *ibid.,* II[2], 112–115.

[57] Marwitz to his fellow deputies, May 29, 1811, *ibid.,* II[1], 334–338. He
still remembered, of course, his experience with the memorandum written
by Adam Müller, for which he was eventually forced to take sole responsibility.

burg aristocrat, for example, declared that the privileges of the nobility had grown historically out of the feudal military relationship between the lord and his vassals and that since this relationship had disappeared with the rise of standing armies there was no longer any justification for maintaining those privileges.[58] Another prominent patrician defended the government's coercive measures on the ground that "the great majority of our noble comrades are so illiberal that they will scarcely be persuaded to make voluntary sacrifices." [59] It is important to remember this progressive group among the nobility, since the temptation is sometimes great to speak about "the nobility" *tout court* as reactionary, without maintaining distinctions within that class.[60]

But if the nobility were not united during the crisis of 1811, neither was the government consistent in its reaction to the opposition. Hardenberg's disciplining of Marwitz and Finckenstein was not simply a logical extension, in response to extreme provocation, of a policy previously applied with greater moderation. On the contrary, it was an unpredictable action, bearing all the marks of a sudden burst of anger on the part of a man whose plans have miscarried.[61]

A review of Hardenberg's policy since the publication of the October decrees will clarify this point. In the first place, the whole scheme concerning the Assembly of Notables had been basically conciliatory in nature. However cynical may have been Hardenberg's idea of using the assembly to prepare

[58] Prittwitz to Marwitz, Dec. 6, 1810, *ibid.,* II[1], 187. Curiously, Prittwitz had been the leader of that faction at the meeting of the Brandenburg Estates in 1809 which fought for the nobility's right to make their own tax assessment, and Marwitz at that time had described this demand as selfish (cf. above, p. 48, n. 12).

[59] Count Arnim-Boytzenburg to Marwitz, Dec. 12, 1810, *ibid.,* II[1], 191. Cf. also Arnim's letter to Stein, summer 1811, Botzenhart, ed., *Stein,* III, 419–423.

[60] Once again it may be wise to recall that most of the reformers themselves were aristocrats.

[61] Hardenberg "sent the most extreme spokesmen of the aristocratic opposition . . . to Spandau; but he met the class as a whole halfway" (Erich Marcks, *Aufstieg des Reiches,* I, 37 f., quoted in Zeeden, *Hardenberg,* p. 110, n. 1).

the ground for executing the fiscal laws, still it implied some degree of deference to public opinion; and even more direct a peace offering was his permission for informal meetings of the deputies of the Kurmark Estates, followed by an expression of "confidence" in the deputies.[62] Yet simultaneously Hardenberg greeted the Assembly of Notables, the potential purveyors of good will for the government, with a lecture on the recalcitrance and selfishness of the provincial Estates and of the nobility in general, which was not likely to dispose the noble members of the assembly favorably toward him.[63] In the course of the succeeding months the chancellor executed two complete reverses of policy toward the opposition, from adamant to conciliatory and back again.[64]

In this vacillating course of action Hardenberg seemed to be able to count on the king's acquiescence.[65] He apparently had no difficulty in obtaining the king's consent to the imprisonment of Marwitz and Finckenstein; on the other hand, at the height of the government's controversy with Marwitz the king issued a Cabinet Order, presumably inspired or at least assented to by Hardenberg, which stressed the injustice of imposing a uniform tax throughout the country in view of local and provincial differences in the price of grain.[66] Here was an official vindication of provincial particularism, in de-

[62] Hardenberg to Pannwitz, Feb. 23, 1811, Steffens, *Hardenberg*, p. 51.

[63] Hardenberg's opening speech to the Notables, Feb. 23, 1811, quoted in excerpts in Meusel, ed., *Marwitz*, II², 135–141.

[64] In June he recommended the imprisonment of Marwitz and Finckenstein. In November, in consideration of the "loyal and liberal behavior of the noble representatives in the recent national assembly" (whom he had studiously ignored), he agreed to confiscate a pamphlet hostile to the nobility (Hardenberg to Count Henckel von Donnersmarck, Nov. 8, 1811, in Steffens, *Hardenberg*, pp. 84–85). In December, as proof of his affability, he suspended a local association of Silesian landlords because it was allegedly tending to become "an association of the entire nobility for selfish ends" (Otto Linke, *Friedrich Theodor von Merckel im Dienste fürs Vaterland* [Breslau, 1907–10], II, 191).

[65] "Hardenberg had the king completely under his thumb" (Schnabel, *Deutsche Geschichte*, I, 462).

[66] Cabinet Order of June 18, 1811, in Mamroth, *Geschichte der preussischen Staats-Besteuerung*, p. 469.

fense of which, in part, Marwitz had written the document for which he was sent to prison.

Hardenberg's own analysis of his policy toward the opposition was that his concessions were merely formal, while on questions of content he did not yield.[67] This analysis implies that by concessions in matters of form he bought the nobles' support in matters of content; or to put it another way, that by concessions to their formal constitutional demands he silenced their material economic demands. If this was indeed his policy, it was a mistaken one, based on the deceptive personal prominence of Marwitz, which concealed the defection of most of his followers; for Marwitz himself was under no delusions that any large numbers of the Prussian or even only of the Brandenburg nobility would, when it came to a test, emulate his willingness to give up economic in return for political privileges. But in fact Hardenberg's own description of his policy does not seem accurate. It was, after all, Marwitz who was a victim of Hardenberg's severest measure of reprisal, taken for constitutional and not for economic demands; and Hardenberg's own report to the king made it clear enough that he was not greatly concerned whether opposition took a constitutional or an economic stand but only whether or not it threatened his authority.[68]

It is, in fact, very easy to show that Hardenberg's concessions to the nobility were by no means confined to formalities. The proof is to be found in the ultimate fate of the financial legislation of October 27 and 28, 1810, which had originally been the cause of the whole oppositional movement. The results of almost a year's pressure against that legislation were embodied in the new law which superseded it, the so-called Additional Edict of September 7, 1811.[69] The most significant provision of this decree was the tacit reaffirmation of noble exemption from the land tax (para. 6), that feature of the old tax system against which the chancellor had most frequently

---

[67] Hardenberg to Stein, July 11, 1811, Botzenhart, ed., *Stein*, III, 427.

[68] Cited above, n. 54.

[69] "Fernerweites Edikt über die Finanzen des Staats und das Abgaben-System," printed in the *Gesetz-Sammlung* for 1810–11, pp. 253–262.

inveighed. The conciliatory purpose of the decree was evident in the tone of the preamble:

We have given much attention to the statements and suggestions submitted to us . . . concerning various changes in the tax system. Always inclined to heed the wishes of our loyal Estates and subjects, . . . we gladly mitigate or abolish altogether those taxes which appear to be most onerous, replacing them with more acceptable ones.

The system of taxation introduced last year, as well as all other recent legislation, rests on the foundations of equality before the law, unrestricted use and free disposition of landed property, freedom of trade, cessation of trading monopolies, taxation on uniform principles for all . . . ; and these foundations will by no means be abandoned . . . ; but we wish to attain our ends, not with shattering blows, not without compensation for the abolition of traditional privileges, but rather by slower and surer means.

Among the other specific provisions of the law, besides recognition of tax exemption for nobles, were the imposition of a capitation tax (para. 6), a fixed sum to be paid by every person over twelve years old, and the abandonment of uniform taxation of town and country in favor of small towns and rural areas (para. 1). In a companion law the brandy monopoly was reinstated.[70]

It can scarcely be maintained that such concessions to the landed nobility were merely "formal," as Hardenberg himself asserted. On the contrary, the Additional Edict represented a retreat from Hardenberg's own fiscal principles. The idea of taxation equitably distributed among all the people, repeatedly affirmed by the chancellor and reiterated in the preamble of the decree, was disregarded in its specific provisions. The edict constituted a peace offering bordering on capitulation.

We must accordingly inquire into Hardenberg's reasons for making such concessions of principle. It will not do to dismiss the matter by saying that he was merely giving in to his own aristocratic predilections or that his devotion to reform was only skin-deep.[71] Even less will it do to beg the question

[70] "Gesetz über die polizeilichen Verhältnisse der Gewerbe, etc.," Sept. 7, 1811, paragraphs 52–53 (*Gesetz-Sammlung* for 1810–11, p. 268).

[71] Hardenberg "was too passionately fond of power to let his actions be directed by his belief in political or economic principles. . . . He, who

by maintaining that for all his concessions Hardenberg remained master of the situation.[72] Capitulation on the central point at issue is not the act of a man who is master of a situation.

Such explanations are superficial. Moreover, any explanation of Hardenberg's behavior in 1811 must remain superficial unless his agrarian policy is taken into account, which we shall do in the next chapter. But in the meantime it is essential, so far as his conduct of the political controversy with the reactionary nobles is concerned, to keep in mind both Hardenberg's political theory and his political position in Prussia. Theoretically, despite a certain ruthlessness, Hardenberg was decidedly not a radical but a moderate. He admired no more than Marwitz the radical aspects of the French Revolution; he admired, if anything, the French Empire of Napoleon. He would have liked to establish in Prussia a suitable counterpart of that regime, stripped of feudal encumbrances but free also of democratic elements. He was therefore quite sincerely unwilling to be counted among those whom Napoleon had called *idéologues*. Hardenberg himself summed up succinctly his position as a moderate: "I have to fight continuously against stupidity, prejudice, and selfishness on the one hand, and against fanaticism, extremism, and the wild play of theory [*la rage des théories*] on the other." [73] He felt himself obliged to curb the legalistic obscurantism of the reactionaries, but not to such an extent as to play into the hands of the idealistic radicals.

The chancellor was deterred from making common cause with the latter, even if he had wanted to, by his own position as an interloper between the king and the nobility, a position which was emphasized further by the fact that he was not a Prussian. In Prussia the rights and privileges of the monarchy were historically linked very closely with those of the aris-

---

came from an old noble family himself, was . . . inclined to give in to the demands of the nobility whenever he could" (Aris, *History of Political Thought in Germany,* pp. 396–397; similarly Steffens, *Hardenberg,* p. 38).

[72] Steffens, *Hardenberg,* p. 70; but elsewhere Steffens takes Hardenberg severely to task for his concessions (pp. 189, 195).

[73] Hardenberg to Stein, July 11, 1811, Botzenhart, ed., *Stein,* III, 427.

tocracy. The right of the Estates to representation and to special consideration, as Marwitz once remarked,[74] was as old
and as sacred as the king's right to rule. Neither the king nor
the chancellor could have failed to perceive this fact or the
inevitable implication that if the rights of the nobility could be
arbitrarily revoked by appeal to the *suprema lex* of the public
good, then the rights of the monarchy also were potentially
in jeopardy. Frederick William III was not the kind of man
to take such alarming possibilities anything but seriously, and
Hardenberg might well have wondered how long he would
continue to enjoy the king's confidence if he campaigned
too relentlessly against the ancient privileges of the nobility.[75]
He had been able to carry the king with him in his reprisal
against Marwitz and Finckenstein, but it was not in the monarch's nature to assent to more than isolated steps of this kind.
If the chancellor persisted, it was possible that he would merely
drive Frederick William into a coalition with the nobility.
Such an alliance would, after all, be a more natural one than
that between the king and the chancellor, with his modern
theories of government; even after the rise of absolutism the
kings and their loyal Estates had usually settled their differences
en famille.[76]

The answer to this kind of reasoning is that nothing could
be gained by not putting the matter to the test. Stein, for
example, would in Hardenberg's position undoubtedly have
stood firm on the question of the land tax exemption. What
the result would have been it is impossible to say with assurance; [77] but it could have been no worse, from the point of

[74] Marwitz' comment, occasioned by Hardenberg's speech opening the
Assembly of Notables, Meusel, ed., *Marwitz*, II[1], 318. Cf. Hardenberg's
own view of the matter, above, pp. 62–63.

[75] In practice, of course, demotion of the nobility was not likely to result
in any direct danger to monarchy. Absolute monarchy had been able, in
western Europe, to supersede feudal monarchy without undermining its
own security.

[76] Cf. the acute analysis of Steig, *Kleist's Berliner Kämpfe,* p. 112.

[77] It may be of value to consider the verdict of a historian who was an
ardent admirer of Stein and an inveterate detractor of Hardenberg: "In
view of the hundreds of personal connections which link the hereditary

view of reform, than Hardenberg's retreat from the principle of uniform taxation. The chancellor no doubt persuaded himself that a better day would come; but it would not, if he did not take steps to bring it. If his purpose in appeasing the nobility was to safeguard his influence with the king, that purpose was foiled, for the nobility used every constitutional concession to build up their own position behind the throne and to render the chancellor ever more powerless. Formally his office remained secure, but it diminished in practical importance; his self-esteem was gratified, but his program of reform gradually began to go by the board. By yielding to the clamor of the nobles over the question of the land tax Hardenberg in effect fatally undermined the future of the reform movement. Stein, who held no small opinion of himself, did at least scorn to hold office without the authority to exercise the powers of that office.

---

nobility to the hereditary monarchy, especially in Prussia, it is very questionable whether such inflexibility would not have led sooner or later to a conflict between Crown and minister" (Lehmann, *Stein,* III, 92–93).

CHAPTER VI

The Price of Emancipation

THE success or failure of Hardenberg's first year as chancellor is commonly assessed in terms of his handling of the constitutional crisis arising out of his tax laws. As a result, a second extremely important aspect of his administration, his policy with respect to agrarian reform, has often been unduly overshadowed. One cause of this comparative neglect may be Hardenberg's own preoccupation with political to the detriment of agrarian affairs; but land reform and improvement of the Prussian peasants' lot were problems still as fundamental as in the time of Stein. Hardenberg's cavalier attitude, therefore, far from justifying superficial treatment of the subject, itself constitutes an important factor in any balanced appraisal of his ministry.

Stein's Emancipation Edict had declared the Prussian peasants free on paper, without in fact enabling them to launch an independent economic existence. They were still subject to onerous obligations and services as a condition of occupancy and use of the land. As a necessary completion of his reform work, Stein, in his "Political Testament," had recommended to his successors abolition of this quasi-manorial system. Such abolition would necessarily imply drastic modifications in the conditions of land tenure, since the peasants' obligations were nothing but a contractual or customary payment to the lords for the use of their land.

Hardenberg committed himself to the general principle of

further land reform as an integral part of his financial plan of August 1810.[1] He contemplated

> freehold property for peasants, preparation for releasing them from their labor obligations in accordance with fixed principles and with allowance for local conditions, . . . abolition of patrimonial justice in favor of appropriate courts, and a suitable police organization.

The detailed problems, of course, were manifold and complicated. It was generally assumed, for example, that the lords were to be compensated for the loss of their servile labor force; but the extent, manner, and duration of such compensation were subjects for detailed and technical discussion. Again, it was questionable whether all the peasants could or should be released from their obligations simultaneously, and if not, no obvious criteria of precedence existed. The degree to which voluntary readjustments between peasant and lord should be encouraged was likewise debatable.

The task of finding solutions to these and many other problems posed by the creation of a freeholding peasant class fell to the young historian Friedrich von Raumer, one of Hardenberg's personal assistants. Raumer devoted himself to his mission with enthusiasm, and all the indications were that his draft law would speedily be enacted. Even the hesitant Dohna, in the changed atmosphere produced by Hardenberg's advent, came out strongly in favor of creating freeholding peasants.[2] But the opposition generated by Hardenberg's fiscal laws of October

[1] Botzenhart, ed., *Stein*, III, 708–717. Stein expressed general approval of Hardenberg's proposals at a secret meeting with him in September: Stein's memorandum dated Sept. 12/13, 1810, *ibid.*, III, 319–331; cf. Haussherr, *Die Stunde Hardenbergs*, p. 179.

[2] See Dohna to Kircheisen, Sept. 21, 1810, in Knapp, *Bauern-Befreiung*, II, 237–238; and his report to the king on Silesia, autumn 1810, in Otto Linke, "Zur Reise des Königs Friedrich Wilhelms III. nach Schlesien 1810," *Zeitschrift des Vereins für Geschichte und Altertum Schlesiens*, XXXIX (1905), 127–130. I cannot reconcile these documents with Rühl's statement (Franz Rühl, ed., *Briefe und Aktenstücke zur Geschichte Preussens unter Friedrich Wilhelm III. etc.* [Leipzig, 1899–1902], II, xxxix–xl) that Dohna was never willing to proceed beyond the principles of the decree of Feb. 14, 1808, in the direction of peasant ownership.

27 and 28, 1810, affected the proposed agrarian legislation as well. The Assembly of Notables that Hardenberg convened in order to make the tax laws more palatable to public opinion was allowed to debate Raumer's plan. Before long the chancellor transferred Raumer's functions to another member of his "kitchen cabinet," Christian Friedrich Scharnweber. It was assumed until recently that the reason for this switch was that Scharnweber was less progressive in his ideas than Raumer; there is evidence, however, that this was not the case but that he was rather, perhaps, more pliable, or simply more acceptable personally to the Notables.[3] In any event, in the course of the succeeding months the Notables obtained a number of important concessions from Scharnweber, with the result that the Edict of September 14, 1811, where the conditions under which the Prussian peasant might be relieved of his burdens were finally laid down, bore but little resemblance to Raumer's draft of October 1810.[4]

One important question at issue was whether the edict should apply to all peasants burdened with servile duties; a second, whether it should contain identical provisions for all those to whom it applied; and, if the answer to the second question was negative, a third question arose as to the nature of the distinctions to be made. On the first two questions Raumer and Scharnweber agreed, but on the third they disagreed. Both excluded from *Regulation* (*Regulation,* which may be rendered "adjust-

---

[3] See the (undated) memorandum of Scharnweber for the king on the question of establishing a model farm, quoted and summarized by Gerhard Wurzbacher, "Studien über den Wandel der sozialen und völkischen Struktur eines Landkreises im pommerschen-westpreussischen Grenzraum zwischen 1773 und 1937," *Zeitschrift für Ostforschung,* II (1953), 197–200. There is no direct evidence as to Hardenberg's motives for this personnel change. In any event, Hardenberg continued to place great confidence in Raumer and was reluctant to allow him to leave government service the following year (Raumer, *Lebenserinnerungen und Briefwechsel,* pp. 164–166).

[4] For expressions of conservative opinion during this period, see Knapp, *Bauern-Befreiung,* II, 257–261, 270–271; Steffens, *Hardenberg,* pp. 113–122. For the edict, see *Gesetz-Sammlung* for 1810–1811, pp. 281–300. For the comparison that follows between Raumer's draft and the edict, see mainly Knapp, *Bauern-Befreiung,* I, 165–169.

ment," was the name given to the entire process contemplated in the legislation) all those peasants who held unlimited hereditary leasehold tenure of the land on which they lived (*Erbpächter, Erbzinsleute*), since such tenure was considered sufficiently secure not to need immediate attention. But the result was anomalous in that this group, who had formerly been the most favored within their class, were now to be relegated to the relatively disadvantageous position of continuing to be leaseholders among freeholders and continuing also to perform the customary services. Raumer and Scharnweber both went on to make further distinctions among the remaining peasants, but the distinctions they made differed from each other. Raumer divided the peasants with whom he proposed to deal into two classes, while Scharnweber divided them into three. Raumer distinguished between peasants who held a right, whether hereditary or not, to use the produce of the land on which they lived (*Lassiten*) and those who held a nonhereditary lease, that is to say a lease of limited duration, on the land itself (*Zeitpächter*). The first group, in order to acquire freeholding status, were to compensate their lord by first ceding to him one-third of the land which they occupied; the second group were required to cede one-half of the land. Scharnweber adopted Raumer's provisions concerning the *Zeitpächter;* but he introduced a further subdivision among the *Lassiten,* distinguishing between those who had hereditary usufruct and those who had nonhereditary usufruct and assimilating the latter to the treatment meted out to the *Zeitpächter.* On paper these variations may sound too technical to be important, but in fact the result was that under the law of September 14, 1811, many Prussian peasants remained as they had been, and of the rest, the majority forfeited half of the land they occupied in order to acquire freehold tenure of the other half. Since many of the holdings were small to start with, this fraction was often totally insufficient for viable farming, especially when funds were lacking for the purchase of equipment.

Nor was this the end of the hardships imposed upon the newly liberated peasantry. The peasant's cession of land was considered as compensation only for the lord's loss of the acreage to which he had formerly possessed legal title. In addition, the lord was to be compensated, in cash or in kind, for the loss of the peasant's compulsory services. Raumer, in his original draft of the law, had proceeded from the principle that the amount of this compensation was to be determined individually for each instance of *Regulation,* according to an assessment of the advantages gained by each party to the transaction. He envisaged instances where the cession of land might be sufficient compensation for the lord's loss of both acreage and services, or even instances where the cession of land would be adjudged excessive payment, so that the peasant might be entitled to some return in cash or in kind in addition to relief from services. Thus Raumer sought to protect the peasant in cases of hardship. But Scharnweber abandoned the principle of individual assessment, substituting inflexible rules for adjustment under which the peasant was invariably liable for some payment.[5] Taken all together, the provisions that Scharnweber inserted into the law were such as to prejudice gravely the economic future of the "regulated" peasants. There was a real danger that many of them would sooner or later find it impossible to make a living on their holdings and would have to hire themselves out as casual labor, and they might consider themselves lucky if they gave up before they sank hopelessly into debt.

Although, therefore, the provisions for the peasants were decidedly unfavorable, it is an exaggeration to assert that the law was written expressly to suit the other party to the transaction, the nobles.[6] The desire to appease the nobles was undoubtedly one of the motives for the government's adoption of Scharnweber's draft, but other factors were also present. For one thing, there were a number of technical and administrative reasons for

[5] Moreover, in fixing the amount of this compensation, Scharnweber, unlike Raumer, included as an item among the lord's losses the exclusion of the possibility of that portion of the land which went to the peasant in freehold reverting to the lord by escheat in virtue of his paramount ownership (*Obereigentum*) thereof.

[6] E.g., Knapp, *Bauern-Befreiung,* I, 165: "The government accepted the recommendations [of the Notables] and completely revised its earlier draft accordingly, thereby virtually fulfilling the wishes of the members of that assembly, most of whom were noble landowners."

Scharnweber's amendments.[7] In the second place, Scharnweber introduced one extremely important reform favorable to the peasant class which Raumer had not advocated: he enforced, against opposition from many nobles, freehold status for *Zeitpächter* whose landlords were unwilling to grant it.[8] Thirdly, the interpretation mentioned does not sufficiently take account of the many demands of the opposition which the government either rejected or ignored.[9]

Perhaps the most convincing refutation of the thesis that the Edict of September 14, 1811, was written so as to be acceptable to the conservative nobles is provided by the large volume of protests against it after publication. With some not unnatural exaggeration, it was said that landowners could no longer enjoy their customary rural life if they could not walk around their land without at every turn encountering land owned by members of other social classes: "Our estates will turn into a hell for us if independent peasant owners are our neighbors."[10] In East Prussia especially the nobles planned programs of resistance and submitted protests to the general effect that the decree was based chiefly on untenable theories and was likely to injure rather than help the country. Local conditions, the opposition contended, were disregarded; the security of property was undermined, for the noble landowners were being arbitrarily deprived of half or two-thirds of the land which they rightfully owned.[11] Ludwig von der Marwitz, leader of the opposition to Hardenberg's fiscal decrees, was equally displeased with his agrarian legislation. The results of the "complete emancipation" of the lower orders, he later wrote, had been unedifying. The master had become the slave of his former workers, discipline and order had become

[7] Knapp's own recording of several such reasons (*ibid.*, I, 169–171) seems inconsistent with his interpretation cited in n. 6 above.

[8] Knapp, *Bauern-Befreiung*, I, 167; Steffens, *Hardenberg*, pp. 116–118.

[9] Steffens, *Hardenberg*, pp. 113, 117, 119–120; Knapp, *Bauern-Befreiung*, II, 270–273.

[10] Knapp, *Bauern-Befreiung*, II, 274.

[11] For various expressions of disapproval of the edict, see *ibid.*, II, 276–282; Zerboni di Sposetti to Stägemann, Sept. 16, and Schön to Gruner, Nov. 2, Nov. 9, and Dec. 11, 1811, Rühl, ed., *Briefe und Aktenstücke*, I, 149–150, 152–155.

things of the past, people jostled each other for advantages, they became slovenly, and there was widespread migration from the country to the towns. "The peasants, so hastily relieved of their obligation to service, did not improve their land, as the authorities, on the basis of their theories, had hoped but became lazy instead." [12]

In summary, the principal agrarian problem facing Hardenberg when he assumed power, that of the status of the peasant on his land and of the duties attached thereto, was solved in the Edict of September 14, 1811, in a manner which neither treated realistically the hazards of the peasant's future nor conformed completely to the wishes of the conservative landowning nobles. But a just appraisal of Hardenberg's achievements in agrarian reform must include his solution of a number of subsidiary problems as well.

The most central of these problems was that of patrimonial justice. Because of his untimely dismissal, Stein had been unable to accomplish its abolition, but he had referred to it specifically, in his "Political Testament," as one of the institutions in need of reform. Theodor von Schön, the actual composer of the "Political Testament," who regarded himself as its foster father, urged upon Hardenberg, when the latter became chancellor, abolition of patrimonial justice and of the lords' police powers. Hardenberg was agreeable at first to the elimination of patrimonial justice but balked, according to Schön's reports, at doing away with the police powers. He himself on his own estate, the chancellor said, could never submit to police regulations administered by other residents of the estate. As Schön sarcastically put it, such an idea ran counter to Hardenberg's "lordly [*freiherrlichen*] conceptions of the need for order in the state." [13] In the end, whether on Hardenberg's orders or merely

[12] Meusel, ed., *Marwitz*, I, 602–603.

[13] Schön actually supplied two slightly variant versions of this episode: Schön, *Papiere,* I, 62–64; *Weitere Beiträge und Nachträge zu den Papieren des Ministers und Burggrafen von Marienburg Theodor von Schön* (Berlin, 1881), pp. 96–97 (hereafter Schön, *Weitere Beiträge*). Cf. also Steffens, *Hardenberg,* p. 142. Note that in his financial plan of August 1810 (see above, p. 89) Hardenberg referred only rather vaguely to improvements in the police organization.

with his tacit consent, both patrimonial justice and the police powers were specifically preserved by the Edict of September 14, 1811.[14]

The edict also left to the nobles another privilege: their hunting monopoly. Much opposition arose against Raumer's plan to abolish it, one Silesian noble fearing the emergence of "a kind of armed peasant corps" and the spread of drunkenness among the peasants if they were allowed to hunt.[15] On the other side of the ledger, Hardenberg preserved more or less intact a number of Raumer's other minor reforms, despite considerable opposition. These included relief of the peasants from obligations to supply horses and fodder on certain occasions, regulation of compulsory domestic service on a basis of voluntary contract, and abolition of monopolies in the production of flour, beer, and brandy.[16] Hardenberg's government quite obviously had the power and the means to drive through reforms when it chose.

This circumstance seems to strengthen the argument of those who see in Hardenberg's concessions to the nobility only weakness, vacillation, and carelessness.[17] These qualities, especially the latter, were no doubt present, but there are also discernible definite lines of policy in the government's position on agrarian reform in 1811. Those reforms in which Hardenberg persisted were designed to achieve primarily economic ends, while those which he was willing to give up under pressure were motivated chiefly by sociopolitical or humanitarian ideas. The chancellor was determined to accomplish the economic recovery of Prussia through the establishment of a free, landowning peasant class without economically unreasonable burdens. But he did not feel obliged to persist in measures which—rightly or wrongly—he regarded as not strictly relevant to that end, if they seemed to

[14] Para. 58: "With respect to jurisdiction and police arrangements this decree institutes no changes."

[15] Steffens, *Hardenberg*, pp. 139–140.

[16] For more information on these measures and on the objections to them, see *ibid.*, pp. 130–131, 144–145, 151–155. The milling monopoly (*Mühlenzwang*) had been abolished in 1808 only in East Prussia and Lithuania.

[17] E.g., the passage from Knapp, cited above, n. 6; Lehmann, *Stein*, III, 90–91.

encroach unduly on the traditional social position of the nobility. In Hardenberg's day it was still possible to distinguish sharply between social and economic problems.

Given the validity of this distinction, it is possible, although not mandatory, to place a less unfavorable construction on Hardenberg's agrarian policy in 1811 than on his fiscal policy. In the face of opposition from the conservative elements among the nobility, he sacrificed the very cornerstone of his fiscal program, abolition of the nobles' exemption from the land tax, whereas in the question of land reform the legislation of 1811 did make substantial inroads into the traditional economic prerogatives of the aristocracy. Was it necessary, Hardenberg may well have asked himself, to pour fuel on the flames of their resistance by pressing at this time for agricultural reforms which he did not regard as absolutely essential? Was it worth while to risk embittering the most important social group in Prussia in the name of a political or humanitarian ideal? [18]

Yet if Hardenberg's agrarian policy in the year 1811 is considered in the light of later events, instead of in isolation, it becomes much more difficult to defend such a charitable interpretation. During the years after 1811 the chancellor displayed such a lack of interest in these matters and allowed them to slip so much out of his control that we are forced to wonder whether, after all, his policy even in 1811 was not guided less by a considered calculation of the risks than by sheer carelessness and lack of concentration.[19] The following pages, by telling the story

[18] Knapp, one of the most outspoken critics of Hardenberg's agrarian policy, concedes that if "a state cannot survive except by depending on some social class—and this was probably true of Prussia in 1811, in her truncated and impoverished condition—it is politically explicable, even though productive of undesirable social consequences, for that state to select the strongest class as its support, and that was the Junker class" (Georg Friedrich Knapp, *Grundherrschaft und Rittergut* [Leipzig, 1897], p. 70).

[19] In support of such a view, one can point to Hardenberg's failure to protect Scharnweber from the assaults of the Notables. Scharnweber himself did not even hold ministerial rank and therefore carried little authority in his own right. Generally speaking, Hardenberg seems to have taken no further personal interest in the progress of agrarian legislation in 1811 after his transfer of Raumer's functions to Scharnweber.

of the ultimate fate of agrarian reform under Hardenberg, will justify this estimate.

Normally, the main problems of agrarian reform would have been disposed of by the Edict of September 14, 1811. But the turbulence of the war years 1812–1815 prevented any effective execution of its provisions, whereas it was exposed throughout those years to the sustained attacks of the opposition. The final result of these circumstances was that the edict was amended out of all recognition by the so-called Declaration of May 29, 1816,[20] a law which does Hardenberg credit with respect neither to its contents nor to the manner of its composition.

As early as 1812 the conservative landowners had persuaded the government to reconsider the edict and to consult with them regarding possible changes. Long preliminary discussions were held, in the course of which the provisional national assembly, the successor to the Assembly of Notables, became the mouthpiece of those landed nobles who were pressing for revision.[21] At one point during these conferences Hardenberg was personally represented by two spokesmen who argued on opposite sides of the same question; the chancellor, who was away from Berlin, blandly ignored two efforts to persuade him to resolve the deadlock. This incident obviously reduced the government to impotence and made Hardenberg himself look ridiculous. Later, the chancellor showed some signs of energy when a group of East Prussian nobles under the leadership of Dohna threatened to gain complete control over the king;[22] in a letter to Dohna Hardenberg declared that "there could be no question of abandoning or altering any integral parts of the Edict of September 14, 1811." But soon he relapsed once more into indifference. First of all, he permitted the provisional assembly to review the entire

[20] The German word *Deklaration*, which I have retained, does not really mean "declaration" but rather "clarification" or "explanation"; hence, by political license, "amendment."

[21] Details on the formation and history of this assembly will be found below, pp. 105–109.

[22] Dohna, who was now chairman of the Committee of the East Prussian-Lithuanian Estates, seems to have entirely abandoned his earlier liberal position on the question of agrarian reform.

law. Then Kaspar von Schuckmann, the minister responsible for agrarian affairs, persuaded Hardenberg to establish a government commission to examine the assembly's recommendations and to exclude from this commission Scharnweber, who as Hardenberg's personal delegate had been responsible in public for his agrarian program, in the interests of "impartiality" and to avoid a "poor reception by public opinion"! [23] Thus did Hardenberg contribute to the undermining of his own former policy. "Integral parts of the edict" were, in fact, abandoned, while the chancellor was occupied in spinning diplomatic webs in Vienna.[24]

Very few Prussian peasants, owing to the unsettled conditions of the war years, had attained their freedom from feudal conditions of land tenure and from servile labor obligations under the Edict of September 14, 1811. In effect, therefore, the Declaration of May 29, 1816, was the basic law under which agricultural property and labor in Prussia were reformed; [25] and its provisions were far less favorable to the peasants than those of the edict, which had already embodied considerable concessions to the landowners. The most incisive changes introduced by the declaration were those restricting eligibility for *Regulation,* i.e., for the process of relief from encumbered tenure and from labor and other obligations, against compensation. Under the Edict of 1811, all peasants (except those with superior tenure) were

[23] It seems questionable, in view of the facts noted, whether Hardenberg continued to place such great confidence in Scharnweber as the latter's biographer (Friedrich Meusel, in *Allgemeine Deutsche Biographie,* LV, 597) asserts. But Hardenberg was steadfast in few things, and the figure of Scharnweber himself is far from clear. Stein, for example, accused him of betraying the cause of agrarian reform (Haussherr, *Die Stunde Hardenbergs,* pp. 180–181). As for Schuckmann, it is impossible to estimate how far his avowed motives for urging Scharnweber's exclusion were sincere and how far he was inspired by jealousy of a man who was encroaching on his administrative domain.

[24] For this paragraph, see Knapp, *Bauern-Befreiung,* II, 345–347; Schön, *Papiere,* VI, 324. For a general narrative of the declaration's genesis, see Knapp, *Bauern-Befreiung,* I, 172–184.

[25] No further important changes were made until 1850, when the hereditary tenants (*Erbzinsleute* and *Erbpächter*) were belatedly freed from their obligations (cf. above, pp. 90–91).

considered eligible; under the provisions of the Declaration of 1816, only those peasants (still with the same exception) were eligible who:

1) were classified as *spannfähig*, capable of supplying draft animals, which meant that their service to their lord included animal as well as human labor;
2) had their farm listed in the tax records;
3) could show that their family's tenure of the land they occupied went back to a fixed date (this date ranged from 1749 to 1774 for the different provinces).

These restrictions tended to operate in favor of the more prosperous and secure peasants to the detriment of those less fortunately placed and deprived the lords of only a portion of the forced labor theretofore at their disposal. In addition to these provisions, the declaration required initiation of the process of *Regulation* in each instance by either the lord or the peasant, which meant that an ignorant or intimidated peasant might never be relieved from his services even though he was eligible; both parties were permitted to apply for adjustment of the normal fixed compensation for special reasons (a clause which was likely in practice to benefit the lords, who were more sophisticated and could hire lawyers); and lords were given increased opportunity to absorb farms devastated by war or vacant for other reasons.[26]

As to the future of those peasants not eligible for *Regulation*, the declaration made no clear provision. In particular, nothing was said about the status of *Bauernschutz* with respect to those peasants who continued to live under the old conditions of tenure and labor. In practice, however, the government ceased to enforce *Bauernschutz*, with the result that large numbers of peasants were, in the decades after 1816, simply evicted from their land and became farm laborers.[27]

The new legislation coincided with a period of economic crisis. Prussian hopes that with the lifting of the Continental System the economy would recover and even exceed its former

[26] The declaration is summarized in Knapp, *Bauern-Befreiung*, I, 184–197 and printed in the *Gesetz-Sammlung* for 1816, pp. 154–180.

[27] See Knapp, *Bauern-Befreiung*, I, 198–199.

level proved illusory. Particularly discouraging was the discovery that Britain, before the revolutionary wars Prussia's best market for agricultural produce, continued to raise high tariffs against continental imports. In the 1820's Prussian agricultural exports dropped catastrophically, and prices followed.[28] In the ensuing depression it was extremely difficult for a small independent farmer to maintain himself. In these circumstances the total result of the Declaration of 1816 was "an extremely severe diminution of medium-sized peasant holdings . . . in favor of the large estates of the nobility and to a lesser extent of the smaller . . . holdings [which continued to be held in leasehold instead of in freehold]." By 1860

those farms whose owners had supplied draft animals but who were excluded from *Regulation* by [other provisions of] the Declaration of 1816 were for the most part absorbed into the larger estates. . . . The old [i.e., otherwise eligible] farms whose owners had not supplied draft animals were . . . [likewise] absorbed, especially the non-hereditary ones.[29]

In short, the consequences were disastrous from the point of view of creating a large independent and reasonably prosperous peasant class, capable of becoming an active and intelligent force in the shaping of Prussia. "The reason why in 1848 so many features of the old structure of society, and therefore so much cause for discontent among the middle and lower classes

[28] On the economic crisis, see A. Sartorius von Waltershausen, *Deutsche Wirtschaftsgeschichte 1815–1914* (Jena, 1920), pp. 39–40.

[29] Hans Goldschmidt, *Die Grundbesitzverteilung in der Mark Brandenburg und in Hinterpommern vom Beginn des dreissigjährigen Krieges bis zur Gegenwart* (Berlin, 1910), pp. 137–138. Cf. also Max Sering, *Die innere Kolonisation im östlichen Deutschland* (Leipzig, 1893), p. 63; Knapp, *Bauern-Befreiung*, I, 274–282. These results contrast unfavorably, from the peasants' point of view, with the consequences of emancipation in western Germany: cf. Werner Conze, "Die Wirkungen der liberalen Agrarreformen auf die Volksordnung in Mitteleuropa im 19. Jahrhundert," *Vierteljahrschrift für Sozial- und Wirtschaftsgeschichte*, XXXVIII (1949), 19. I do not find convincing the attempt of Henning Graf von Borcke-Storgardt, "Zur preussischen Agrargesetzgebung der Reformzeit," in *Mensch und Staat in Recht und Geschichte, Festschrift für Herbert Kraus* (Kitzingen/Main, 1954), pp. 315–318, 323–324, to interpret the Declaration of 1816 far more favorably.

on the land, still persisted is to be found in the indulgence of the landowners' wishes in the year 1816." [30]

It would, of course, be incorrect to infer that these consequences were necessarily foreseen by those responsible for the declaration. Nevertheless, it cannot be denied that the government allowed itself to be maneuvered into turning the Declaration of 1816 largely into an instrument for amending the Edict of 1811 in favor of the landed nobility. The latter continued to dispose of compulsory manual peasant labor, and they were tacitly permitted to absorb lands hitherto protected by *Bauernschutz* and to convert the former occupants into a completely dependent labor force, without rights of any sort.

The ultimate responsibility for this situation lay with Hardenberg. Although he had said in 1814 that he would permit no important changes in the Edict of 1811, in fact he did not lift a finger to save that edict from attack. True, Hardenberg had been busy at the Congress of Vienna with matters no doubt more important as well as more enjoyable for him and had therefore been obliged to delegate his authority; but he had delegated it capriciously and allowed himself to be taken in by transparently partisan arguments when he excluded Scharnweber from participation in drafting the declaration. No diplomatic or military crisis existed any longer in 1816 as an excuse for preserving internal unity at all costs; on the contrary, Hardenberg offered even less resistance to the pressure of the landed nobility in the relaxed atmosphere of 1816 than he had done in the first strenuous year of his chancellorship.

Hardenberg's weakness in time of peace is bound to reflect

---

[30] Knapp, *Bauern-Befreiung*, I, 191. Some diehard landowners were not satisfied even with the concessions of 1816: see e.g., the complaint of Winterfeld, in Alfred Stern, "Die preussische Verfassungsfrage im Jahre 1817 und die Rundreise von Altenstein, Klewiz, Beyme," *Deutsche Zeitschrift für Geschichtswissenschaft*, IX (1893), 78–79; and the views of Dohna and Farenheid, Rühl, ed., *Briefe und Aktenstücke*, II, 327–330, 332–338. Cf. also Hein, *Geschichte der ostpreussischen Landschaft*, p. 93. Still, in general, the landowners after 1816 devoted themselves to exploiting rather than attacking Hardenberg's agrarian legislation: F. Lenz, *Agrarlehre*, p. 69, and cf. e.g., Jachmann to Stägemann, Jan. 29, 1819, Rühl, ed., *Briefe und Aktenstücke*, II, 321.

back unfavorably on his position in time of anxiety. If one considers the course of agrarian reform under Hardenberg as a continuous whole, it is impossible to escape the conclusion that, by faults of both commission and omission, unduly great concessions were made to the interests of the landed nobility, interests which at least in part were selfish. At the same time, we can interpret the outcome in these exclusively negative terms only at the risk of ignoring some of the most powerful intellectual forces of the period. At least three elements ought to be distinguished among the causes of the betrayal of Stein's program of agrarian reform: the international exigencies of Hardenberg's first five years in office, especially the need for domestic unity to support the diplomatic and later the military offensive against France; Hardenberg's tendency to become impatient with, and therefore to neglect, the many technical problems of domestic reform; and his consciousness of his own aristocratic birth and consequent reluctance to become a complete apostate from his class—all these were significant factors.

Finally, it is almost impossible to overestimate the impact of the doctrines of economic liberalism on the entire agrarian reform movement. Among all the reformers only Stein was relatively untouched by the idea that those best able to promote production and trade should be left free to do so and that the state, once it had established the conditions under which this freedom existed, had neither right nor cause to interfere in the economic life of the nation. This theory had already left its mark in 1807 in the projects of Schroetter and Schön, modified by Stein at the eleventh hour.[31] In Hardenberg's time the most prominent exponent of the doctrine was the economist Albrecht Thaer. Although it was Scharnweber who took official responsibility for the agrarian legislation of 1811, much of the actual drafting of the decrees seems to have been the work of Thaer.[32]

[31] See above, p. 20. For Schön's later views, see his remarkable attack on the Edict of September 14, 1811, in his memorandum of July 13, 1817, Schön, *Papiere*, IV, 403–404.

[32] Schnabel, *Deutsche Geschichte*, I, 464; Wilhelm Körte, *Albrecht Thaer: Sein Leben und Wirken, als Arzt und Landwirth* (Leipzig, 1839), p. 291. The legislation with which Thaer chiefly concerned himself was, however,

Adam Müller, for instance, accused him of rationalizing a relationship which was essentially personal (that between lord and peasant) and of defiling the sanctity of agriculture by treating it like any other pursuit.[33] Thaer contended that it was perfectly reasonable and fair for all landowners, large and small, to face the same dangers and enjoy the same opportunities; that there was no justification for continued enforcement of *Bauernschutz;* and that if any peasant should find that he could not maintain himself, then he was free to become a laborer if he so desired.[34]

It is easy to point out the paradox in the respective effects of these conflicting theories. "Despite their romantic trappings and their feudal inclinations, the spokesmen of the [conservative] opposition had in fact the better economic understanding. . . . The noble owners of the large estates were the last defenders of the Prussian . . . tradition of *Bauernschutz.*"[35] The doctrines of Thaer, as put into practice by Hardenberg's government, were in the end even more favorable to the noble landowners than

---

the breaking up of common land (*Gemeinheitsteilung*). The law effecting this step was not issued until 1821. While *Gemeinheitsteilung* was in some respects connected with the measures taken in the Edict of September 14, 1811 (since it involved the cessation of certain duties and rights, e.g., the right of pasturage, which overlapped with those dealt with in the latter law), it is of significance more for technical than for social reasons; therefore I cannot take space to elaborate further on this aspect of Thaer's official activity. For further information, see Walter Simons, *Albrecht Thaer* (Berlin, 1929), chap. vi; Ludwig Elster, ed., *Wörterbuch der Volkswirtschaft* (Jena, 1906–7), article "Gemeinheitsteilung."

[33] Cf. the interesting National Socialist formulation (Joachim Frhr. v. d. Goltz, *Auswirkungen der Stein-Hardenbergschen Agrarreform im Laufe des 19. Jahrhunderts* [Berlin, n.d.], p. 8): "Thaer's conception of agriculture was a trade carried on for money profit, like any industrial trade. Darré [the Nazi minister of agriculture] always defines agriculture as a means of employing and sustaining a particular class of society on the land entrusted to them [by the people]."

[34] For Thaer's arguments with the conservatives, see chiefly F. Lenz, *Agrarlehre,* pp. 46–60; also Schnabel, *Deutsche Geschichte,* I, 467–470; Körte, *Albrecht Thaer,* p. 269.

[35] Lenz, *Agrarlehre,* p. 62.

those of Adam Müller, who wrote in their name. The nobles easily made the transition from manorial to capitalistic agriculture, while large numbers of the peasantry were permitted to drown in the cleansing waters of economic freedom.[36]

[36] It is, of course, erroneous to magnify the power of economic liberalism into a kind of irresistible *Zeitgeist* and to regard the fate of the peasants as inevitable; e.g., Winter, "Zur Entstehungsgeschichte des Oktoberedikts," p. 33: "The reform of the status of the peasants and of agriculture was bought with sacrifices which, given the historical environment, were predestined, one might say, to be borne by the economically weak." Such a statement is sheer mysticism and explains nothing, least of all why a "reform of the status of the peasants" was undertaken in the first place if the peasants were predestined to gain nothing by it.

— transition from manor to economic liberalism
really helped the lords Bauernschutz
convenient only where it helped them

CHAPTER VII

Toward a

Constitutional Monarchy

IN FOLLOWING agrarian reform under Hardenberg through to its ultimate fate, we have moved far ahead of the chronological development in constitutional affairs. We left this subject with the dissolution of the Assembly of Notables after its enforced acquiescence in the agrarian Edict of September 14 and in the Additional Edict of September 7, 1811. This latter law contained the important assurance that the idea of representative government was not being abandoned: "It is still our intention, as declared in the . . . Edict of October 27 of last year, to grant to the nation an appropriately constituted representative body [*zweckmässig eingerichtete Repräsentation*]." But since, the decree continued, there had not been time to make the necessary preparations for calling into existence a permanent parliament and since the king wished to have the benefit of immediate consultation "with respected men from all classes in our provinces," a provisional national assembly was to be established.

The Provisional National Assembly

In order to avoid the necessity of creating new machinery for the calling of a parliament, the expedient was adopted of adding the function of a national assembly to a body already contemplated: namely, a commission for regulating the national and provincial debt arising from the war. The members of this commission doubling as a national assembly were for the most part to be elected, though a few were to be appointed. The manner of election was strictly regulated: from each province were to be chosen two noble landowners, one representative of the large towns, and one for the rural districts, including the smaller towns. In addition, the three cities of Berlin, Königsberg, and Breslau were each to elect a representative of their own.[1]

It was very plain that this assembly could, indeed, be only a stopgap. Such a very small group of men, whose general functions as a representative body were, moreover, from the first subordinated to its specific function in connection with a definite technical problem,[2] could not be truly representative of the nation and could not command the respect and attention required in the western parliamentary tradition. To be sure, in constrast to the Notables, most of the members were to be elected; but even this line of progress was severely limited by the electoral regulations that assured to the nobility almost half the seats in the assembly. Furthermore, the provincial governments were given power to supervise the elections and to nullify the choice of anyone not acceptable to the government; and finally, the government reduced the prestige of the deputies by forbidding them to accept mandates from their constituents.

In view of all these restrictions, there is room for doubt whether this assembly was really to be "consulted." The indications were clear that the government proposed to keep it under strict control and that Hardenberg, at least, was inclined to respect its status as a genuine representative body as little as that of the Notables. The provisional national assembly was a product of mixed and fundamentally contradictory motives, and consequently it was only a "semiparliamentary mongrel creature which was in the long run incapable of sustaining life." [3]

---

[1] Announcement of, and regulations for, the provisional national assembly, Additional Edict of September 7, 1811, *Gesetz-Sammlung* for 1810–1811, pp. 260–262.

[2] This problem occupied much of the members' time; see, e.g., their concern with the capital tax of May 24, 1812, described in Mamroth, *Geschichte der preussischen Staats-Besteuerung*, pp. 629–633, 648–651.

[3] Zeeden, *Hardenberg*, pp. 162–163; cf. Stern, *Abhandlungen und Aktenstücke*, pp. 174–175. On pp. 123–124, Zeeden lists some of the reasons why,

The rulers betrayed their contempt for the provisional assembly by at first totally ignoring it. The government failed to prescribe the procedure or even the competence of the assembly, and it was only by their own energetic efforts that the members finally succeeded in obtaining recognition. After nearly two months of floundering and aimless existence, the deputies voted to request Hardenberg to appoint a royal commissioner in consultation with whom they might establish the organization, procedure, and jurisdiction of the assembly. Hardenberg expressed his customary displeasure at any suggestions that did not emanate from his office and declared that since the assembly had only advisory powers its internal organization, until the government might find time to prescribe it, was "a matter of indifference." But the chancellor nevertheless seized on the idea of a royal commissioner and converted it to his own use by appointing a president of the assembly to act as intermediary between the deputies and the government.[4]

The provisional assembly, then, was clearly no more suitable to promote the idea of parliamentary government than the Notables had been. Its members, moreover, were acutely conscious of its shortcomings, and many of them regarded themselves merely as caretakers for the promised permanent assembly, which would presumably emerge after the war was over. This feeling culminated on April 7, 1815, in a vote of 22 to 13 in favor of a motion to request speedy completion of the government's plans for a permanent national assembly and for a constitution.[5]

---

in his opinion, this assembly was, nevertheless, significant in Prussian constitutional history: destruction of the old class hierarchy; promotion of the idea of citizenship; strengthening of national unity; the role of the representatives as legislators instead of assistants in the executive department of government. Only the last of these factors appears to me to be both true and important.

[4] For these developments see Stern, *Abhandlungen und Aktenstücke*, pp. 177–191. The assembly by this time had its own ideas about the extent of its powers, some members even demanding a veto power over legislation. Finally, they submitted an address on the matter to the king over Hardenberg's head. The king's reaction is not known.

[5] The debate in the assembly and the resulting petition are printed *ibid.*, pp. 216–222.

Unfortunately, an analysis of the vote is not available; but it is clear that some of the affirmative votes must have come from noble members of the assembly. To anyone familiar with the bitter struggle of Marwitz and his Brandenburg colleagues in 1811 against a constitution, it might at first glance be surprising to find a group of men dominated by the nobility voting four years later to jostle the government in the direction of a constitution. The explanation probably lies in the ambiguity of the word "constitution." We are too apt to connect the word with "constitutional government" and with democracy, whereas of course a constitution may be the basis of almost any kind of government. Even Marwitz was in favor of a constitution: namely, the feudal one which he conceived to be still in force. The noble members of the provisional national assembly, in demanding a new constitution, were less rigidly conservative than Marwitz, but assuredly they were very far from envisaging a limited monarchy on the model of Britain or even the states of the Rhenish Confederation. What they probably had in mind was a government in which certain political rights were constitutionally guaranteed to a national assembly composed for the most part of nobles. They showed their hand by passing a motion in the provisional assembly, immediately following the vote for a constitution, to remind the rulers of the existence of provincial constitutions.[6] Evidently they did not favor a form of government which would limit the privileges of the nobility in provincial and local administration.[7]

[6] *Ibid.,* pp. 220–221.

[7] Examples can be multiplied of demands for a constitution whose originators had nothing farther from their minds than ideas of democracy or popular government. See Dohna's letter to the king on behalf of the Committee of the East Prussian–Lithuanian Estates, April 5, 1815, Bezzenberger, ed., *Aktenstücke,* pp. 52–53, and compare it with his ideas, reminiscent of Marwitz and Adam Müller, on the representation of quality and of "corporations" rather than of mere numbers, in Dohna to Schön, May 14, 1814, Schön, *Papiere,* VI, 331–332; cf. Marwitz to Quast, Dec. 25, 1812, Meusel, ed., *Marwitz,* II², 168–169. An even more striking instance is the request for a national assembly by the Silesian nobles, the most reactionary group in the country (memorandum to the king, Jan. 3, 1811, in Röpell, "Zur inneren Geschichte Preussens," pp. 348–349, and cf. above, pp. 23–24). Others are in Haake, "Verfassungsfrage," XXVI, 563–568.

The full import of the ambiguous meaning of the word "constitution" was brought out with exemplary clarity some years later by Friedrich von Gentz,[8] but the discovery that the promise of a constitution might be differently interpreted was made within a few months of the provisional national assembly's vote. On July 8, 1815, the government published a decree signed on May 22 which definitely proposed the establishment of a regular national assembly; and in view of this decree, the provisional assembly was dissolved on July 10.[9]

The Decree of May 22, 1815

The royal decree of May 22, 1815, seemed to leave little doubt as to what kind of constitution was contemplated. In a few short, clipped sentences, which contrast strangely with the involved phraseology of many of the laws of the day, it provided:

1. A representation of the people is to be formed.
2. For this purpose:
   (a) provincial Estates, wherever they still survive with more or less efficacy, are to be restored and adapted to the needs of the times;
   (b) where no provincial Estates exist at present, they are to be created.
3. The assembly of national deputies is to be elected from among [*aus*] the provincial Estates and is to sit in Berlin.
4. The competence of the national deputies includes consultation on all matters of legislation which concern the personal and property rights of citizens, including taxation.[10]

It further stated that a commission under the chairmanship of the chancellor was to meet not later than September 1, 1815, to organize both the provincial and national assemblies and to draft a constitution according to the principles contained in the decree.

Two important decisions concerning the nature of the prospective constitution were implied in this brief order: as to the

[8] See below, pp. 212–213.

[9] Stern, *Abhandlungen und Aktenstücke,* p. 213.

[10] "Verordnung über die zu bildende Repräsentation des Volks," May 22, 1815, *Gesetz-Sammlung* for 1815, pp. 103–104.

powers of the national assembly, it was to be only an advisory body; as to its composition, it was to be chosen "from among" the provincial Estates. The first of these decisions preserved the absolute power of the monarch, while the second allowed considerable special influence to the aristocracy who dominated the provincial Estates. The inference is clear that the government— the king, or Hardenberg, or both—was unwilling to introduce any of the elements of limited monarchy into Prussian public life. It was, no doubt, not feasible to launch manhood suffrage, which was in any event suspect as a Jacobin principle; but it would have been possible to moderate the class basis of the new assembly by means of a restricted franchise, perhaps analogous to that prevailing in Great Britain before the Reform Bill. This latter idea would presumably have guided Stein in creating a national assembly.[11]

The very limited progress represented by the decree of May 22, 1815, from the point of view of Prussia's evolution toward a constitutional monarchy, becomes even clearer in the light of the genesis of this decree. A Cabinet Order issued on June 3, 1814, in Paris, after the triumphant entry of the allies following the first defeat of Napoleon, had expressed the king's desire for both a council of state [12] and a *ständisch* constitution and representative assembly.[13] Shortly afterwards Hardenberg delegated Friedrich von Stägemann, a junior minister, to draft a proclamation of the king's intention of granting a constitution. Stägemann

---

[11] See his "Political Testament" (Botzenhart, ed., *Stein*, II, 548): "In so far as we have hitherto had representation of the people, it has been most imperfectly organized. It was therefore my plan to give every active citizen the right to be represented, whether he possess a hundred acres or ten thousand, whether he be engaged in agriculture or manufacture or trade, or in a professional or intellectual calling." In 1815, although he had in some respects turned more conservative than in the days of his ministry, he specifically disapproved of the idea of the national assembly emanating from the provincial Estates (Lehmann, *Stein*, III, 476).

[12] It will be recalled that Stein's plans for a council of state were frustrated after his dismissal. For further developments in the matter, see below, pp. 123–124.

[13] Cabinet Order of June 3, 1814, *Gesetz-Sammlung* for 1814, p. 43. This order was inspired by Hardenberg, according to Haake, "Verfassungsfrage," XXVI, 551.

went busily to work studying the constitutions of other German states and various plans submitted to him by others. He himself declared that he opposed the creation of assemblies on traditional lines, either for the provinces or for the nation, and that he favored manhood suffrage for a unicameral national assembly.[14] In view of the ultimate wording of the decree, the conclusion is inescapable that Stägemann's ideas were overruled, presumably by Hardenberg. There is definite evidence that the chancellor intervened in another connection, replacing Stägemann's word *Reichsstände* with the more traditional-sounding *Landes-Repräsentanten*.[15] This action is difficult to reconcile with Hardenberg's statement, a short time earlier, that birth was no longer important in public life.[16] Apparently it was another of the chancellor's stratagems of soothing ruffled tempers with honeyed words.

It is possible, on the other hand, that it was the king, rather than Hardenberg, who determined the final form of the decree of May 22. Frederick William III had had disagreements with Hardenberg at the Congress of Vienna over questions of foreign policy [17] and may therefore have been the readier to insist on his own constitutional views rather than accept the chancellor's. Always cautious and desperately determined to preserve his sovereignty, he was prepared in principle to have an advisory national assembly so long as there were safeguards against its grasping more power.[18] Moreover, Hardenberg was no longer the king's only trusted adviser, as he had been in 1810. A new circle of intimates was forming around the throne, men without office who nevertheless were beginning by their personal influence to wield considerable power over public affairs.

Prominent among this group was Friedrich Ancillon, the

---

[14] Stägemann in 1815, quoted without date by Rühl, ed., *Briefe und Aktenstücke*, II, 52; cf. *ibid.*, II, xv–xviii, 40–45, 50–51.

[15] See the textual analysis of the decree by Edmund Richter, *Friedrich August von Staegemann und das königliche Verfassungsversprechen vom 22ten Mai 1815* (Schweidnitz, 1913), pp. 29–41, 81–90.

[16] Hardenberg to Dorow, 1814 (no further date), in Wilhelm Dorow, *Erlebtes aus den Jahren 1790–1827* (Leipzig, 1843–45), III, 167.

[17] See below, p. 133, n. 58.

[18] See Haake, "Verfassungsfrage," XXVI, 539–540.

Huguenot tutor and friend of the crown prince.[19] It was Ancillon who procured the delay until September 1 of the first meeting of the constitutional commission, instead of Hardenberg's proposed date of July 1.[20] Delay, however, was not his principal aim; he merely hoped to use it to frustrate any attempt to shape the new constitution on a "popular" model. Ancillon was an ardent supporter of absolute monarchy: "To desire to change the Prussian constitution is to desire to impose limits and barriers on the existing sovereign authority," he wrote to Frederick William III.[21] He was not, indeed, opposed to the proclamation of a constitution; in fact, early in July, with Napoleon finally defeated, he urged the king to issue the decree of May 22 at once, in the full flush of victory, as a gift to his people from a triumphant monarch.[22] But Ancillon firmly maintained that Prussia already possessed a constitution and that it would be impossible to ignore it while proclaiming a new one; his version of a "new" constitution included most of the traditional conservative concepts, such as divine-right monarchy, the nobility as a socially stable "intermediary class," and special consideration for the historic institutions evolved in the various provinces.[23]

In all his constitutional writings Ancillon was especially fond of attacking the *Zeitgeist,* which he said was responsible for all the ideas about a "modern" constitution. The *Zeitgeist,* Ancillon asserted, did not really represent the will of the majority in Prussia but was the product of intensive propaganda by "a few shrill voices" capitalizing on the excitability of a people in arms.

[19] On Ancillon, see Paul Haake, *Johann Peter Friedrich Ancillon und Kronprinz Friedrich Wilhelm IV. von Preussen* (Munich and Berlin, 1920). The fact that Ancillon was Haake's special subject may have influenced the latter in his more general works to overestimate the extent of Ancillon's influence with the king, but his documentation is on the whole convincing.

[20] Richter, *Staegemann,* pp. 48, 52.

[21] Haake, "Verfassungsfrage," XXVI, 573.

[22] *Ibid.,* XXVIII, 196–197.

[23] This is the sketchiest possible summary of Ancillon's political thought, as expressed in his memorandum to the king of June 1815 (*ibid.,* XXVIII, 182–193), and at greater length in his book *Ueber Souveränität und Staats-Verfassungen: Ein Versuch zur Berichtigung einiger politischer Grundbegriffe* (2nd ed., Berlin, 1816, first pub. 1815), especially pp. 11–13, 27, 35–36, 46, 52–56, 63–66.

It must not be followed blindly but weighed judicially "from a superior vantage point." The French monarchy had fallen because it had yielded to the *Zeitgeist* instead of mastering it.[24]

The agitators who, according to Ancillon, were artificially exciting public opinion were to be combated, not appeased. As early as 1813 Ancillon had warned of the menace of the "few shrill voices":

There is present in the kingdom a ferment which may easily become dangerous if it is not speedily calmed or moderated. . . . Doubtless in a well-organized monarchy one ought not to pay too much attention to public opinion. . . . Doubtless the number of overexcited minds . . . is small. . . . The great mass of the nation is sound, . . . but this mass may easily be led astray in a critical moment. . . . The primary task . . . is to balk any kind of attack directed against the majesty of the throne; above all else the fountainhead of the public weal [*l'ancre du salut*], the royal authority, must be preserved. . . . The people must wait submissively and in respectful silence for the king in his great wisdom to declare his decision.[25]

Thus the very desire of the people for a modern constitution was for Ancillon an additional, and perhaps the most powerful, argument against such a constitution. The "few shrill voices" soon turned into the "demagogues" who were allegedly perverting the country's social and political morals and against whom Ancillon and many of like mind launched after 1815 the systematic persecutions which have come to be known as the *Demagogenverfolgungen*. This phenomenon came to have a direct bearing on the constitutional problem in Prussia; for by smearing all aspirations for a limited monarchy with the taint of Jacobinism, Ancillon and his fellow conservatives effectively prevented the assimilation of Prussia to the western political pattern, hurling the country instead toward the barricades of 1848 and toward Bismarck.

[24] *Ibid.,* pp. 69–76. See also Ancillon's interesting letter to his pupil, the crown prince, in Haake, *Ancillon,* p. 82.

[25] Max Lehmann, ed., "Ancillon's Denkschrift vom 4. Februar 1813," *Historische Zeitschrift,* LXVIII (1892), 277–278. But cf. the strangely contrasting note in Ancillon's letter to the crown prince, Oct. 28, 1813, in Haake, *Ancillon,* p. 61.

CHAPTER VIII

The Constitution

and the Demagogues

ANCILLON was not the first to raise the specter of "demagoguery" and revolution in Prussia. Others had seen the special dangers of a people in arms. As early as 1808 there had been much agitation against the so-called *Tugendbund* (League of Virtue), a secret society dedicated to the cause of liberating Germany from the yoke of Napoleon. General York, for example, while ardently supporting this cause, nevertheless opposed the *Tugendbund* on the grounds that it was secret, more German than Prussian, and created "enthusiasm" among junior officers.[1] But most of the opposition to the league came from those who preached submission to or even co-operation with the French. Since Stein was known to favor resistance to the French, it was easy to draw the erroneous conclusion that he must be a member of the *Tugendbund;*[2] the problem of internal unrest became bound up with that of external resistance, and Stein was accused of fostering both. Thus the former minister, Otto von Voss, whom Stein had replaced, wrote to the king concerning complaints he had received from the French representative in Berlin:

[1] Droysen, *York,* I, 135.

[2] On the *Tugendbund* and Stein's relations with it, see August Fournier, "Zur Geschichte des Tugenbundes," in his *Historische Studien und Skizzen* (Prague and Leipzig, 1885), pp. 301–330; Paul Stettiner, *Der Tugendbund* (Königsberg, 1904); Stern, *Abhandlungen und Aktenstücke,* pp. 3–41.

The continuing administration of Stein . . . was certainly his principal [grievance], but, according to him, Your Majesty is surrounded,
apart from this minister, by a number of other persons with more or
less influence in public affairs, who all share an inveterate animosity
against France and political leanings quite incompatible with the
system which Your Majesty has solemnly chosen to adopt henceforth.

Voss went on to urge the king to give France full satisfaction "as
demanded by our circumstances":

This is the only way to save our kingdom from harm from without
and the only way also to suppress the internal agitation of factions
[*l'effervescence de l'esprit de parti*] which is beginning to make itself
felt everywhere.[3]

A year later Adam Müller also linked radicalism in domestic
and foreign affairs. In his prospectus of the official paper he
wanted to edit,[4] he wrote:

Of course it would be necessary to prevaricate for the time being so
far as foreign affairs are concerned; indeed, the regrettably large
party of our native *Enragés* supplies the best of reasons for speaking
for a while the language of those at present in power.[5]

And Ancillon's own reflections in 1813 were linked to recommendations for concluding peace with Napoleon.[6]

---

[3] Voss to the king, Nov. 15, 1808, Botzenhart, ed., *Stein*, II, 601–604. Voss
was, incidentally, an interesting case. One of the most violent opponents of
Stein, he later became the candidate for chancellor of the Brandenburg
nobles during the struggle with Hardenberg in 1811 (Merckel to Stein,
July 23 and 29, 1811, *ibid.*, III, 441–442, 445) and continued to oppose
Hardenberg's constitutional plans until the latter's death. In his earlier days,
however, he had been one of the most prominent figures in the agrarian
"reform before the reform" as a provincial minister (see article by H. v.
Petersdorff in *Allgemeine Deutsche Biographie*, XXXIX, 355–359).

[4] See above, p. 71.

[5] A. Müller to Stägemann, Aug. 29, 1809, in Baxa, *Adam Müller*, p. 125.

[6] Lehmann, ed., "Ancillon's Denkschrift," *passim;* cf. Gebhardt, *Hum-*
boldt, I, 458–468; Niebuhr to Gneisenau, Feb. 2, 1816, Dietrich Gerhard
and William Norvin, eds., *Die Briefe Barthold Georg Niebuhrs* (Berlin,
1926–29), II, 669.

The "Demagogues"

Such, then, was the background for the systematic efforts made after 1815 not only to minimize the role of the people and of the common soldier in the victory over Napoleon and to change the character of the war from a *Freiheitskrieg* (war for freedom) to a mere *Befreiungskrieg* (war of liberation) but also to undermine the movement toward constitutional government by representing that movement to be dangerous and revolutionary. The situation in 1815 was summed up by General Gneisenau: "The so-called high society in Berlin consists mostly of former partisans of France, and these are now the big noises. We others are considered Jacobins and revolutionaries." [7]

Gneisenau was, indeed, accused of being the leader of the alleged revolutionary movement in the army; [8] but it was his superior, the forthright Marshal Blücher, who supplied more ammunition for the attack on this movement. The famous "Marschall Vorwärts" was the commander of the victorious Prussian troops in France, and he soon began to clash with the government in Berlin over occupation policy. Thereupon Blücher submitted his resignation to Hardenberg under protest: "It is held that I have no business in these matters, but I believe that it is my duty to make them my business; for nobody but I will speak for the army." [9] The apparent defection of a beloved general made a deep impression on the sensitive nature of Frederick William III, who felt personally aggrieved by Blücher's flouting of the government's policy. From that time on he began to regard participation of the public and of the army in political

[7] Gneisenau to Gruner, April 10, 1815, in G. H. Pertz and Hans Delbrück, *Das Leben des Feldmarschalls Grafen Neithardt von Gneisenau* (Berlin, 1864–80), IV, 492.

[8] *Ibid.*, V, 25.

[9] For these developments, see W. v. Unger, *Blücher* (Berlin, 1907–8), II, 322–343. For Hardenberg's unfavorable attitude toward Blücher in the matter, see H. Ulmann, "Die Anklage des Jakobinismus in Preussen im Jahre 1815," *Historische Zeitschrift*, XCV (1905), 442. Blücher's resignation was refused, but he continued to obstruct the government's occupation policy.

matters as undesirable. In this incidental way, therefore, an opening was made for those who, like Ancillon, sought to impress the king with the existence of a revolutionary movement in Prussia fomented by the egalitarian tendencies of a conscript army.[10]

Besides Ancillon, two other men took leading roles in this campaign to suppress the *Zeitgeist:* one was a courtier, like Ancillon, while the other was a professor. Prince Wittgenstein had the easiest possible access to the king's person, for he was the royal chamberlain (*Hofminister*), while in his capacity as minister of police he had excellent sources of information and considerable power. Wittgenstein was a die-hard legitimist, but at the same time he had, like Stein, been a direct subject of the Holy Roman Emperor (*reichsunmittelbar*) and hence felt allegiance to no particular sovereign. Just as Stein had gone into the service of the Emperor of Russia, Wittgenstein felt no hesitation about serving the Emperor of Austria; his position, however, was somewhat different, in that he omitted the formality of first resigning from the Prussian government. Theodor Anton Heinrich Schmalz was professor of law at the University of Berlin; his weapon was not court intrigue but propaganda directed at public opinion.

Wittgenstein and Schmalz agreed that the principal source of danger to the Prussian state was to be found in the new nationalism which had grown out of the War of Liberation and which was a German rather than a Prussian nationalism. In 1808 the foes of the *Tugendbund* had closely associated radical (anti-French) nationalism with internal radicalism and had almost automatically attacked one whenever they attacked the other; analogously, after 1815 the conservatives assumed that nationalism implied republicanism or some other form of opposition to the domestic *status quo* of the existing states. Historians still commonly assume a connection between liberalism and nationalism in early nineteenth-century Europe; but in fact the connection was by no means universal. In the polyglot Habsburg empire there was, indeed, a potential connection, and it was therefore

[10] Pertz and Delbrück, *Gneisenau,* V, 16.

the cornerstone of the policy of the Austrian minister, Prince
Metternich, to stifle both liberalism and nationalism.[11] But the
special conditions of Austria did not apply to the rest of Germany, and by extending his identification of the two movements
beyond his own borders, Metternich merely drove Prussian liberals into a spirited defense of Prussian sovereignty.[12]

It was the special thesis of Professor Schmalz (although Metternich and Wittgenstein soon came to share it) that the dangerous
new radical nationalism was being propagated by some of his
colleagues in the universities who were inciting the students in
the *Burschenschaften* (fraternities) to action and who aimed
ultimately at winning over public opinion at large. To Schmalz
it was the university professors who were the "few shrill voices,"
the "demagogues," and against them he launched a campaign
of counterpropaganda which soon led to the persecutions known
as the *Demagogenverfolgungen*.

Schmalz linked the agitation of the alleged "demagogues"
with the earlier activities of the *Tugendbund*. He rehearsed the
old stories about the subversiveness of that organization and
declared that its principles were being carried on by clubs which
took its place after its suppression.

These clubs [Schmalz asserted] are the sources . . . of those insen-
sate orations about the union of all Germany under one government
(in a parliamentary system, as they call it . . .), in favor of which
allegiance to the several dynasties is to be extinguished in every German breast by derision and agitation. . . . They preach German nationalism, as formerly the Jacobins preached cosmopolitanism [*die
Menschheit*], to make us forget the oaths which bind each of us to his
sovereign.[13]

[11] That this was not the only possible policy even for Austria is shown
by the reform program of Count Stadion, Metternich's predecessor.

[12] For the machinations of Metternich see below, pp. 137–139. For the con-
sequences and for elaboration on the issue of nationalism, see my article,
"Variations in Nationalism during the Great Reform Movement in Prussia,"
American Historical Review, LIX (1953–54), 305–321.

[13] Schmalz, *Berichtigung einer Stelle in der Bredow-Venturinischen
Chronik für das Jahr 1808: Ueber politische Vereine, etc.* (Berlin, 1815),
pp. 11–14.

The demagogues, wrote Schmalz, "seek constitutions to destroy the power of the princes." [14] Constitutions, to Schmalz, immediately suggested the French Revolution, and the French Revolution suggested Jacobinism. Therefore he asked, in the manner of Adam Müller:

Are we Germans or Frenchmen? This accursed hatching of constitutions has been a characteristically French vice for twenty-six years. Bonaparte created them by the dozen, like decrees: our political scribblers create them by the dozen, like newspaper articles. . . .

I regard . . . every constitution as good . . . which has formed itself out of the special characteristics of a nation, spontaneously, gradually, and unostentatiously; and I regard every constitution as absolutely bad which a man takes it into his head to write down. . . . The real constitution of the state . . . is the totality of all public institutions. And who is the man who can grasp them all, their interrelation and their relation with countless private situations, so completely that he can destroy and change without injustice? Or is a constitution to appear annually, after the French fashion, like a calendar? [15]

Schmalz's original pamphlet was published in August 1815; in October of the same year the king conferred a medal on the author.[16] Presumably the medal was in the nature of a reward for his defense of the monarchy. Against this official endorsement of Schmalz's denunciation of nationalist "demagogues," i.e.,

[14] Schmalz, *Ueber des Herrn B. G. Niebuhrs Schrift wider die meinige, politische Vereine betreffend* (Berlin, 1815), p. 8. See in a similar vein the contemporaneous anonymous pamphlet *Die deutschen Roth- und Schwarz-Mäntler* (Neubrandenburg, n.d.), pp. 9, 14–15.

[15] Schmalz, *Letztes Wort über politische Vereine* (Berlin, 1816), pp. 5, 10. In view particularly of this passage, I find it difficult to follow Max Lenz (*Geschichte der königlichen Friedrich-Wilhelms-Universität zu Berlin* [Halle, 1910–18], I, 540–541) in describing Schmalz as a liberal. Knapp, *Bauern-Befreiung*, I, 137, seems to dispose of his liberalism in economic matters. Lenz may have based his judgment on the authority of Schön, *Papiere*, I, 50.

[16] Evidently on the advice of either Ancillon or Wittgenstein. See Haake, "Verfassungsfrage," XXVIII, 211; Justus von Gruner, "Die Ordensverleihung an den Geheimen Rat Professor Schmalz 1815," *Forschungen zur brandenburgischen und preussischen Geschichte,* XXII (1909), 169–182.

those who were in favor of a constitution, a storm of protest arose, and by no means only among Schmalz's victims. In fact, the man who took issue with Schmalz most directly was the historian Barthold Georg Niebuhr, certainly no Jacobin and if anything a conservative.[17] Also prominent was General Gneisenau, who expressed his position thus:

If, now that the French overlordship over us has been removed, a secret society still exists, then it can have only revolutionary or treasonable purposes, and in that event its members should be severely punished. But to encourage indefinite conjectures, and thus to foster and to increase mistrust of those suspected of secret illegal activity, is unjust.[18]

The result, thought Gneisenau, was to introduce a feeling of bitterness into Prussian affairs.

And this condition . . . has been brought about by a phantom. . . . I do not believe in the existence of a secret society. In fact, I suspect that those who have made it their business to spread this notion, with the exception of one or two, do not believe in such a secret society themselves but have merely been trying to arouse alarm as a tool for their persecutions.[19]

Hardenberg had been away from Berlin at the time of the award of Schmalz's medal, and Niebuhr and his followers presumed that on his return he would take steps to rescind it or to make sure that no further such incident occurred. "We can certainly count on the good will of the chancellor," wrote Niebuhr.[20] But his optimism was disappointed; Hardenberg refused to undertake an investigation of the award because it

[17] Niebuhr published a pamphlet in rebuttal to Schmalz, entitled *Ueber geheime Verbindungen im preussischen Staat, und deren Denunciation* (Berlin, 1815). For Niebuhr's constitutional views, see Niebuhr to Dahlmann, Feb. 17, 1816, Gerhard and Norvin, eds., *Briefe Niebuhrs*, II, 675, and I, lxxx. Another conservative who rejected the demagogue scare was Marwitz: see Meusel, ed., *Marwitz*, I, 621–626.

[18] Gneisenau to Boyen, Nov. 19, 1815, Karl Griewank, ed., *Gneisenau: Ein Leben in Briefen* (Leipzig, 1939), p. 332.

[19] Gneisenau to Thile, April 9, 1816, *ibid.*, pp. 342–343.

[20] Niebuhr to Gneisenau, Dec. 18, 1815, in Pertz and Delbrück, *Gneisenau*, V, 63.

"would only serve to exacerbate factional agitation," and subsequently he prohibited any further public discussion of Schmalz's pamphlet, though he did not prevent Schmalz from publishing another one. Niebuhr wrote: "For some incredible reason Hardenberg believes in the continued existence of secret societies. One must assume that our opponents . . . have constructed for his benefit a whole edifice of forged papers and fictitious oral disclosures." [21]

Even this, however, was too generous an interpretation of Hardenberg's attitude. The chancellor was not the unsuspecting victim of a conspiracy of deception; on the contrary, he was well aware what he was doing, and he had personal reasons for doing it. It has been established that Hardenberg himself had, only a few months earlier, given his approval to a secret society whose aim was the unification of Germany (though, to be sure, a Germany "linked to the Hohenzollern dynasty and to the Prussian monarchy"). Its leading spirit, Justus Gruner, had written to Hardenberg to ask his support "for the German people against their governments," and the chancellor had specifically given it.[22] It was, from Hardenberg's point of view, in the highest degree undesirable that an investigation into the secret societies should be held. If his connection became known, he would have to defend himself against charges of Jacobinism.

Thus Hardenberg's attitude, not only in the matter of the Schmalz medal but toward the whole question of the "demagogues" and the agitation about a constitution, becomes explicable. To cover his own tracks he tacitly endorsed Schmalz and

[21] Niebuhr to Gneisenau, Jan. 13, 1816, *ibid.*, V, 70. Nevertheless this touching faith in Hardenberg persisted as late as 1818 in Clausewitz, another opponent of the persecutions: Clausewitz to Gröben, Jan. 4, 1818, in Eberhard Kessel, "Zu Boyens Entlassung," *Historische Zeitschrift*, 175 (1953), 48–49.

[22] Documentary proof is given by Justus von Gruner, "Justus Gruner und der Hoffmannsche Bund," *Forschungen zur brandenburgischen und preussischen Geschichte*, XIX (1906), esp. pp. 491–497; Gruner to Gneisenau, June 18, 1815, in Pertz and Delbrück, *Gneisenau*, IV, 566. See further, on Hardenberg's relations with Gruner, Walter Obenaus, *Die Entwicklung der preussischen Sicherheitspolizei bis zum Ende der Reaktionszeit* (Berlin, 1940), pp. 104–105.

later threw Gruner and many others sympathetic toward a constitution to the wolves.[23] Only by so doing, he felt, could he remain in office and preside over the installation of a constitutional regime. But in fact, by so doing he played into the hands of the opponents of a constitution and sealed the doom of Prussian constitutional evolution.

The Constitution in the Balance

There can be no question that the demagogue scare, through its effect on Hardenberg, was one of the principal causes of the defeat of constitutionalism in Prussia. But despite the best efforts of Ancillon, Wittgenstein, and their cohorts, the hysteria did not reach its full force until after the famous celebration on the Wartburg in 1817, of the tercentenary of the Reformation; and in the meantime other factors also played their part in thwarting Hardenberg's undoubtedly sincere desire to crown his career by establishing a constitution.[24] Basic among these was the formidable problem of digesting the extensive new territories acquired by Prussia under the settlement of 1815; administrative adjustment was necessarily a more urgent task than the promulgation of a constitution.[25] The delay imposed by this circumstance allowed time for other forces hostile to a constitution to make themselves felt.

The constitutional commission contemplated in the decree of

[23] Prominent among the victims was Stein's friend Sack, who was transferred away from the governorship of the Rhineland because of conservative pressure—Hardenberg would not risk any association with unpopular liberals. See Sack's complaint, Sack to Stein, Jan. 27, 1816, Botzenhart, ed., *Stein*, V, 291–293; cf. Pertz, *Stein*, V, 44.

For general views on Hardenberg and the Schmalz affair, see Gruner, "Justus Gruner," pp. 485–489, 503–506; Ulmann, "Die Anklage des Jakobinismus," pp. 445–446; and the contemporary judgments of Dorow, *Erlebtes*, I, 159, and K. A. Varnhagen von Ense, *Denkwürdigkeiten des eigenen Lebens* (Leipzig, 1871), V, 124.

[24] The chancellor expressed this desire too often to too many different people to admit of any reasonable doubt of his sincerity: see Haake, "Verfassungsfrage," XXIX, 310, 315–316.

[25] See Hardenberg to Gneisenau, March 15, 1816, in Pertz and Delbrück, *Gneisenau*, V, 92.

May 22, 1815, whose date of meeting had already been twice postponed to September 1, 1815, had not met by the end of that year, nor yet by the end of the following year. Stägemann, the author of the May decree, wondered whether "perhaps the constitutional commission is awaiting the *Zeitgeist*." [26] The same observer also noticed a gradual lessening of interest in the constitution on the part of the king,[27] a judgment which was scornfully confirmed by Sack:

The king has sunk into complete apathy, approves everything and lets everyone do what they please, concerns himself with nothing except petty military affairs, and merely transmits incoming papers to the chancellor and the ministers without caring what becomes of them, happy and content to hear no more about them.[28]

If this had been the situation, it might at least have had the virtue of leaving Hardenberg a clear field. But in fact, Frederick William III was becoming increasingly the instrument through which the conservative court faction exerted its influence on Prussian politics. A clear symptom of this relationship is provided by the manner in which a Prussian council of state was finally established. Originally, a council of state had been conceived by Stein as the supreme executive organ of the state, serving both to co-ordinate and to transcend the spheres of activity of the various ministers. The creation of such a body had been prevented, after Stein's departure, on the combined initiative of the king and Altenstein. The project had then been revived in the familiar decree of October 27, 1810, with the important difference that the council was now envisaged as an advisory and no longer as an executive body, in deference to Hardenberg's own position as the highest executive officer after the king; but even in this altered form the council did not take shape, the king belatedly announcing on April 24, 1812, that there would be further delay. The next step had been the Cabi-

[26] Stägemann to Varnhagen, Aug. 28, 1816, Varnhagen von Ense, *Aus dem Nachlass: Briefe von Stägemann, Metternich, Heine und Bettina von Arnim* (Leipzig, 1865), p. 39.

[27] Stägemann to Varnhagen, Feb. 4, 1817, *ibid.*, p. 41.

[28] Sack to Stein, May 8, 1816, Botzenhart, ed., *Stein*, V, 310.

net Order from Paris of June 3, 1814, which placed the question
of the council of state once more on the agenda.[29]

Concrete progress began to be made during 1816, and various
suggestions were finally incorporated into a draft decree by
Humboldt. But Frederick William III allowed himself to be
persuaded by the conservatives, especially Wittgenstein, Schuckmann, and the finance minister, Count Bülow, to make several
important changes in the draft.[30] The most significant concession
consisted in the elimination of all passages tending to give the
council of state a status superior to the ministers. Since the council's function had already been reduced from that of a supermin-
isterial executive body to that of an advisory group to the king,
this concession removed the last vestiges of Stein's political
philosophy from the new organ. Other important changes included a reduction in the chancellor's powers of convening the
council and arranging its agenda and elimination from the Order
of all references to a future national assembly. All these concessions were wrung from Hardenberg after he had been obliged,
by the king's orders, to submit his plans for the council to Wittgenstein and to others of his party.[31]

The establishment of the council of state seemed for the
moment to augur well for a Prussian constitution, for within
ten days the constitutional commission provided for in the decree of May 22, 1815, was created, composed entirely of members
of the council. Its first meeting took place in an aura of optimism

[29] For the earlier events here recapitulated, see above, pp. 44–46, 110;
Gesetz-Sammlung for 1810–1811, pp. 3–4; *Gesetz-Sammlung* for 1814, p. 43;
Schneider, "Entstehung des preussischen Staatsrats," pp. 500–506. Haussherr,
Die Stunde Hardenbergs, p. 194, asserts that Hardenberg did not intend to
institute the council in 1810 at all.

[30] Cabinet Order of March 20, 1817, establishing the council of state,
Gesetz-Sammlung for 1817, pp. 67–76; Gebhardt, *Humboldt*, II, 233–235.
For what follows and for further details on this episode, see Paul Haake,
"Die Errichtung des preussischen Staatsrats im März 1817," *Forschungen
zur brandenburgischen und preussischen Geschichte*, XXVII (1914), 247–
265, where copious documentation is provided; and Schneider, "Entstehung
des preussischen Staatsrats," pp. 506–529.

[31] It should be observed, however, that Wittgenstein demanded still
further alterations, which Hardenberg refused to make. This raises the
question of whether the chancellor could have resisted the pressure entirely.

on July 7, 1817, when it was addressed by Hardenberg in glowing terms:

History teaches us that the old Prussian Estates [*Landstände*] did not operate for the benefit of the state but were in fact merely the guardians of the privileges of certain sections of the population and constituted veritable obstructions to the working of the state machinery. . . . Being persuaded that the existing . . . situation of the state cannot continue without severe harm being done and that a better regulated constitution, working for the benefit of all classes of the population and adapted to the needs of the times, is necessary; guided by the knowledge that the Prussian nation is ready for and worthy of a permanent constitution and representation . . . , His Majesty has been moved to the voluntary decision to grant such a [constitution].

But then Hardenberg went on to reveal that it was the king's "unalterable desire" that the future assembly (referred to here only vaguely as *Stände*) was to have only advisory powers in legislation and no powers in administration; and the commission was directed to take this principle as its point of departure.[32]

The king's unalterable desire had been communicated to Hardenberg in an earlier memorandum together with a second one: namely, that the organization of the provincial assemblies must be completed before discussion about the national assembly could begin. (This second proviso, despite its importance, appears not to have been mentioned to the commission by Hardenberg, and one may speculate whether he hoped to be able to modify it. Certainly he was not in favor of it.[33]) The king had explained that he did not wish these two matters to become subjects of discussion in the constitutional commission, since experience in other states had shown that public discussion of constitutional fundamentals led to a manifestation of selfish interests.[34] Frederick William evidently had in mind recent

[32] Heinrich von Treitschke, "Der erste Verfassungskampf in Preussen. (1815–1823.)," *Preussische Jahrbücher,* XXIX (1872), 350–351 (hereafter Treitschke, "Verfassungskampf").

[33] *Ibid.,* p. 348.

[34] The king to Hardenberg, April 12, 1817, in Haake, "Verfassungsfrage," XXIX, 347–348.

events in Württemberg, where a Diet convened to consider the king's draft of a new constitution had proved most untractable.[35] Because of this painful example, the government adopted a peculiar method of fulfilling a provision of the decree of May 22, 1815, which called for consultation on the matter of the constitution with "well-informed . . . residents of the provinces." The obvious way to do this would have been to invite selected well-informed residents to Berlin to meet with the commission, but now it was feared that such a gathering would display untoward recalcitrance, on the Württemberg model. Instead, it was decided that agents of the government would tour the provinces to consult the wishes of the inhabitants.

The person responsible for this decision was a new member of the government, Wilhelm von Klewiz, who held the title of secretary of state, a position created to provide an intermediary of ministerial rank between the king and the council of state.[36] But even more far-reaching was his second recommendation: namely, that no national assembly be created at all but only provincial assemblies, and that therefore those undertaking the tour of inquiry should ascertain not only the wishes of the inhabitants with respect to a national constitution but also the precise status of the existing constitutions of the provinces. The inference is inescapable that Klewiz and other adherents of unrestricted provincial politics regarded the tour of inquiry as a potential means of killing the idea of a national assembly. Presumably provincial particularism would receive stronger expression by residents of the provinces when questioned individually

---

[35] For Württemberg, see Schnabel, *Deutsche Geschichte*, II, 80–81; Albrecht List, *Der Kampf um's gute alte Recht (1815–1819) nach seiner ideen- und parteigeschichtlichen Seite* (Tübingen, 1912), pp. 5–6. Cf. Schuckmann's reference to Württemberg as a deterrent example, Schuckmann to Hardenberg, June 4, 1817, in Haake, "Verfassungsfrage," XXIX, 353; and Stägemann's comment, Stägemann to Varnhagen, May 16, 1817, Varnhagen, *Aus dem Nachlass*, p. 47.

[36] Klewiz' memorandum of April 28, 1817, in Treitschke, "Verfassungskampf," pp. 349–350. As an undersecretary, Klewiz had been one of Humboldt's supporters in the fight for a council of state in 1809; see above, pp. 44–45, and Schneider, "Enstehung des preussischen Staatsrats," pp. 492, 507–508.

—especially if, as it turned out, most of those questioned were nobles—than by a gathering of "Notables" from all provinces assembled in Berlin. One can only marvel at an administration which allowed control over a major political undertaking to fall into the hands of an official who was avowedly opposed to its principles. Klewiz himself, moreover, was one of the designated poll takers; the others were Altenstein, who appears to have abandoned his earlier anticonstitutional views, and Beyme, the king's cabinet secretary before Stein had had him dismissed, whose political views were not then clearly known. Thus, of these three observers, who divided up their task on a geographical basis, one was opposed to Hardenberg's ideas, one was friendly, and the position of the third was uncertain—an eloquent commentary on Hardenberg's execution of his plans.[37]

The results obtained by the three agents were, not surprisingly, in accord with their own constitutional views.[38] Klewiz heard most sentiment against a national assembly and in favor of old-style provincial assemblies or else, where the need for a national assembly was acknowledged, in favor of election of its deputies from among the provincial deputies. This latter view was expressed by the former minister Voss, among others.[39] But a different view was taken by another of Stein's old enemies, Field Marshal York, who declared with an air of resignation:

The constitution dearest to me is the monarchical one, as it used to be under Frederick the Great. However, a constitution and repre-

[37] On Altenstein, see above, p. 45; Varnhagen von Ense, *Denkwürdigkeiten*, V, 7. On Beyme, see *ibid.*, V, 178–179; Gneisenau to Clausewitz, Dec. 23, 1817, in Pertz and Delbrück, *Gneisenau*, V, 278–279; and, most important, Beyme's ambiguous letter to Varnhagen, Dec. 2, 1815, in Dorow, *Erlebtes*, III, 205–206. Later events were to prove that, in fact, Beyme was one of the staunchest advocates of a constitution for Prussia (see below, p. 220).

[38] For the tour of inquiry, see chiefly A. Stern, "Die preussische Verfassungsfrage"; but for the results obtained by Klewiz, more detailed information on the province of Brandenburg is available in Müsebeck, "Die märkische Ritterschaft," pp. 168–173. Accordingly my remarks in the case of Klewiz are based on Brandenburg alone (Klewiz' territory included three other provinces).

[39] Treitschke, "Verfassungskampf," p. 358.

sentation have been promised the country, and the promise must be kept, and that as soon as possible, too, because the continued existence of heavy burdens is causing discontent which may easily become dangerous when a people is armed.

York favored a small national assembly, voting by classes, which was to consult the provincial assemblies on all proposed legislation.[40] Others besides York conceded that since a national assembly had been promised, it must be formed. In fact, though the opposition to a constitution was widespread, it was by no means concerted.[41]

Beyme, on the basis of a distribution of opinion much like that in Klewiz' territory, declared that the old Estates were recognized as obsolete and that "the ideas of common citizenship and civil liberty" had greatly developed and were expressed in a desire for a parliamentary constitution. Prussia, Beyme thought, must not lag behind other nations in her political development.[42] Public opinion seemed friendliest to the idea of a national assembly in Altenstein's area, the western provinces, where revolution and foreign occupation had done much to weaken traditional institutions. Altenstein found the general sentiment to be in favor of new provincial assemblies together with an influential national assembly independent of them.[43]

If it was almost a foregone conclusion that the results of the tour of inquiry would reflect the political opinions of each of the three poll takers, it was equally predictable that those results would carry little weight with Hardenberg, who had made up his mind long ago what he wanted in the way of a constitution. In fact, he wrote to Altenstein: "I am not much concerned with the existing conditions, but I am eager to know *your* ideas about

[40] Stern, "Die preussische Verfassungsfrage," pp. 81–82. York's allusion to an armed people referred to the Landwehr, for which see below, pp. 186–187.

[41] Cf. Müsebeck, "Die märkische Ritterschaft," p. 173.

[42] For Beyme's results, see Stern, "Die preussische Verfassungsfrage," pp. 96–98.

[43] For Altenstein, see *ibid.*, pp. 66, 71–72. A somewhat different emphasis on the basis of the same data is suggested by Jakob Roebers, *Die Einrichtung der Provinzialstände in Westfalen und die Wahlen zum ersten westfälischen Provinziallandtag* (Münster, 1914).

the new ones to be introduced." The chancellor was in practice little interested either in the old provincial constitutions or in the desires of the "residents of the provinces" but wanted only to produce a constitution as soon as possible.[44]

But many of his contemporaries were most doubtful whether Hardenberg's actions were adequate to his purpose. Sack wrote to his mentor Stein that the entire state administration would be beyond repair unless fundamental changes were made soon. "The chancellor has visibly deteriorated both in body and mind"; his memory was bad, he grasped no connections between related matters, and he was entirely in the hands of his "wicked entourage."[45] From this and other reports Stein concluded: "I admire the chancellor's skill in frustrating the work of all vigorous and able men. The spirit of the Lord has left him, . . . nothing that he does succeeds."[46]

Hardenberg did, indeed, seem to have a remarkable talent for weakening his friends and strengthening his enemies.[47] Humboldt observed that all of Hardenberg's ministers except Boyen, the war minister, were worse than useless; the chancellor was aware that he had surrounded himself with men either inefficient or hostile to him, but "he seems to lack the resolution to make a change."[48] This judgment was confirmed almost at once. Hardenberg complained to the king about the inadequacy of Schuckmann, Bülow, and Kircheisen, the ministers of interior, finance, and justice, respectively;[49] but instead of having the courage of his convictions and dismissing these three, he adopted a half measure characteristic of his whole career. He divided two of the ministries concerned into two unequal parts each, giving both of the smaller parts to a liberal. Thus Schuckmann lost the education section of his ministry, Altenstein becoming minister of education; Kircheisen lost juris-

[44] Hardenberg to Altenstein, Feb. 12, 1818, and Hardenberg's marginal note, in Haake, "Verfassungsfrage," XXIX, 358–359 (italics mine).

[45] Sack to Stein, May 8, 1816, Botzenhart, ed., *Stein,* V, 310–311.

[46] Stein to Gagern, Sept. 16, 1818, *ibid.,* V, 516.

[47] Cf. Clausewitz to Gneisenau, Nov. 7, 1818, in Pertz and Delbrück, *Gneisenau,* V, 358.

[48] Humboldt to Stein, Sept. 16, 1817, Botzenhart, ed., *Stein,* V, 409.

[49] Hardenberg to the king, Oct. 10, 1817, in Meinecke, *Boyen,* II, 326–327.

diction over the Rhineland, Beyme heading a special ministry of justice for that province.[50] Bülow was, indeed, replaced in the finance ministry by Klewiz—an improvement from the point of view of efficiency if from no other; but at the same time some sections of his old ministry were detached and given to Bülow as a new ministry of commerce. On this timid handling of the situation Boyen, the liberal minister of war, offered the only possible comment:

The day is past when one could throw together a ministry out of heterogeneous elements and regard it as a loose association. Such a child born of caprice will die of consumption if not of apoplexy. Nothing except unity of purpose, and above all a plan logically executed in all its details, can control public opinion and create confidence in a stable government.[51]

In the meantime, no progress was being made toward a constitution in Prussia. The whole autumn of 1817 was taken up with the tour of inquiry; then there was a delay in the reports of the three observers. During a large part of the following year either the king or Hardenberg was away from Berlin, and Frederick William had stipulated that during such intervals no action was to be taken with respect to the constitution.[52]

One of these trips, however, was to carry an even greater significance than the delaying of the constitution. On January 12, 1818, Hardenberg, vacationing on the Rhine, granted an audience to Joseph Görres, a Rhenish publicist of democratic leanings, who had been collecting signatures for a petition reminding the government of the promise of May 22, 1815. This petition, the so-called *Koblenzer Adresse,* Görres gave to Hardenberg. In a subsequent pamphlet reporting on his audience with the chancellor, Görres took the occasion to add

[50] There was some justification for this apparently arbitrary arrangement, since the Rhineland posed the special problem of integrating the existing Roman law with the Prussian system.

[51] Boyen to Schön, Oct. 26, 1817, in Meinecke, *Boyen,* II, 327–328. For Schön's reaction, cf. Schön, *Papiere,* VI, 426–427; Treitschke, "Verfassungskampf," p. 417.

[52] In his instructions to Hardenberg of April 12, 1817, cited above, n. 34.

some general reflections on the political situation in which he emphasized the role of the demagogue scare in the successful resistance to the promised constitution. The fires of liberty, he declared, could not be extinguished: "those who are supposed to put them out will themselves go up in flames, and in the end the just cause will triumph according to the inevitable demands of history." [53]

To the Ancillon-Wittgenstein faction, Görres, his petition, and his pamphlet came like a heaven-sent gift: for not only could they point to Görres as the very model of a modern demagogue,[54] but they had the further satisfaction of seeing Hardenberg involved in a quarrel over Görres with his sovereign. In his report to the king of his meeting with Görres, the chancellor expressed his conviction that the latter should be censured for his violent language and for his collecting of signatures, an act which betrayed distrust in the king's word. Hardenberg also sent to the king for his endorsement a draft reply to the petitioning Rhinelanders advising them to await with confidence the consummation of the promise of May 22, 1815.[55] But Frederick William III brusquely rejected this draft, asserted that Görres' pamphlet was renewed evidence of subversive activities in the Rhineland designed to force concessions from the government, ordered a reprimand issued to implicated officials, and finally declared that "demonstrations of this sort to hold the sovereign to a promise" were "reprehensible and improper":

I will determine when the promise of a constitution shall be fulfilled, and I will not be swayed by untimely remonstrances from steadily progressing towards this goal. . . . The duty of the subjects is to

[53] Haake, "Verfassungsfrage," XXIX, 364; cf. Schnabel, *Deutsche Geschichte*, II, 285.

[54] Görres himself was, indeed, forthwith hounded out of Prussia; see Schnabel, *Deutsche Geschichte*, II, 262–263, and cf. Karl Alexander von Müller, *Görres in Strassburg 1819/20: Eine Episode aus dem Beginn der Demagogenverfolgungen* (Stuttgart, Berlin, and Leipzig, 1926).

[55] Hardenberg to the king, Feb. 19, 1818, in Haake, "Verfassungsfrage," XXIX, 364–365.

await, with confidence in my sovereign discretion, . . . the time which I, guided by my grasp of the whole situation, shall find suitable for its fulfillment.[56]

One is reminded of that notorious pronouncement by one of the king's ministers when the French were about to occupy Berlin in 1806: "The first duty of a citizen is to remain calm" (*Ruhe is die erste Bürgerpflicht*). The king reasserted his power as an absolute monarch who would brook no disagreement even from his chancellor. The effects of the Görres affair were thus twofold: not only were Hardenberg's power and prestige impaired, with the result that he felt less than ever free to proceed with directness in the matter of the constitution, but also the king's desire for a constitution, never very robust, was further weakened because he was made to feel that the granting of a constitution would be a concession to those who were intent on limiting his sovereignty.

By itself the Görres affair might not have had these effects, at least not permanently; the episode took place, however, against a historical background which greatly enhanced its importance. In the first place, Frederick William's confidence in Hardenberg had been weakened for other reasons; in the second place, the demagogue scare had been revived with a vengeance following the proceedings on the Wartburg in October 1817. The first of these occurrences resulted from a speech by Hardenberg on February 5, 1818, to the Diet of the German Confederation on the progress of the Prussian constitution. Hardenberg had there stated that, on the basis of the materials gathered by the three investigators on the tour of inquiry, it would be possible soon to institute provincial assemblies, "whereby the most essential step will have been taken in the execution of the decree of May 22 [1815]." Subsequently, he had said, the government, giving due weight to provincial requirements, would proceed with "whatever it may deem necessary and suitable to create a bond between all the provinces." Finally, he had promised a further statement in a year's

[56] The king to Hardenberg, Feb. 23 and March 21, 1818, *ibid.*, XXIX, 365–368.

time.[57] But Frederick William III, in the strong language of a sovereign monarch to a subservient minister reminiscent of his dismissal of Stein in 1807, took Hardenberg severely to task for issuing a declaration without his assent on the highly important matter of the constitution, on which he, the king, had specifically requested to be kept fully informed. He did not expect, he wrote, to read about such speeches in the newspapers. In any event, he disapproved of Hardenberg's undertaking to report progress in a year's time: he could not permit "this extremely difficult and involved matter to be hurried, just because it appears to have been delayed"; perhaps a year would not be sufficient, and then Prussia would be humiliated in the Diet. "The promise will be fulfilled; but people will have to wait patiently for the proper time [*der Zeitpunkt muss aber abgewartet werden*]." [58]

The second element in the background of the Görres affair, the resurgence of the persecution of the demagogues, deserves more detailed treatment.

The Wartburg, the Hofburg, and the Constitution

The year 1817 was named by the legatee of Stein's reform program, Theodor von Schön, as marking the beginning of the

[57] Treitschke, "Verfassungskampf," p. 412.

[58] Cabinet Order to Hardenberg, Feb. 18, 1818, in Haake, "Verfassungsfrage," XXIX, 361–363. It will be appropriate to take note here of the much earlier disagreement between Hardenberg and his royal master over foreign affairs at the Congress of Vienna in the winter of 1814–1815. At that time, partly under pressure from Tsar Alexander, Frederick William ordered Hardenberg to withdraw from negotiations with Austria and Great Britain directed against Russia and intended to secure Saxony for Prussia. It is noteworthy, however, that on that occasion, according to the available evidence, no diminution of the king's confidence in Hardenberg resulted. Hardenberg appears to have kept his grumbles to himself, complaining, indeed, about the aggressive Prussian generals rather than about the timid king. In general, there is no reason to believe that Hardenberg lost prestige at Vienna. The best account of these matters is by C. K. Webster, *The Foreign Policy of Castlereagh 1812–1815: Britain and the Reconstruction of Europe* (London, 1931), pp. 342–384; cf. Hans Delbrück, "Friedrich Wilhelm III. und Hardenberg auf dem Wiener Kongress," *Historische Zeitschrift*, LXIII (1889), 242–265, and Karl Griewank, "Preussen und die

triumph of reaction in Prussia.[59] The most significant turning point of that year was the celebration on the Wartburg, Luther's refuge, of the tercentenary of the Reformation.[60] This was an occasion sponsored by the *Burschenschaften* (fraternities) of all the German universities. Under the auspices of the great reformer, the delegates glorified the idea of German nationality and of medieval "liberty." Someone was reminded of Luther's burning of the papal bull and, in the tradition of undergraduate pranks the world over, promoted the burning of the books of some of the worst enemies of academic freedom and of German unity (among those honored was Professor Schmalz).

Modern scholars are agreed now that these events on the Wartburg were innocent enough, representing little more than undergraduate exuberance. But the demagogue hunters—the Ancillons, the Wittgensteins, and of course the Schmalzes—regarded, or professed to regard, the proceedings as no mere pranks but on the contrary as symptomatic of sedition and revolution. Even Gneisenau, only recently an advocate of a constitution, now wrote: "The demand for a constitution is getting dangerously out of hand, and some Jacobin yeast is mixed in with it." [61] Obviously, the Wartburg celebration offered excellent ammunition for those who asserted that the chief danger to the Prussian monarchy was to be found among the "demagogues," the teachers at the universities, and especially

---

Neuordnung Deutschlands 1813–1815," Forschungen zur brandenburgischen und preussischen Geschichte, LII (1940), 250–257.

[59] Eduard Wilhelm Mayer, "Politische Erfahrungen und Gedanken Theodors von Schön nach 1815," *Historische Zeitschrift,* 117 (1917), 435.

[60] On the events on the Wartburg and their background, see Schnabel, *Deutsche Geschichte,* II, 231–247; for more detailed discussions see Herman Haupt, ed., *Quellen und Darstellungen der Burschenschaft und der deutschen Einheitsbewegung,* especially Volume VI: Paul Wentzcke, *Geschichte der deutschen Burschenschaft,* Vol. I (Heidelberg, 1919).

[61] Gneisenau to Clausewitz, Dec. 23, 1817, Griewank, ed., *Gneisenau,* p. 354. Cf. also Gneisenau to Gibsone, Dec. 19, 1817, in Pertz and Delbrück, *Gneisenau,* V, 274. This stand did not even rescue Gneisenau from the reputation of being a demagogue himself: Clausewitz to Gröben, Jan. 4, 1818, in Kessel, "Zu Boyens Entlassung," p. 48.

in their tendency to ignore the existing states in favor of a united Germany. For example, Duke Charles of Mecklenburg, a relative of the king and one of the group at court intent upon influencing the king against granting a constitution, wrote to him: "The mischief on the Wartburg assaults all sovereigns, great and small, promotes terrorism, intolerance, and demagogic despotism; from there it is only a few steps to outright revolutionary actions." [62] The effect of such suggestions on the suspicious nature of Frederick William III can be imagined. To Altenstein, the new minister of education, he wrote: "It is the urgent duty of all governments and of your ministry to counteract vigorously the highly dangerous and criminal state of mind which has gained ascendancy among the inexperienced youth in the German universities." [63]

This revived atmosphere of suspicion and persecution brought back to the king's first minister, Hardenberg, all the embarrassments which he thought he had dispelled by suppressing agitation of the issue of Schmalz's medal early in 1816. First, Hardenberg felt himself obliged, because of his unfortunate involvement with a nationalistic secret society, to sacrifice many liberal professors accused of being "demagogues"; later, the situation forced from him concession after concession in the matter of the constitution itself.

The two most prominent university men affected by the new persecutions were the famous (or notorious) *Turnvater* Jahn, and the poet and novelist Ernst Moritz Arndt. Having taken Jahn under his wing as late as December 1817, the chancellor a bare two months later described him as "a highly dangerous man" against whom it was urgently necessary to take measures.[64] Arndt, formerly a companion of Stein's at the court of St. Petersburg during the Prussian alliance with Napoleon in 1812, had been nominated by Hardenberg to a professorship at the new university in Bonn. The appointment

---

[62] Duke Charles to the king, Nov. 3, 1817, in Haake, "Verfassungsfrage," XXX, 325.

[63] Cabinet Order to Altenstein, Dec. 27, 1817, *ibid.*, XXX, 327.

[64] Hardenberg to Altenstein, Dec. 8, 1817, and Feb. 5, 1818, in M. Lenz, *Geschichte der Universität Berlin*, II¹, 39–40.

was attacked by Wittgenstein on the ground that Arndt was
not "a true friend of lawful monarchical tranquillity and
order." Finally, Wittgenstein forced the government to choose
between himself and Arndt by threatening to resign unless
Arndt's appointment were rescinded. Hardenberg immediately
abandoned his nominee and wrote to Wittgenstein: "Steps
must be taken against Arndt." It is true that later Wittgenstein
was formally removed from the police ministry, and Arndt's
appointment was confirmed. Nevertheless, the chancellor had
capitulated in principle to the faithless servant of Metternich.
Wittgenstein remained in his influential position as lord
chamberlain, and in a Cabinet Order of January 11, 1819,
Altenstein was ordered to caution Arndt against further utterances of sentiments unsuitable for a teacher of the young.[65]

Altenstein himself was deeply disturbed by these problems
which confronted him so soon after taking office as minister
of education. He found it difficult, he admitted, to draw a
line between legitimate discussion on the one hand and expression of radical views dangerous to existing governments
on the other, and he stressed his anxiety not to throw out the
baby with the bathwater. His rather lame conclusion was that
the government should support the good cause of a representative constitution and should develop the nation's spiritual
values, while rejecting and punishing all forms of perversion
(*Entartung*), of which one of the most important was the perversion of the nation's youth, manifested in slack academic
discipline and premature involvement of students in politics.
Concretely, he recommended both the removal of Arndt from
his professorship and the dismissal of Karl von Kamptz, one of
Wittgenstein's chief lieutenants at the police ministry. In a
later memorandum Altenstein attributed "the current excesses" to "incomplete education in defective schools and in
universities which have been afraid to tackle these phenomena."
Again he recommended "severe punishment of every per-

[65] For the case of Arndt, see *ibid.*, II¹, 42–43; Ernst Müsebeck, "Die Einleitung des Verfahrens gegen E. M. Arndt: Eine Untersuchung zur
Geschichte der Reaktion in Preussen nach 1815," *Historische Zeitschrift*,
105 (1910), 516–529.

version . . . while at the same time respecting and encouraging as much as possible the pursuit of true learning." Such a procedure would, he thought, enlist scholarship itself in the cause of eliminating undesirable excesses.[66]

This position, though vacillating and logically untenable, was far from hostile to the academic or even the journalistic professions as such. Its main thesis was that "pure" scholarship should isolate itself from political entanglements and cultivate its own garden. Such scholarship by its very achievements would then subserve the constitutional idea by engendering confidence in the intellectuals, who would presumably be the leaders of the newly enfranchised masses. While it cannot be denied that even for Altenstein scholarship was more a means than an end, still it retained its integrity and within broad limits its independence. Furthermore, Altenstein did not seek to capitalize on the possible danger from the "demagogues" in order to prevent progress toward a Prussian constitution.

Just this, however, was the purpose of Wittgenstein and of his master, Metternich. The Austrian minister saw students, professors, universities, and scholarship as hostile forces which had to be subdued if the liberal constitutional movement in Germany was to be halted and turned back. In the southern German states and in Weimar, this movement was in Metternich's view already dangerously far advanced; but the key to the problem lay in Prussia, for Prussia was Austria's only serious rival for the leadership of the German Confederation. If Prussia could be prevented from turning to liberal constitutionalism, she was unlikely to capture the allegiance of the smaller liberal states, and conservative Austria would continue to exercise her primacy in the Diet. Metternich wrote in this sense to Hardenberg directly: "Political tranquillity rests on the basis of fraternity among the monarchs and of the principle of the preservation of the *status quo;* to act contrary to these principles would be to rock the political edifice to its

[66] Altenstein's memoranda of November 1818 and April–May 1819, in Ernst Müsebeck, *Das preussische Kultusministerium vor hundert Jahren* (Stuttgart and Berlin, 1918), pp. 196–198, 280, 286–287.

foundations." [67] Much of Metternich's campaign in Prussia was conducted for him by Wittgenstein, who as early as February 1818 was in a position to write to his master that his "friendly suggestions" were having a "salutary effect" on Hardenberg.[68]

In his efforts to keep Prussia in line, Metternich concerned himself both with the specific problem of the "demagogues" / and the universities and with the larger question of the constitution with which it was connected. He insisted on Prussian action to suppress "the various agitating groups," among which he included the *Burschenschaften,* the professors, and also the free press.[69] He took advantage of a meeting with Frederick

[67] Memorandum of November 1818, Fürst Richard Metternich-Winneburg, ed., *Aus Metternich's nachgelassenen Papieren* (Vienna, 1880–84), III, 173 (hereafter *Aus Metternich's Papieren*).

[68] Wittgenstein to Metternich, Feb. 6, 1818, in Haake, "Verfassungsfrage," XXX, 329. Metternich's biographer (Heinrich Ritter von Srbik, *Metternich: Der Staatsmann und der Mensch* [Munich, 1925], I, 527) protests against the historians' references to his subject's "machinations" and "insinuations," but the evidence supports them. Besides the obvious fact that Wittgenstein was in Metternich's service, see for instance the commissioning of a certain Karl von Woltmann by Metternich and his imperial master to send intelligence reports on Prussia to be used in Vienna for the purpose of countering Prussian attempts to assert primacy in Germany (reported in Franz Hadamowsky, ed., "Beiträge zur Geschichte Preussens zur Zeit der Befreiungskriege: 'Über den Tugendbund' und 'Preussische Charaktere' von Karl v. Woltmann," *Forschungen zur brandenburgischen und preussischen Geschichte*, XL [1927], 88–93). But Srbik is right to point out that Metternich's ascendancy over Prussian statesmen was a sign either of their weakness or of their agreement. Cf. also above, pp. 117–118.

[69] Metternich's essay "Ueber Erziehungswesen, Turnwesen und Pressfreiheit," sent to Hardenberg in November 1818, *Aus Metternich's Papieren,* III, 178–181. Cf. Gentz to Metternich, April 25, 1819, *ibid.*, III, 241. It is, however, not beyond all dispute that Hardenberg was not genuinely predisposed to agree with Metternich's interpretation, and did not really believe in the existence of dangerous currents of public opinion. Thus he wrote to Metternich (Dec. 6, 1817) that Austro-Prussian co-operation was necessary to obtain from the federal Diet a law "to place limits on the wild license of our propagandists and journalists" (in Haake, "Verfassungsfrage," XXX, 329–330, and cf. Srbik, *Metternich*, I, 583). See also the Cabinet Order to Wittgenstein of July 17, 1813, drafted by Hardenberg (in Maximilian Blumenthal, *Der preussische Landsturm von 1813* [Berlin, 1900], p. 53), and his attitude

William III at the Congress of Aix-la-Chapelle in September 1818 to put his case to him personally.[70] Then, in the spring of 1819, fresh impetus was provided by the celebrated assassination of the writer and propagandist August von Kotzebue by Karl Sand. Sand, a student, was alleged (falsely, as later investigation showed) to have acted on behalf of a conspiracy of university "demagogues" led by the radical Karl Follen.[71] Metternich commented: "In this instance some good will come out of evil, since poor Kotzebue stands as an *argumentum ad hominem* which not even the liberal duke of Weimar will undertake to defend. My concern is to turn the affair to good account." [72]

Through Wittgenstein, Metternich also offered unsolicited advice on Prussia's constitutional position:

A national assembly composed of representatives of the people would mean the dissolution of the Prussian state . . . because such an innovation cannot be introduced in a great state without revolution or preparing revolution; because the Prussian state, in view of its geographical situation and of its composition, is not suited to a national assembly properly speaking; and because it requires above all a military force of power and prestige, which can never be maintained by the side of a purely representative system.

His personal recommendation would be to institute provincial assemblies only; but since, unfortunately, the king had already promised a national assembly, Metternich conceded that perhaps an assembly emanating from the provincial institutions might stop short of being revolutionary.[73]

---

toward democratic forms of military organization in general (cf. below, p. 179). But one should always remember Hardenberg's unfortunate involvement with nationalist "demagoguery" in 1815 and his consequent anxiety to cover his own tracks (cf. above, pp. 121–122).

[70] Srbik, *Metternich*, I, 586–588; Otto Hintze, *Die Hohenzollern und ihr Werk* (Berlin, 1915), p. 498.

[71] For this episode, see Schnabel, *Deutsche Geschichte*, II, 253–255; for a highly colored but accurate version, see Karl Alexander von Müller, *Karl Ludwig Sand* (Munich, 1925).

[72] Metternich to Gentz, April 9, 1819, *Aus Metternich's Papieren*, III, 227.

[73] Metternich to Wittgenstein, Nov. 14, 1818, *Aus Metternich's Papieren*, III, 171–172. For military considerations connected with the constitutional question, see below, pp. 189–192.

Metternich's was by far the most potent influence on Prussia from beyond her borders, but in any matter relating to international conservatism in these years the originator of the Holy Alliance cannot be left out of account. Tsar Alexander I confined his explicit comments to the "demagogue" question, but the implicit relation of this issue to the larger one of the constitution was undoubtedly as clear to him as it was to Metternich. The tsar acted on the basis of advice from his Corsican minister, Count Pozzo di Borgo. During the late summer of 1815 the latter had addressed to Alexander an astonishing document in which he developed the idea that governments, and especially the Prussian government, were in the hands of the armies and that the armies were hotbeds of revolutionary agitation and conspiracy. The Prussian king, Pozzo declared, "was no more than tolerated by the leaders among his generals." [74] Evidently Alexander was impressed: the story reached Berlin that he had spoken of the possibility of having to rescue Frederick William III from his own army.[75] But he confined his actions to sending notes approving of the award of a medal to Professor Schmalz and of the government's subsequent silencing of the discussion on the affair. Alexander congratulated the king on "the success of the wise and vigorous measures which you have taken to control the secret societies, whose excesses might have given good grounds for anxiety." [76]

[74] Pozzo di Borgo to Tsar Alexander, undated, Comte Charles Pozzo di Borgo, ed., *Correspondance diplomatique du comte Pozzo di Borgo . . . et du comte de Nesselrode, etc.* (Paris, 1890–97), I, 217–218; cf. the brilliant analysis of this memorandum by Meinecke, *Boyen*, II, 72–73: "Pozzo di Borgo felt instinctively . . . that Prussian power in Germany was irresistibly growing as a result of the struggle with France, that the convenient European balance of power which he was trying to establish, in concert with Castlereagh and Metternich, was threatened by the might of this youthful country; but he felt all this only in a manner peculiarly characteristic of statesmen of the old school, in that he converted the spokesmen of a rising national power into ambitious, scheming members of a secret society, a classification more intelligible to his understanding."

[75] Gneisenau to Boyen, Sept. 16, 1815, in Pertz and Delbrück, *Gneisenau*, IV, 631.

[76] Zichy to Metternich, Nov. 11, 1815, in Haake, "Verfassungsfrage,"

After a lapse of some years Pozzo di Borgo resumed his concern with Prussian internal affairs. He submitted to the tsar, and then with the latter's approval to the Congress of Aix-la-Chapelle, a memorandum in which he declared that peace was in double jeopardy from the revolutionaries on one side and on the other side from governments which persisted in "arbitrariness in domestic policy and partial alliances in foreign policy." [77] Pozzo was still seeing the "demagogues" as an international issue, but he allotted some blame to the governments as well. Another protégé of Alexander's, the Rumanian Count Stourdza, published in November 1818 a pamphlet in the tsar's name condemning the excesses of the German students on the Wartburg; and when Metternich submitted to him plans for the Carlsbad Decrees,[78] Alexander gave his approval. After their promulgation, however, the quixotic Alexander attacked the decrees, fearing the increased power which they gave to Metternich.[79] Alexander was trying his hand at balancing power in Germany.

Frederick William III, despite his hero worship of Alexander since the dark days of Tilsit, seemed less impressed with the latter's advice than with that of the scheming Metternich. In 1816 the king issued what might even have been construed as a rebuff to Alexander's congratulations, declaring that the current agitation was merely "a natural consequence of the disturbed state of the political scene." [80] The Prussian ambassador

XXIX, 324, n. 2; Alexander to Frederick William III, Jan. 27, 1816, Paul Bailleu, ed., *Briefwechsel König Friedrich Wilhelms III. und der Königin Luise mit Kaiser Alexander I.* (Leipzig, 1900), p. 269.

[77] Pozzo di Borgo to Alexander, June 24, 1818, F. de Martens, ed., *Recueil des traités et conventions conclus par la Russie avec les puissances étrangères* (St. Petersburg, 1874–1919), VII, 293.

[78] For details concerning these decrees, see below, pp. 211–212.

[79] See K. Waliszewski, *La Russie il y a cent ans: Le règne d'Alexandre Ier* (Paris, 1923–25), III, 43–47; Andrei A. Lobanov-Rostovsky, *Russia and Europe 1789–1825* (Durham, N.C., 1942), pp. 377–379; C. K. Webster, *The Foreign Policy of Castlereagh 1815–1822: Britain and the European Alliance* (2nd ed., London, 1934), p. 193.

[80] Frederick William III to Alexander I, Bailleu, ed., *Briefwechsel*, p. 271.

in St. Petersburg was instructed to give a reassuring impression in Russia of affairs at home.[81]

Although Metternich was far more successful than Alexander or anyone else outside Prussia in bringing pressure to bear on the rulers of that country, the fact remains that even Metternich could not have achieved the results that he did if the ground had not been prepared from within. Whether we are concerned only with the persecution of the demagogues or with the ultimate question of the constitution, in both respects Metternich could build on strong foundations of domestic Prussian sentiment. Marwitz, for example, would probably have been annoyed at the suggestion that he was promoting a foreign power's interests, but obviously such utterances as the following were grist to Metternich's mill:

The great question is whether a representative assembly ordered according to the ideas now prevalent would not be a great misfortune? Land has been made mobile, the old landowners no longer exist or have taken up new ways [*haben eine andere Richtung erhalten*]. No feeling of community remains in the cities; the dominant forces are the masses, numbers, and money. Of whom, then, would the new assembly be composed? Certainly only of . . . innovators, . . . who have no notion of tradition [*Geschlecht*], of the past, or of the future, and who value nothing except the present moment, money, theories, and their own esteemed persons.[82]

Marwitz and many of the others who objected to Hardenberg and to his "newfangled" constitutional ideas were not, however, primarily politicians but soldiers. They became involved in politics (if for no other reason) because the reform movement begun by Stein and carried on, though differently, by Hardenberg had its military side, too; in fact, the very core of the feudal state to which Marwitz looked back with longing had been the army, the feudal levy, in which Marwitz' illustrious ancestors had done battle for their feudal lord, the king, at the head of their own band of soldiers.

[81] Hardenberg's instructions to General von Schöler, June 19, 1816, in Haake, "Verfassungsfrage," XXIX, 330–331.
[82] Marwitz in 1818, Meusel, ed., *Marwitz*, II², 134.

PART THREE

Military Reform
and Reaction

CHAPTER IX

Scharnhorst and the Reorganization of the Army (1807-1813)

AFTER the collapse of the old Prussia at the battle of Jena, which, whatever it may have been besides, was first and foremost a crushing military defeat, the structure of the army inevitably came within the purview of the reformers. This was the more true in the light of the inseparable links which existed between the old army and the entire social edifice of *ancien-régime* Prussia.

It is no accident, therefore, that the collapse of the reform movement should have been signalized, twelve years after Stein's recall to office, by the virtually simultaneous dismissal of the symbols of constitutional and of military reform respectively: Humboldt and Boyen. It had become almost inevitable during the preceding months that the fall of one of them would involve the fall of the other; they stood, in their two different spheres, for the same principle. But before the melancholy events of the year 1819 can be told, the congruence of Humboldt and Boyen must be traced back to the congruence of Stein and Scharnhorst in 1807. In that and the following years Boyen's great predecessor and mentor achieved under Stein's aegis the military regeneration of Prussia, while Stein himself was aspiring after her civil regeneration.

The Old Army

The Prussian army which lost the battle of Jena was an army based on a semifeudal social structure but adapted to the needs of the national warfare of the eighteenth century between enlightened absolute monarchs.[1] Recruitment for the army, in so far as it was not composed of volunteers or of foreign mercenaries, was accomplished under the canton system. This system, though undergoing numerous changes in the course of the eighteenth century, did not lose its essential character. It meant in practice, despite prefatory declarations about the obligation of all subjects to defend their country, exemption from military service of all classes of citizens except the peasants: "the Prussian canton system became merely an administrative device for selecting reservists from the lowest classes of the population."[2] The nobility, voluntarily and by tradition, supplied the overwhelming majority of the officers. It was extremely difficult for sons of middle-class families to gain commissions, and even then they were restricted to a few branches of the service, especially artillery, where some studious types were needed who had enough mathematics to compute trajectories. The nobility jealously guarded this exclusive privilege of officering the army and pointed with justifiable pride at the long line of their ancestors who had led the king's troops into battle.

Even if such an army was suitable for fighting the dynastic wars of the eighteenth century, it was no match for Napoleon's troops. Napoleon's were not dynastic wars; he had inherited from the French Revolution the *levée en masse,* and he fought with the resources of the entire nation behind him. By contrast, the forces of Frederick William III, commanded by a senile hero of the wars of Frederick the Great, were composed of ignorant peasants and mercenaries officered by petty noblemen

---

[1] For the army before the reforms, see chiefly Max Lehmann, *Scharnhorst* (Leipzig, 1886–87), II, 67–83, and William O. Shanahan, *Prussian Military Reforms 1786–1813* (New York, 1945), chaps. i, ii. For earlier attempts at reform, see *ibid.,* chap. iii.

[2] *Ibid.,* p. 60.

whose arrogance all too often expressed itself in brutality. In turn, the men became so resentful of the army that only the strictest discipline could hold them in line. It was said that Prussian officers dared not maneuver in dense woods for fear of losing half their men.

But the old Prussian army was nothing more than a faithful reflection of the civil society from which it emanated. The gulf between the officer and the soldier was at least as much a social as a military one, and it could be secured only by maintaining a corresponding gulf in civil society as well. The civilian counterpart of officer and common soldier was seigneur and serf. Frequently, because of the regional emphasis of the canton system, a peasant would serve his term in the army under the same man whose fields he had worked before; and "the peasant who was not whipped in the army would not have let himself be whipped for neglecting his servile duties." [3] Consequently, any thoroughgoing reform of the Prussian army presupposed civil reforms; and such military reform would, in turn, have profound repercussions throughout the whole fabric of society.

Indeed, Stein's formula for restoring the country to health —education of all citizens to active interest and participation in the country's affairs—had an obvious military application. It did away with the notion that only certain segments of the population were obliged to perform military service, while the rest of the nation took no part or interest in its own defense.[4] Specifically, it would mean the abolition of class exemptions in recruiting and the substitution of a close approximation to universal service. It would mean a change in the system of reserves as well as in the active ranks. In the old army, in peacetime, most conscripted soldiers were furloughed for the greater part of every year, though liable to recall to the colors in the event of war. With the more inclusive system of conscription and the shorter term of service projected by the reformers, a

[3] Lehmann, *Scharnhorst*, II, 82.

[4] Cf. as illustrative of the passivity of the civilian population toward military matters the ministerial dictum quoted above, p. 132; also Lehmann, *Stein*, II, 64.

new type of reserve in the form of a national guard (*Land-wehr*), composed of men who had completed their service, was evolved. The *Landwehr* was planned so as to create a bond of sympathy between the civilian population and the army.

The central aims of the military reform movement were, then, substitution of universal service for recruitment with wholesale class exemptions, opening of officer careers to classes other than the nobility on the basis of merit, and replacement of the furlough system by a Landwehr.[5] It was only to be expected that the fulfillment of these aims would encounter at least as much resistance as reform in the agrarian and constitutional structure of the state. Opposition would stand on the dual grounds of principle and self-interest. To large sections of the nobility the old army represented an honorable though not a lucrative career; they had a vested interest in it. But on the other hand, the old army represented also an essential part of the social structure of Prussia to which some of the nobles, at least, were quite genuinely devoted for reasons higher than personal convenience. They would therefore be opposed to the principle of universal service, which broke down class barriers, and to the idea of a Landwehr, which seemed likely to expose the army to civilian influence and infiltration.

The argument most readily available to the nobles in their resistance to the proposed reforms of Stein and Scharnhorst consisted of a methodical defense of the old army.[6] They were willing to concede that minor improvements were necessary to bring the organization of the army up to date, but they contended that in principle it was sound. General York held that not new military institutions but better leadership to operate them was needed;[7] though he might have reflected that the leaders were themselves products of the institutions. Another

[5] I shall in future refrain from italicizing the word Landwehr, which will occur too frequently to inflict this disruption on the reader. The same will apply to the word Landsturm, when it makes its appearance. If we were to be consistent, we should have constantly to italicize Reichstag.

[6] We are reminded inevitably of the defense of the *ancien régime* undertaken by the opponents of the French Revolution, both at the time of the Revolution and ever since.

[7] Droysen, *York*, I, 128.

general cautioned that if one aspect of the military organization were tampered with, the whole system would suffer a blow;[8] though this warning did not lead him to ask whether such sensitivity might not be a sign of weakness.

The catastrophe of Jena was too telling a blow to the prestige of the army for these defenders of the old system to obtain much of a hearing during the first stages of the movement toward reform. Stein himself did not take an active part in the military aspects of this movement. He was content to entrust military matters to his chosen deputy, Scharnhorst, and to support him in every way. Scharnhorst was one of the rare exceptions to the practice of reserving army commissions to the sons of the nobility, and even he was not only a mere artillery officer (the artillery being an unfashionable branch of the service) but a product of non-Prussian training to boot. A serious student of history and politics as well as of military matters, he was nevertheless also an outstanding strategist and field commander. His advocacy of army reform was therefore based on both theory and practical experience. In this respect he had much affinity with Stein: there was about him nothing of the doctrinaire reformer. He could say honestly that his principal objective was to restore a balance of power between France and Prussia by offsetting the superior physical resources of France through a release of Prussia's "moral resources"; yet he was aware also that his proposals were aimed at the very foundations of the Prussian monarchy. But although in his studiousness and in his shyness Scharnhorst was unique among the military reformers, his zeal, and above all his conviction that spiritual as well as material remedies were in order, were shared by them all. As a group of military men, Scharnhorst, Gneisenau, Clausewitz, and Boyen had a range of vision all too rarely to be found.[9]

[8] General von Rüchel, in Meinecke, *Zeitalter der deutschen Erhebung,* p. 37. Cf. the official rejection, earlier, of the idea of a national militia on the ground that it would have subversive effects on the military establishment (Reinhard Höhn, *Scharnhorsts Vermächtnis* [Bonn, 1952], p. 157).

[9] The principal biography of Scharnhorst is Max Lehmann, *Scharnhorst;* more recently, excellent though on a more modest scale, there is Rudolf Stadelmann, *Scharnhorst: Schicksal und geistige Welt* (Wiesbaden, 1952),

Scharnhorst and the Military Commission

As was true with agrarian reform, the machinery of military reform was already established when Stein returned to office in October 1807. In July the king had appointed a Military Reorganization Commission, with Scharnhorst at its head. The commission was to survey the whole range of Prussia's military problems, but the king urged immediate consideration of the following subjects: investigation of the conduct of officers in the recent campaign and punishment of those guilty of negligence or incompetence; investigation of the possibility of opening the commissioned ranks to the middle classes; elimination of mercenaries; reduction of exemptions in recruiting; and revision of the army penal system to conform to this reduction.[10]

Scharnhorst was well pleased with the king's agenda, but he was much less enthusiastic about the other members of his commission with whom he would have to discuss these problems.[11] Most of Scharnhorst's colleagues were adherents of the old order; it was characteristic of the vacillating king to check his own reformist suggestions by appointing men to consider them who were likely to oppose them.

The special difficulties that Scharnhorst experienced with one of the other members are worth a moment's consideration.

---

see especially pp. 73–74. For a sound and perceptive essay, see *id.*, "Scharnhorst und die Revolution seiner Zeit," *Das innere Reich,* V¹ (April–September 1938), 44–65; for a good concise summary of Scharnhorst's career and personality, see Schnabel, *Deutsche Geschichte,* I, 365–373. For the views of Gneisenau and Clausewitz on the necessity of "spiritual regeneration," see respectively Gerhard Ritter, *Gneisenau und die deutsche Freiheitsidee* (Tübingen, 1932), pp. 30–32 and Hans Rothfels, *Carl von Clausewitz. Politik und Krieg: Eine ideengeschichtliche Studie* (Berlin, 1920), *passim.* For Boyen, see below, p. 181.

[10] Memorandum of the king, July, 1807, Rudolf Vaupel, ed., *Das preussische Heer vom Tilsiter Frieden bis zur Befreiung 1807–1814,* I (Leipzig, 1938), 8–15.

[11] Scharnhorst to Goltz, Aug. 8, 1807, and to Clausewitz, Nov. 27, 1807, Karl Linnebach, ed., *Scharnhorsts Briefe* (Munich and Leipzig, 1914), I, 324, 334–335. Cf. also Meinecke, *Boyen,* I, 209. For a descriptive roster of the members of the commission, see Lehmann, *Scharnhorst,* II, 10–19.

General von Borstell held views which were by no means the
farthest removed from Scharnhorst's own. He was the author
of a recent memorandum recommending recruitment under a
principle of conscription "which imposes on all classes of the
population, rich and poor alike, the duty of personally defending the state." [12] Borstell also advocated a change in the reserve
system, as well as other reforms urged by Scharnhorst. The only
major point on which he differed from Scharnhorst was in his
opposition to opening officer cadet schools to all qualified candidates regardless of birth. It was, indeed, not over a question
of substance at all that the clash between the two men occurred
but over a matter of procedure. Borstell insisted that Scharnhorst's position as chairman of the commission did not empower
him to reject the suggestions of other members and that all
members equally should have the right of direct access to the
king.

This episode, perhaps trivial in itself, is nevertheless significant for its implications. In the first place, it indicates that
the Prussian reform movement was obliged to contend with
quite irrelevant sources of opposition. In the second place, it
suggests an incipient uncertainty about the constitutional position of the monarchy. The absolute monarchs of Prussia in
the eighteenth century had exercised, or attempted to exercise,
personal rule; but the corollary had been that they were in
theory accessible in person to any of their subjects with a
suggestion or grievance. With the reform period, such men as
Stein and Scharnhorst, and later Hardenberg, began to be-
have at times as though the government were in reality in the
hands of the ministers with the king being, if not yet exactly
an ornament or a symbol, at least a remote personage who was
above politics. Such a theory precluded appeals to the king
from a minister's decision. With Stein this theory was designed
to promote ministerial responsibility on the English model;

[12] Borstell's memorandum of Sept. 20, 1807, Vaupel, ed., *Das preussische
Heer*, I, 87–90. On the Borstell episode in general see Lehmann, *Scharnhorst*,
II, 19–20, 143, n. 2, now considerably modified by Rudolf Stadelmann, "Das
Duell zwischen Scharnhorst und Borstell im Dezember 1807," *Historische
Zeitschrift*, 161 (1939–40), 263–276, which rehabilitates Borstell; also Mei-
necke, *Boyen*, I, 172–173.

with Hardenberg it was designed to prevent it by substituting the strong autocracy of the chancellor for the weak autocracy of the king, and on this rock the whole reform movement, in the persons of Humboldt and Boyen, eventually foundered. In the incident between Scharnhorst and Borstell, nothing more momentous occurred than the granting of Borstell's request for a transfer; though Frederick William III may have perceived the larger constitutional issues at stake when he informed Scharnhorst: "Every member of the commission has the right, without regard to seniority, to submit his ideas and suggestions to the full commission." [13]

Borstell was replaced by an officer sympathetic to Scharnhorst's views; soon Boyen replaced another of the conservatives, and the cause of reform had the upper hand in the commission. Only one major obstacle remained for Scharnhorst: not he but Count Lottum, the conservative adjutant general, made the official reports of the commission to the king. In June 1808, apparently at the instigation of Stein, this last hindrance was removed when Scharnhorst himself became adjutant general.[14] This event signified a considerable personal sacrifice on the part of the king, who, as Boyen remarked, liked Lottum much better than Scharnhorst but saw that in the circumstances "pleasant manners were no substitute for Scharnhorst's talents." [15]

Scharnhorst's alleged lack of elegant manners was, of course, one of the objections against him of those who resented the elevation to a position of power of a quiet, studious, bourgeois artillery officer who was not even a Prussian. Marwitz, who had much more respect for Scharnhorst than he had for Stein or Hardenberg, nevertheless could not forbear in later years to stress the differences marking Scharnhorst off from the traditional Prussian officer: "He was no hero, not even an outstanding chief of staff in the field. . . . Scharnhorst was

---

[13] Cabinet Order to Scharnhorst, Dec. 16, 1807, Vaupel, ed., *Das preussische Heer*, I, 204. Some days later, referring to the cavalry officer Borstell, the king admonished Scharnhorst to stop the silly rivalry between infantry and cavalry (the king to Scharnhorst, Dec. 22, 1807, *ibid.*, I, 235).

[14] Lehmann, *Scharnhorst*, II, 26, 38.   [15] Boyen, *Erinnerungen*, II, 12.

entirely unmilitary in his appearance and in his behavior, he looked more like an old and pensive writer." Marwitz was particularly incensed at the fact that a statue of Scharnhorst was erected in Berlin: "He is surely the first man whose statue has been placed among those of generals merely for the good institutions that he created." And then the final outburst of pique: "And he had quite mediocre thighs, not nearly so splendid as . . . [the sculptor] has given him." [16] Scharnhorst personified for men of Marwitz' stamp a new and alien force operating within their special preserve, the army. His disrespect for traditions which he himself had not enjoyed infuriated them. Thus it was possible for Borstell and for others like him to shy away from Scharnhorst's reformist zeal as from "a sinister phenomenon which they feared would bring about the internal disintegration of the army," [17] even if they had no objection to many of Scharnhorst's specific proposals. General Bülow, for example, no opponent of army reform in principle, "feared radical innovations and the so-called learned officers, the theorists and planners." [18] York declared himself in favor of changes in the system of recruiting, yet in a famous phrase he ridiculed "that scrupulous 'democratic partiality' which suspects a hidden talent under every peasant's jacket and, because Pope Sixtus V had been a swineherd in his youth, takes anxious care of all such possible candidates, lest some divine swineherd perish unnoticed." [19]

[16] Meusel, ed., *Marwitz*, I, 504–505; cf. *ibid.*, I, 527.

[17] Meinecke, *Boyen*, I, 171.

[18] K. A. Varnhagen von Ense, *General Graf Bülow von Dennewitz* (Vol. VIII of his *Biographische Denkmale;* Leipzig, 1874), p. 69. Cf. the comment of Boyen, *Erinnerungen*, I, 294.

[19] Droysen, *York*, I, 130. Contrast the use of the same idea in the opposite sense by the reformer Gneisenau: "In the breasts of thousands upon thousands of people lies hidden a great genius, whose aspiring wings are clipped by misery and poverty. While an empire wastes away amid weakness and shame, in its most squalid village a Caesar may be following his plow and an Epaminondas subsisting on the product of the work of his hands" (Ritter, *Gneisenau und die deutsche Freiheitsidee*, p. 6; cf. Gray's "Elegy," "Some mute inglorious Milton"). In these two quotations is reflected the essential contrast between the mentality of the reformer and that of his opponent.

Scharnhorst in the Years of Peace, 1807–1812

Of the two important military reforms designed to adapt the army to the new kind of state planned by Stein, recruitment without exemptions (universal service) and a Landwehr, the latter, in peacetime at any rate, depended on the former and could not well be considered before something decisive was done in the matter of conscription. This question, therefore, was the dominant one throughout Scharnhorst's term of office. But an urgent preliminary problem was that of the officer corps: its purging of those found derelict in their duties during the campaign of 1806 and its opening on a large scale to classes other than the nobility.

Such proposals, naturally, provoked enraged opposition on the part of that very class. Marwitz called the opening of officer careers to the bourgeoisie a substitution of cleverness for courage and of the profit motive for honor.[20] York called it "feeble yielding to the views of the cosmopolites and theorists" and pointed out that the son of a noble family was well suited to command peasants in the army whom he had formerly supervised as children.[21] Both York and Marwitz ridiculed the idea that the aristocratic officer corps had been responsible for the defeat at Jena. And York made a telling point (which Marwitz also used later in his clash with Hardenberg[22]) when he asked one of the princes of the royal house who was friendly to the reformers: "If Your Royal Highness deprives me and my children of our rights, on what foundations will yours rest?"[23]

Scharnhorst and his commission, however, had other views. In a draft of a law which they sent to the king, and which the latter accepted without significant changes, the preamble read:

Officer commissions shall henceforth be awarded in peacetime only for knowledge and education and in wartime for outstanding bravery and comprehension of situations [*Überblick*]. Therefore all individuals in the whole nation who possess these qualities may aspire to positions of highest military honor. All hitherto prevalent class priv-

[20] Meusel, ed., *Marwitz*, I, 513.   [21] Droysen, *York*, I, 129.
[22] See above, p. 86.   [23] Droysen, *York*, I, 130.

ileges are to cease entirely in the army, and everyone has equal duties and equal rights.

A system of competitive examination was therefore to be introduced to select qualified candidates.[24]

Marwitz attributed the entire military reform movement to a "passion for equality." He applied this term to another of Scharnhorst's preliminary reforms, that of military justice and the penal system. For Scharnhorst a more humane penal code was a prerequisite for any attempt to reduce exemptions for conscription; but for Marwitz it represented nothing but an attempt to indoctrinate soldiers with "demagogic and egotistical ideas of equality." Boyen suspected that one motive for resistance to a milder penal system was an instinctive feeling on the part of the old peacetime drill soldiers that under such a system more effort would be required in enforcing discipline. But here also Scharnhorst succeeded in getting the king's approval for a new set of articles of war providing, among other reforms, for the abolition of whipping except for severe or repeated offenses.[25]

But he was not so successful with respect to the cornerstone of the military edifice that he hoped to build, the introduction of the principle of universal military service by abolishing class exemptions. It used to be thought that the famous *Krümper* system, whereby the intent of Napoleon's numerical limitation of the Prussian army was evaded by instituting a rapid turnover of personnel undergoing military training, was the answer to Scharnhorst's prayers. But apart from the fact that the scope of the *Krümper* system has been greatly over-

[24] The military commission to the king, July 30, 1808, Vaupel, ed., *Das preussische Heer*, I, 533–536. Cf. *Gesetz-Sammlung* for 1806–10, pp. 275–277 (law of Aug. 6, 1808). Later Scharnhorst was able to supplement this reform, though still imperfectly, with a reorganized system of military education; see Vaupel, ed., *Das preussische Heer*, I, 187–191; Shanahan, *Reforms*, pp. 133–135.

[25] For this paragraph, see Shanahan, *Reforms*, pp. 135–138; Vaupel, ed. *Das preussische Heer*, I, 361; Meusel, ed., *Marwitz*, I, 514; Boyen, *Erinnerungen*, I, 294; *Gesetz-Sammlung* for 1806–10, pp. 253–264, esp. para. 3, p. 253 ("Krieges-Artikel für die Unteroffiziere und gemeinen Soldaten," Aug. 3, 1808). Cf. also Höhn, *Scharnhorsts Vermächtnis*, p. 205.

estimated, it did not, in fact, provide for any reductions in exemptions from service; indeed, the system was not adopted by Scharnhorst until he had failed in his efforts to introduce · universal service.[26] These efforts spanned almost Scharnhorst's entire career as war minister. As early as the spring of 1808 the king approved of a memorandum in which universal service was recommended, but soon afterwards he withdrew to a characteristically cautious position, permitting allusion to universal service in a law relating to other matters without commitment to the principle itself.[27]

The question of universal service was, to be sure, not a clear-cut issue between the friends and enemies of reform. Besides soldiers like York and Marwitz, a number of influential men, without personal interest and with reformist sympathies, for a variety of reasons opposed Scharnhorst's proposals. Baron Vincke, a famous jurist and an admirer of English political institutions, described to his friend Stein the consternation which universal service would cause among the educated classes. Conscription on this basis meant "the death of culture, learning, and trade, of civil liberty and of all human happiness." It would waste years in the lives of the country's educated youth.[28] The historian Niebuhr, an enlightened conservative, eloquently stigmatized universal service as a Jacobin principle, as "a kind of equality that must enrage the true friend of liberty. . . . No privilege, no tradition sacred, no property except the money-bag." Universal service made no allowance for differences of trade, of locality, or of aptitude and treated all men equally as ciphers; without regard for "spiritual requirements, for the stamp of divinity on a man, it counts only the animal in him." Peasants, since their labor was seasonal, could be conscripted with a minimum of inconvenience, and anyway "the rough peasant will not mind the service much." The rich must be left with the right to buy their sons' exemption from

[26] Shanahan, *Reforms,* pp. 11–13 and chap. vi.

[27] Vaupel, ed., *Das preussische Heer,* I, 332 ff (memorandum of Major von Lossau, March 21, 1808) and editorial note, p. 332; Lehmann, *Scharnhorst,* II, 98–99.

[28] Vincke to Stein, July 8 and Sept. 30, 1808, Vaupel, ed., *Das preussische Heer,* I, 598–601.

service, "for in this class wealth is of great significance, as the means of climbing into a more cultured sphere."[29] (Much of the opposition to universal service came, indeed, from the rich merchants and from the middle class generally, as well as from the aristocracy.[30] In a way, the middle classes had even more at stake; for while the nobility wished merely to preserve their traditional way of life in the army, the middle classes wished to avoid any kind of life in the army.)

A formulation similar to Niebuhr's was that of Colonel Boguslawski, though his was more influential since he worked in the war ministry and addressed his thoughts to the king himself. All classes and all individuals, he said, were not equally suitable for military service, for example, a healthy farm boy and a sickly tailor's apprentice. "Young men from the upper classes," intellectuals, and artists were all unsuited. In view of this situation, a system of buying off one's service by hiring a substitute was advisable. Boguslawski admitted that even under this system some of the unsuitable persons would not have the means to buy a substitute and would have to go themselves, but that could not be helped. He further admitted that for his part he thought the principle of universal service entirely sound, but he argued that there were many who disagreed and that it would be unwise to antagonize them.[31]

No doubt Boguslawski had little understanding for the philosophy of the reform movement, but his was a sincere, moderate, and well-reasoned argument. Not as much could be said about some of the efforts of the nobility to avert universal service. The nobles had a much better case than some of them knew: they had always served in the army voluntarily and could with some reason object to a system which would submerge this fact in a general obligation to serve. But some of the aristocracy chose to take up different ground. A group of East

[29] Niebuhr to Altenstein, Aug. 30, 1808, Gerhard and Norvin, eds., *Briefe Niebuhrs*, I, 497–502.

[30] Cf. Götzen to Gneisenau, Dec. 1, 1808, Vaupel, ed., *Das preussische Heer*, I, 749.

[31] Boguslawski to the king, July 20, 1809, Max Lehmann, ed., "Preussen und die allgemeine Wehrpflicht im Jahre 1809," *Historische Zeitschrift*, LXI (1889), 98–104.

Prussian nobles, for example, alarmed by a reference to universal service in a government decree, wrote to the king protesting their theoretical right of exemption as one of the traditional rights and privileges of their class:

> General conscription extended to the nobility is a principle which first saw the light of day as a product of revolution [i.e., the French Revolution], . . . which by its very nature can rest only on the concept of universal equality and which would lead to . . . the complete destruction of the nobility. They would be left with nothing but empty and useless titles.[32]

To this document the king replied with considerable firmness that universal service was "a measure which derives from the obligation of every subject to defend his country and which is inescapably imposed by the passage of the years. . . . I cannot allow myself to be swayed by one-sided objections." [33] Not long afterwards the Pomeranian nobility also submitted a memorandum in which they called universal service a result of "the French fraud about freedom and equality." This time, however, the king replied graciously, promising to heed their desires.[34]

No satisfactory explanation of this reversal suggests itself (though the dimming of Stein's influence after his exile may have been a factor). But in any event, exchanges of this sort were unimportant in view of the fact that the monarch had already rejected the proposal of Scharnhorst's committee to institute conscription without class exemptions and was to reject it twice more within two years.[35]

---

[32] Thirteen nobles of Kreis Mohrungen to the king, Nov. 17, 1808, Vaupel, ed., *Das preussische Heer*, I, 748–749. In fact, universal service had been on the books since 1733 and had been repeatedly reaffirmed since that time without being enforced; so that its inclusion in the decrees of Aug. 3, 1808, was not necessarily of great significance. Cf. Lehmann, *Scharnhorst*, II, 99, n. 1, Shanahan, *Reforms*, pp. 41–42, 45–47.

[33] Cabinet Order to the thirteen nobles, Vaupel, ed., *Das preussische Heer*, I, 749.

[34] For this episode see Lehmann, *Scharnhorst*, II, 295–296.

[35] For a narrative of the failure of Scharnhorst's efforts to institute universal service in peacetime, see *ibid.*, II, 98–99, 201–202, 289–296, 330–342. Documents setting forth the views of Scharnhorst and his commission can be

Scharnhorst had not even the united support of the ministry. The two leading ministers, Altenstein and Dohna, both decided against universal service. Altenstein stressed the cultural losses that would result. What was needed in the army, he declared, was mainly physical strength, and military manpower should therefore be drawn from that section of the population where physical strength abounded. "By means of the admission of substitutes from the lower classes, or from the physically stronger classes if the former phrase sounds offensive, military needs would be filled and the burden of general conscription lightened." Indiscriminate use of manpower would mean unwarranted neglect of culture, "without which lasting strength is impossible." Altenstein agreed, however, that universal service would be necessary in wartime.[36] After the fall of the Altenstein-Dohna ministry, Scharnhorst hoped at last to achieve his aim, but Hardenberg and some of his advisers were no more sympathetic than the leaders of the previous government.[37] Thus, for the last time before the outbreak of the War of Liberation put an end to the argument, the principle of universal service, the first article of the reformers' military creed, was submerged.

The motives of those who opposed the principle have for the most part appeared in the preceding account of their victory. But they do not, perhaps, account fully enough for the failure of Scharnhorst's efforts. The king himself, after all, had

---

found in Vaupel, ed., *Das preussische Heer,* I, 817–822; Lehmann, ed., "Preussen und die allgemeine Wehrpflicht im Jahre 1809," pp. 98–104; Max Lehmann, ed., "Preussen und die allgemeine Wehrpflicht im Jahre 1810," *Historische Zeitschrift,* LXIX (1892), 432–437; Max Lehmann, ed., "Vier Denkschriften Scharnhorst's aus dem Jahre 1810," *Historische Zeitschrift,* LVIII (1887), 102–105.

[36] Memorandum of Altenstein, Feb. 12, 1810, Lehmann, ed., "Preussen und die allgemeine Wehrpflicht im Jahre 1810," pp. 437–440. Dohna supported his colleague without adding any significant new arguments: see his memorandum of Feb. 14, 1810, *ibid.,* p. 440.

[37] See Lehmann, *Scharnhorst,* II, 201–202, 341–342. Contrast Hardenberg's opposition to exemptions from military service in 1807: Hardenberg's "Riga Memorandum," Ranke, ed., *Denkwürdigkeiten des Staatskanzlers Fürsten von Hardenberg,* IV, Appendix, pp. 31–46.

originally suggested reduction in military exemptions as part of the agenda for Scharnhorst's commission.[38] Possibly the most imperative reason for Frederick William's abandonment of this idea was the pressure of considerations of foreign policy. To be sure, the Treaty of Tilsit limited the Prussian army to 42,000 men without specifying how they were to be recruited. Nevertheless, an army formed according to the principle of universal service might have seemed to Napoleon to answer the purposes of nationalism and national revival much more closely than an old-fashioned army composed of peasants and mercenaries; Napoleon had only to reflect on the military legacy of the revolution to which he himself was heir. In short, such an army might have been too bold an augury of aggressive intentions for the cautious Frederick William III to risk announcing to the world; it might have betrayed the ultimate designs which reformers like Stein and Scharnhorst did, in fact, secretly harbor.[39]

Universal service was, however, only half, and perhaps the less vital half, of the reformers' military program of national regeneration. A reserve force, not subject to military discipline except when called to active service, would have helped to promote the idea that the army was not an autonomous organization without claims on the loyalty of the citizens but rather an organization which prospered or languished in proportion to the interest and support accorded to it by the nation as a whole. Such a force would truly have been a "people's army." But this idea faced even greater obstacles than the conception of universal service. Scharnhorst himself had in mind a militia composed only of the middle classes, since a force which included members of the lower classes might "cause misgiv-

[38] In fact, the king had subsequently created a second commission exclusively for the purpose of studying the problem of exemptions (Shanahan, *Reforms*, p. 154).

[39] See Meinecke, *Zeitalter der deutschen Erhebung*, pp. 109–110. Conversely, when in 1814 Prussia wanted to impress the diplomats at the Congress of Vienna with her power, universal service was employed to that end (*ibid.*, p. 129).

ings." [40] Even this plan, however, was abhorrent to the king. Frederick William had a genuine attachment to the precision and glitter of a professional army; he delighted in details of uniform. He could be expected to acquiesce in almost any other military reform before assenting to the creation of a popular force whose emphasis was not on discipline. Even in his most generous moods, said Boyen, when his distrust of "the people" was at a minimum, Frederick William III contemplated reform only "within the framework of a well-drilled regular army clothed according to his canons of military taste; he distrusted anything that tended toward arming the nation, any development of a broader martial spirit outside of the traditional confines." [41]

In any event, the subject of a reserve contingent could not even be broached until the system of exemptions was first removed from the regular army. To this step Scharnhorst was unable to move the king throughout the five years of peace between 1807 and 1812. But early in 1813 the initiative was seized by the popular revolt against the French in East Prussia, which signalized the beginning of the War of Liberation and which at the same time provided an instrument for fighting it. The East Prussian Landwehr, established by the provincial assembly on its own initiative in circumstances in which communication with the national government was impossible, was the first armed force in Prussia ever to call upon all citizens for service; and thus it was a forerunner not only of the Landwehr which was decreed for the whole kingdom on March 17, 1813, but also indirectly of the principle of universal service enunciated, at long last, on February 9.

To be sure, the East Prussian Landwehr of 1813 was in important respects different from the one instituted in the following years by the reformer Boyen, Scharnhorst's successor. Boyen's force was to be composed for the most part of veterans

[40] Scharnhorst's military commission to the king, March 15, 1808, Vaupel, ed., *Das preussische Heer*, I, 323. This passage had been omitted in previous publications of the document.

[41] Boyen, *Erinnerungen*, I, 295.

of the regular army who had been retired to the reserve and taken up civilian pursuits and who were to go on maneuvers for a few weeks each summer. The Landwehr of 1813, on the other hand, had no considerable body of veterans on which to draw; it partook, therefore, much more of the nature of a makeshift auxiliary force, to be used only in defense of the province and composed of men without previous military experience. But it did employ the principle of conscription instead of relying on volunteers, as such bodies frequently do; conscription, moreover, without exemptions. Under the stress of war, the two issues of Landwehr and universal service became all but merged. The spirit of reform breathed in both; and it was perhaps a form of historical justice that the Russian proconsul who sponsored the East Prussian provincial Diet should have been Baron Stein. But the real founder of the East Prussian Landwehr was none other than the man who as Stein's successor in 1808 had dissipated the momentum of his civil reforms: Count Alexander Dohna.

Dohna and Scharnhorst, 1813

The position of Prussia after the Convention of Tauroggen of December 30, 1812, in which General York agreed to withdraw his corps of Prussian troops from Napoleon's army, was neutral as between France and Russia. But since York's corps occupied all Prussian territory east of the Vistula, this region was now, in effect, free from French control; and Stein, who had been Tsar Alexander's adviser on Prussian affairs since the spring of 1812, was sent as Russian plenipotentiary for the purpose of mobilizing the region's resources for the continuing Russian struggle against France. First and foremost among these resources was, of course, manpower. Many East Prussian officials were fearful of committing themselves to any major action, in view of Frederick William III's failure to confirm the Convention of Tauroggen; the governor of the province, Auerswald, steadfastly refused to assume responsibility for formally convening the provincial Diet to hear Stein's proposals. Stein finally succeeded in gathering together an informal "assembly of deputies of the Estates." To this group he suggested the enactment of a decree calling on the whole population to join in the fight against Napoleon.[42]

The population in general, and particularly the nobility, was decidedly favorable to energetic action against the French. One nobleman had even attempted, before Stein's arrival, to call a meeting of deputies on his own initiative, only to be arrested for his pains.[43] There were, however, dissenting voices, even among the nobility. A certain Count Dönhoff confided to his diary that the purpose of the assembly engineered by Stein was a *levée en masse* (*allgemeines Aufgebot*) but that those who spoke most eloquently of sacrifices were those who had nothing to sacrifice. Resentment against Stein lived on from his reform ministry: Dönhoff called him "the dictator . . . whom fate has unfortunately brought back to Prussia." As for the principle of a Landwehr: "I do not see how one can endorse the idea of making men who are essential for work on the land go out to fight." This was a "fantastic notion" of the "egotistical despot," Stein.[44]

The leading advocate of the Landwehr was the chairman of the provincial Committee of the Estates, the former minister, Count Alexander Dohna. But, significantly, he inserted into the proposal which he steered through the assembly a provision that those conscripted were permitted to send substitutes. This clause, of course, represented a restriction on the principle of equal obligation to defend one's country so tenaciously advocated by Scharnhorst. Nevertheless, it was in this form that the assembly on February 7, 1813, approved a proclamation

[42] For the background of the East Prussian rising, see chiefly Ritter, *Stein*, II, 163–178; Lehmann, *Stein*, III, 215–222, 224–227, 236–238; and for Schön, Görlitz, *Stein*, pp. 364–365. Cf. also throughout "Errichtung der Landwehr und des Landsturms in Ostpreussen, Westpreussen am rechten Weichsel-Ufer und Litthauen im Jahre 1813," *Beihefte zum Militair-Wochenblatt*, January–October 1846.

[43] Lehmann, *Stein*, III, 222–224. For the patriotism of the East Prussian nobility see also Ernst Müsebeck, "Freiwillige Gaben und Opfer des preussischen Volkes in den Jahren 1813–1815," No. 23 in *Mitteilungen der K. Preussischen Archivverwaltung* (Leipzig, 1913), pp. 2–4, 115 ff.

[44] Quotations from Maximilian Schultze, *Königsberg und Ostpreussen zu Anfang 1813: Ein Tagebuch vom 1. Januar bis 25. Februar 1813* (Berlin, 1901), pp. 21, 22, 27, 23.

calling for the formation of a Landwehr.[45] It was partly for this reason that when the decree was taken to the king at his temporary headquarters in Breslau for his approval, Scharnhorst was not altogether pleased with it. But the brother of Alexander, Ludwig Dohna, who was the East Prussian envoy, reported back flatly that Scharnhorst was placing difficulties in the way of the Landwehr.

The biographer of Alexander Dohna concluded, on the basis of this report, that Scharnhorst was opposed to the idea of a Landwehr in principle.[46] This interpretation, though honest, proved to be wrong. The real reason for Scharnhorst's hesitation in approving the East Prussian Landwehr was not that he thought it strayed too far from the traditional military organization but that he thought it did not go far enough. This fact is attested by Boyen, who was not only an intimate friend of

[45] York, as the military governor of the province, had been consulted on the details of the projected Landwehr and had submitted a draft (based in turn on a draft by Clausewitz, at that time, like Stein, in the employ of the tsar) which barred substitutes. Dohna's scheme replaced this one. The two plans are in Adalbert Bezzenberger, ed., *Urkunden des Provinzial-Archivs in Königsberg und des gräflich Dohnaschen Majorats-Archivs in Schlobitten betreffend die Erhebung Ostpreussens im Jahre 1813 und die Errichtung der Landwehr* (Königsberg, 1894), pp. 15, 19.

[46] Johannes Voigt, *Das Leben des königlich preussischen Staatsministers Friederich Ferdinand Alexander Reichs-Burggrafen und Grafen zu Dohna-Schlobitten* (Leipzig, 1833), pp. 25–31, where Ludwig Dohna's reports are also quoted. Voigt's disparagement of Scharnhorst started a controversy which soon called into question the relative patriotism of the East Prussians, symbolized by Dohna, and of the reformers, symbolized by Scharnhorst. In this controversy Theodor von Schön, an East Prussian, took the side of Dohna (Schön, *Papiere*, VI, 57–59). Subsequently the argument began to turn on the veracity of Schön as a historian, the initial attack being delivered by Max Lehmann in his first book, *Knesebeck und Schön: Beiträge zur Geschichte der Freiheitskriege* (Leipzig, 1875). This called forth an impassioned anonymous defense of Schön: *Zu Schutz und Trutz am Grabe Schön's: Bilder aus der Zeit der Schmach und der Erhebung Preussens* (Berlin, 1876). The controversy was, it is to be hoped, ended by M. Baumann, *Theodor von Schön: Seine Geschichtsschreibung und seine Glaubwürdigkeit* (Berlin, 1910) (where the rest of the literature is cited), who offers a moderate and wholly convincing arbitration vindicating the integrity of Scharnhorst as well as of Schön and Dohna. (See also the text following.)

Scharnhorst's but also an eyewitness to the developments in Breslau during February and March 1813. Scharnhorst, Boyen relates, had himself already drafted a Landwehr decree for the entire kingdom, so that the East Prussian *fait accompli* disturbed his plans. Not only did the East Prussian proclamation permit substitutes, a provision unpalatable to him, but it also stipulated that the Landwehr could not be used beyond the limits of the province; [47] finally, a more technical drawback, the East Prussian Landwehr was to have only infantry, no cavalry. In these respects Scharnhorst found the East Prussian measure wanting from the point of view of the mobilization of the whole kingdom.

To the extent [wrote Boyen] that Scharnhorst had thus to fight for great ideas and to discharge his official responsibilities, he sometimes seemed to Count Dohna an enemy of the Landwehr, whereas on the contrary he was not only its real originator and defender, but sought, besides, to place it on a higher spiritual plane.[48]

In the end, Scharnhorst grudgingly decided to permit substitutions in East Prussia to continue when he established a Landwehr for the whole kingdom on March 17, 1813.[49] He had already committed himself to the principle of universal service without exemptions and without substitutions in the decree of February 9 concerning conscription for the regular army.[50] While it is erroneous to count Scharnhorst among the opponents of a Landwehr, neither was Scharnhorst justified in claiming sole credit for the idea of such an auxiliary force.[51] Even Boyen acknowledged that the efforts of Dohna and the East Prussian example constituted valuable support for Scharn-

[47] Cf. Ritter, *Stein,* II, 373, n. 26.

[48] Boyen, *Erinnerungen,* II, 331–334; see also Boyen's *Beiträge zur Kenntnis des General von Scharnhorst, etc.* (Berlin, 1833), written in direct rebuttal of Voigt's biography of Dohna (see above, n. 46); and cf. Ritter, *Stein,* II, 181.

[49] For this decree, see *Gesetz-Sammlung* for 1813, pp. 36–37, 109–119; and cf. Lehmann, *Scharnhorst,* II, 538.

[50] For this decree, see *Gesetz-Sammlung* for 1813, pp. 13–14.

[51] Scharnhorst to his daughter, March 19, 1813, Linnebach, ed., *Scharnhorsts Briefe,* I, 462.

horst in overcoming the resistance of the king and of some of his advisers to the idea of a people's army.[52]

The picture of virtue in Königsberg and iniquity in Breslau painted by Ludwig Dohna was misleading in another respect. The middle-class population of both cities expressed immediate concern over the effects of conscription on them. The municipal authorities of Breslau protested officially against Scharnhorst's conscription decree of February 9, 1813. The citizens of Breslau, they declared, had enjoyed exemption for six hundred years; its suspension now was a grievous blow, threatening ruin for many careers. Only volunteers, they urged, should be taken from the cities.[53] The citizens of Königsberg (together with those of two other East Prussian cities) requested special consideration for city dwellers in conscripting for the Landwehr, stressing the fact that farmwork was seasonal, and in off-season periods farmworkers were not hard hit by being conscripted. These representatives of the East Prussian bourgeoisie proposed exemption of all civil servants and establishment of a committee in each city to rule on individual cases of hardship.[54] Such protests demonstrated that the bourgeoisie by no means lagged behind the nobility in defending their personal interests when they were at stake.[55]

[52] As to the identity of these advisers, the nature of their resistance, and the means by which it was overcome, little is known. Schön mentions Knesebeck as one of the king's military aides opposed to the Landwehr (Schön to Droysen, March 16, 1851, Franz Rühl, ed., *Briefwechsel des Ministers und Burggrafen von Marienburg Theodor von Schön mit G. H. Pertz und J. G. Droysen* [Leipzig, 1896], p. 174). Ludwig Dohna in his reports mentions some others (Voigt, *Dohna*, p. 29). For comment see Pertz, *Stein*, III, 307.

[53] Hans Helfritz, *Geschichte der preussischen Heeresverwaltung* (Berlin, 1938), pp. 298–299. Hardenberg rejected this protest, pointing to the enthusiastic response elsewhere in Prussia. Nevertheless, Breslau was slow in complying with the law, there were continual protests from the rank and file, and few offered themselves as candidates for commissions.

[54] Document quoted in Robert Müller, ed., "Urkunden zur Geschichte der ständischen Versammlungen zu Königsberg im Januar und Februar 1813 betreffend die Errichtung der Landwehr," *Altpreussische Monatsschrift*, N.S. XIV (1877), 124–127. For later developments, including Scharnhorst's rejection, see Lehmann, *Scharnhorst*, II, 537–538.

[55] Cf. also Ritter, *Stein*, II, 178.

These evidences of recalcitrance notwithstanding, it was undeniable that the exigencies of war had accomplished in a few weeks what Scharnhorst had striven in vain for years to achieve. Although the Landwehr was a vital part of the reform program, its establishment reflected not the triumph of reform principles but the imminence of war. For the moment, the warnings and objections of the cautious went unheeded in the popular enthusiasm generated by the prospect of liberation from the thralldom to Napoleon.

CHAPTER X

Boyen and the Struggle over a Citizen Army (1813-1818)

IN THE days before Jena the characteristic attitude of the Prussian civilian toward the army was apathy; he was acquiescent equally in victory and in defeat. In 1813 there had come into being a Landwehr, a national reserve army based on the liability and willingness of every able-bodied citizen to serve. The difference represented a development of tremendous importance; but, paradoxically, by the time it was completed events had already overtaken it. To Scharnhorst and his advisers the Landwehr no longer seemed adequate in the spring of 1813, when the country was girding itself to eject the invader. What these conditions required, in their opinion, was a *Landsturm*, or local citizens' militia. The Landwehr, when mobilized, was to be treated for purposes of discipline, pay, and administration analogously with the regular army, and its members, apart from volunteers, were to be selected by lot. On the other hand, the Landsturm, as conceived by Scharnhorst, was to include every citizen who was not physically incapable of performing some useful function in local defense. Its members, armed with clubs, pitchforks, perhaps some discarded shotguns, but mostly with determination and ingenuity, were to harry the enemy troops, interfere with their communications, scorch the earth, and generally act, within the limits of German topography, like the Spaniards of 1808 who had originated the concept of "guerrilla warfare." Perhaps the most crucial difference between Landwehr and Landsturm was that the latter would go into action only as a last resort, when the enemy was actually approaching a given locality. The Landsturm could not, therefore, be subjected to the routine administrative and disciplinary machinery designed for regular military units. Above all, the Landsturm would draw its members and assign them to tasks without regard to social status. With the enemy at the gates, social distinctions were to be ignored.

It was evident that the Landsturm was likely to arouse strong opposition both for its military and for its social significance. Military men would object to its raggedness; civilians of the upper and middle classes would object to its leveling tendencies. In the towns especially, those who were accustomed to giving orders would suddenly find themselves obliged to take them from people who were lower on the social scale but who happened to be more capable of organizing an incendiary raid or the building of barricades.

The Landsturm of 1813

The Prussian Landsturm was established by royal decree on April 21, 1813,[1] and was to last only three months in its original form. Its purpose, according to the preamble of the decree, was to show the enemy that, regardless of the possible vicissitudes of the army, "a people united with its king can never be defeated." "Every citizen," the decree continued, "is obliged to resist the approaching enemy with any kind of weapon" and to employ any and all effective means of hampering his movements, cutting his supply lines, and destroying the value of conquered territory. The Landsturm could be mobilized in local or provincial units on orders of army and corps commanders or military governors and also, in local units only, by local commanders. These were the only officials authorized to mobolize it: "Any assembly [of the Landsturm] without mobi-

---

[1] "Verordnung über den Landsturm," *Gesetz-Sammlung* for 1813, pp. 79–89. The Landsturm had been referred to in a preliminary way in the Landwehr law of March 17.

lization will be punished as mutiny." The country was divided up into Landsturm districts coinciding with the civil unit *Kreis* and also into subdistricts. Local commanders were to be named by the military and civil governors of the provinces. Towns of a population over two thousand were to appoint defense committees headed by the mayor; in rural areas the land-owners (of any class) of a *Kreis* were to elect from among themselves one deputy for each subdistrict, the deputies composing district defense committees. These committees *(Schutz-deputationen)* in both town and country were to plan and execute local defense measures in consultation with the district commanders and with the military. They were responsible for drawing up lists of all available able-bodied men between fifteen and sixty and for disciplining malingerers. They were also to read in their communities, and to require everyone to swear an oath to obey, the following article of war:

Any attack on, or robbery or looting of, property in friendly territory without orders from commanding generals and military governors, any attempt to evade taxes, duties, compulsory labor [i.e., servile duties on the land], or due obedience to local authorities resulting from, or aided by, the arming or mobilization of the Landsturm, will be mercilessly punished by death.—Likewise inciting to mutiny.[2]

The king ordered all civil, military, and ecclesiastical authorities to pay very special attention to preventing such occurrences. "What is an emergency measure against the enemy should not be perverted into destructive unruliness [*verderbende Zügellosigkeit*]." [3]

There were also specific provisions as to personnel. During the first three months Landsturm captains (commanding about one hundred men) were to be appointed by district commanders. Thereafter vacancies were to be filled by vote of the "troops," and lieutenants and noncommissioned officers were to be chosen by the "troops" throughout, with the reservation that "to begin with" only landowners, state and local officials, teachers, and so forth were eligible. Military rank and subordination were to be in force only during actual drill and during action against the enemy.   /

[2] *Ibid.,* para. 25, p. 82.   [3] *Ibid.,* p. 88.

It is quite evident from all these stipulations that the government feared the possibility of the Landsturm's degenerating from a citizenry in arms against the enemy into a peasantry in arms against the well-to-do—in other words into a threat to property—with or without the connivance of their officers. This fear, naturally, was shared by those who saw themselves as the potential victims of hypothetical bands of marauding peasants. They were often joined by local officials who regarded the defense committees and the leaders of the Landsturm in the light of rival administrators; alternatively, others saw in the offing not so much dual authority as anarchy, a dissolution of all authority. Another source of opposition to the Landsturm was the officer corps, especially the old-style generals who could not grasp the idea of a supposedly military organization with such lax discipline. One general saw in the Landsturm "a complete desecration of all military ideals." [4] Boyen tells the story of how once, at a military parade, he had had occasion to speak to the king in praise of the high morale of the people, especially among the lower classes. Suddenly "the horse of General Knesebeck, who was usually in the habit of riding quite sensible horses, became restless; the general rode between the king and me, apologized to the former, and our conversation was over—was not that a strange coincidence?" [5]

In addition to those who feared the Landsturm as subversive of social and military discipline, there were others who doubted its military effectiveness, and others yet who declared that while it might be effective, it would make incommensurately large demands on the time and economy of the nation. These

[4] Boyen, *Erinnerungen,* III, 74. A conspicuous exception to the generally hostile sentiment of high-ranking officers was Marwitz, who called the Landsturm "a necessary and indispensable measure" and possibly the country's only source of hope (Kayser, *Marwitz,* p. 264). Cf. also Meusel, ed., *Marwitz,* II¹, 225–227. In later years, to be sure, Marwitz viewed democratic military organizations with a more jaundiced eye: see his comment on the Landwehr in 1835, Friedrich Meusel, ed., "Aus Marwitz' Memoiren: Der Zusammenbruch des preussischen Staates 1806," *Deutsche Rundschau,* 162 (1915), 449, and see also below, p. 188 and n. 47.

[5] Boyen, *Erinnerungen,* III, 76. Cf. for Knesebeck above, p. 166, n. 52; and Haake, "Verfassungsfrage," XXVIII, 180, n. 1.

latter questioned the value of the scorched-earth policy and pointed out that to cripple the entire economy in order to send everyone off to fight was to undertake an unwarranted gamble on a war of short duration. There were legal minds who called attention to the fact that establishment of the Landsturm enabled the enemy to treat every Prussian male between fifteen and sixty as a spy. The author of the only full study of the Prussian Landsturm of 1813 tends to minimize the effectiveness of conservative attacks on the "revolutionary" social and military tendencies of the Landsturm and maintains that it was a technical military reason which did most to undermine its existence: namely, that the Landsturm was conceived for use in a defensive war and was therefore discarded when Prussia took the offensive.[6] But the documents cast serious doubt upon this conclusion. Undoubtedly there were serious drawbacks in the general idea of a Landsturm and *a fortiori* in the specific form in which it was rather hurriedly decreed in the spring of 1813, and undoubtedly there were men who were objectively concerned to remove those faults; but the documentary evidence, combined with contemporary comment, leads unmistakably to the inference that the opposition of those who thought of the Landsturm as a revolutionary organization was the dominant factor in bringing about an amendment to the establishing decree within three months of its promulgation. Naturally, furthermore, the objective and technical arguments against the Landsturm were adopted for their own purposes by those who acted on grounds of personal or political prejudice.[7]

The vocal and effective resistance to the Landsturm was centered in Berlin.[8] Here there was the largest concentration of

---

[6] Blumenthal, *Der preussische Landsturm,* pp. iii–iv. Other significant treatments of the question may be found in Meinecke, *Boyen,* I, 287–300, who advances the opposite interpretation; M. Lenz, *Geschichte der Universität Berlin,* I, 509–511; Rothfels, *Carl von Clausewitz,* p. 180.

[7] This fact is admitted by Blumenthal himself in *Der preussische Landsturm,* pp. 74–75.

[8] In the provinces, with the exception of Silesia, resistance was rather spasmodic; see *ibid.,* pp. 22–31, 127–134, 140. Schön's reference to the Silesian Landsturm (Schön, *Papiere,* IV, 30) is evidently based on a misapprehension.

property and hence the greatest fear of its destruction, if not by the scorched-earth policy, then by the mobilized Landsturm itself.[9] Women, children, old and sick people, a petition from the Berlin municipal government to the king declared, must be protected not only from the enemy, but also from the "unruly rabble" within the city. If supplies were removed, mills burned, wells buried, as the Landsturm law contemplated if the enemy approached, "the fury of the people, especially of the rabble, would be boundless in the consequent disorder and anarchy."[10] The chief of police in the capital, Paul Ludwig Lecocq, who was himself the chairman of the city commission on Landwehr and Landsturm, protested to the military government of Berlin against its use of Landsturm men for guard duty: the Landsturm, he wrote, was not yet mobilized and its use was therefore unconstitutional, interfering with the operation of municipal government and threatening the tranquillity and security of the city. It had caused certain elements of the population, "especially among the craftsmen and those who work with their hands," to harbor notions "about the equality of Landsturm men as such," and as a result it was becoming increasingly difficult for the authorities to exact the obedience and respect necessary for the efficient performance of their duty. The "common man" was being tempted to excesses under the cover of patriotism. Respected citizens were being humiliated for petty infringements of Landsturm regulations. The police would be helpless in the event of a riot by the Landsturm. In conclusion, Lecocq asked for power to veto the majority decisions of the Landwehr-Landsturm committee over which he presided if in his opinion they conflicted with the rights and interests of the king.[11]

But Sack, the head of the military government to which

[9] Cf. Meinecke, *Boyen,* I, 290; reports of the Brandenburg military government (headed by Sack, who was friendly to the Landsturm) in Blumenthal, *Der preussische Landsturm,* pp. 32–33.

[10] Petition of May 15, 1813, Blumenthal, *Der preussische Landsturm,* pp. 34–36. Boyen wrote to Hardenberg concerning the petitioners: "The scoundrels should lose their civic rights and their positions" (Meinecke, *Boyen,* I, 297).

[11] Reports of Lecocq to the military government, June 26 and 29, 1813, Blumenthal, *Der preussische Landsturm,* pp. 39–42, 48–52.

Lecocq addressed these remarks, was a determined advocate of the Landsturm and was tireless in pointing out its advantages to the king and in labeling its opponents as cowards and enemies of the good cause and as unwitting accomplices of the enemy.[12] Lecocq, going over Sack's head, in turn presented his case directly to the king. In a report endorsed as representative of all respectable public opinion by his superior, Wittgenstein, the minister of police, Lecocq rephrased and expanded his argument in a manner calculated for the king's special susceptibilities. He described the steps of the military government in making use of the Landsturm as "actually dangerous to the authority of the sovereign." Most men still in Berlin, according to Lecocq, were unfitted for Landsturm duty by long years of regular work and family life and by "various other comforts of life such as are available to the well-to-do, especially in a capital city." The small military value of a Landsturm composed of men whose morale would be so low must be balanced against possible severe reprisals against the city by the French. This was the view, Lecocq assured his monarch, of all citizens except "the common class of the rabble, who have nothing to lose [and] hope to benefit by general confusion and disorder."

Then Lecocq turned his attention to the committee of which he was chairman, and it becomes apparent why he wanted the veto power. The committee was controlled, he asserted, by

a few men who, to be sure, are enthusiastic supporters of the present political condition of the nation [*gegenwärtigen politischen Verhältnisse des Staats*], but who for that very reason are devoid of all moderation and of proper conceptions of obedience and submissiveness to Your Majesty's sovereign decisions.

Lecocq continued:

This class of people . . . , especially at the present time, is as dangerous to the welfare of the state and throne as the foreign enemy can ever be. The more the nation's political organization is in accord at present with their overriding aim, which completely disregards the

[12] Sack to the king, June 30 and July 5, 1813, *ibid.*, pp. 67–71.

constitution and the authority of the sovereign, and the more the mobilization of the nation's resources, necessary for carrying on this struggle, is related to their principles . . . , the more carefully and energetically must the government maintain its authority and enforce its will . . . , in order to suppress for the future their increasingly dangerous attempts at rebellion.[13]

It would hardly be possible to express with greater clarity the fear prevalent among influential people that the Landsturm represented dangerous egalitarian tendencies—represented, indeed, as Lecocq unmistakably insinuates, merely the culmination of the egalitarian tendencies inherent in the reform movement from the very beginning.

On the basis of these arguments, Lecocq recommended to the king outright exemption of Berlin from the Landsturm decree or else mobilization of the Landsturm on orders of the king alone; alternatively he insisted on the removal of two members of his committee whom he described as "not born subjects of your Majesty." Exactly a week before Lecocq wrote this report, General Scharnhorst, the Hanoverian-born founder of the Landsturm, had died of wounds sustained in battle for his adopted sovereign. Lecocq's remark was hardly in the best of taste.

In the meantime, while Sack valiantly attempted to defend the Landsturm against the imputations of "cowards and weaklings" that it would breed disorder and revolution,[14] other prominent members of what Schön called the "aristocratic party," including government ministers, began to "smell Jacobins."[15] Kircheisen, the minister of justice, protested to the king against the usurping of judicial functions by Landsturm leaders and the defense committees.[16] The most influential recruit for the opposition was Hardenberg's confidant,

---

[13] Lecocq to the king, July 4, 1813, *ibid.,* pp. 43–48.

[14] *Ibid.,* pp. 36–37, 58–63, 143–144.

[15] Schön, *Papiere,* IV, 65. Wittgenstein reacted to the publication of a popular pamphlet on the Landsturm by demonstrating the Landsturm's unsettling effect on public opinion (Paul Czygan, *Zur Geschichte der Tagesliteratur während der Freiheitskriege* [Leipzig, 1911], I, 274–275).

[16] Blumenthal, *Der preussische Landsturm,* pp. 53–58; see also the opinion of the minister Bülow, *ibid.,* p. 39.

Scharnweber, who during the summer of 1813 produced, reportedly in collusion with members of the "aristocratic party" in Berlin,[17] a series of memoranda against the Landsturm. In these lengthy documents the author of the agrarian edict of September 1811 advanced a number of different arguments.[18] He declared that the Landsturm was entirely ineffective as a military institution; that the scorched-earth policy would frighten off allies who did not want their earth scorched; that it was not feasible suddenly to impose martial law on hitherto undisciplined civilians; that excessive punishments were meted out which violated personal integrity and honor. Finally, he argued that both private and national economy were rendered insecure, especially "by releasing the common people from all obedience to authority whenever the enemy arrived." Scharnweber made it plain, however, that he had not abandoned his reformist ideas; on the contrary, he declared that the danger in arming the people was so great only because "the rural population is oppressed by burdens which recent legislation was designed . . . to relieve," but which it had not yet done owing to "wrong-headed ideas in the government." Scharnweber referred particularly to the absence of the constitution promised in the laws of October 1810 and September 1811.

As soon as Scharnweber submitted these suggestions to his mentor, Hardenberg, events moved rapidly. Impressed with the force of Scharnweber's arguments, Hardenberg ordered him to confer first with Theodor von Hippel, the author of the Landsturm edict, and then with General Gneisenau. Scharnweber did not fare well at these meetings: Hippel was a political enemy of his,[19] and Gneisenau became so incensed with him that he ordered him out of the room, a duel being averted only by the king's personal intervention. Nevertheless, Hardenberg persisted in supporting Scharnweber and commissioned him to draft an emendation of the Landsturm decree

---

[17] *Ibid.*, pp. 74–75.   [18] *Ibid.*, pp. 76–96.

[19] Scharnweber and Hippel had clashed over the amendment of the agrarian edict of September 1811 (Theodor Bach, *Theodor Gottlieb von Hippel, der Verfasser des Aufrufs: "An mein Volk"* [Breslau, 1863], pp. 234–235); cf. above, pp. 98–99.

of April 21; Hardenberg himself subsequently adapted Scharnweber's document into a draft of his own which the king signed into law on July 17.[20]

Most of Scharnweber's recommendations were incorporated into this amending decree. Motivated by the desire "to demand only such efforts and sacrifices as are really necessary and to disturb trade as little as possible," the king rescinded the total mobilization ordered in the original decree of April 21, placing various limitations on, and allowing exceptions to, the universal obligation to serve in the Landsturm. The defense committees were dissolved; in Berlin the Landsturm was suspended entirely, as demanded by Lecocq; elsewhere the authority to mobilize it was vested solely in the military governments, on orders from the king; administration of justice by Landsturm authorities was forbidden; the guerilla-warfare measures and the scorched-earth policy which had been stressed in the decree of April 21 were to be undertaken only on specific orders from the military governments. The general effect of the law of July 17 was to leave the Landsturm formally in force but to cripple the spontaneous enthusiasm and ingenuity which are the essential qualities of such makeshift defense forces. As Schön put it, "the fine military spirit, the inspired enthusiasm for king and country" had been mistaken for "Jacobinism and sansculottism." [21]

We are now in a position to review again the reasons for the speedy extinction of the Landsturm idea and to decide who was ultimately responsible for it. Schön, Clausewitz, and Gneisenau, among interested contemporaries, were of the opinion that it was Hardenberg who had tipped the scales in favor of the opponents of the Landsturm.[22] Boyen, although he by

---

[20] For this paragraph, see Blumenthal, *Der preussische Landsturm,* pp. 96-103, 108–122; Pertz and Delbrück, *Gneisenau,* III, 137, 684–688. For the law of July 17, see *Gesetz-Sammlung* for 1813, pp. 89–92, and cf. Blumenthal, *Der preussische Landsturm,* pp. 146–147.

[21] Schön, *Papiere,* IV, 70; cf. Meinecke, *Boyen,* I, 299.

[22] Schön, *Papiere,* IV, 70; M. Lenz, *Geschichte der Universität Berlin,* I, 513; Gneisenau to Eichhorn, Aug. 6, 1813, Griewank, ed., *Gneisenau,* p. 242. Gneisenau was confident that Hardenberg would recover from what he regarded as a temporary lapse. His disappointment did not prevent him

no means exonerated Hardenberg completely, thought that Frederick William III had had a considerable share in the matter as well.[23] In support of his contention Boyen related an incident which, minor in itself, may have had important consequences. On July 14, 1813—three days before the emasculation of the Landsturm became law—the king had returned to his palace at Charlottenburg from a trip to the provinces. During the evening some of the Charlottenburg residents had demonstrated their affection for the monarch by staging a small but loud celebration, in the course of which some rifles had been fired in the air. When the king commented unfavorably on this episode at a conference of high-ranking officers the following morning, the commandant of Berlin had declared that such an incident could have happened only as a result of the Landsturm, which had destroyed all discipline and respect for authority. Boyen himself, who was present, had objected to this conclusion but had received the impression that the king had been struck by it. In recalling the whole affair Boyen remarked that the residents of Charlottenburg were normally very sensitive to the king's dislike of public demonstrations, and he speculated on the possibility that the unusually vociferous welcome accorded the king on this occasion had been deliberately engineered by opponents of the Landsturm.

Any decision as between the responsibility of the king and of his chancellor for the decree of July 17 will in part contain a decision as to the importance of antirevolutionary agitation against the Landsturm on the one hand and of practical and technical drawbacks in the Landsturm on the other.[24] This is so because presumably the king would have been most impressed with warnings of impending revolution at the hands of the Landsturm, while Hardenberg would have listened more readily to the technical arguments of Scharnweber. No definitive judgment, of course, can be rendered; but I would

---

from entertaining, in common with Niebuhr, similar hopes with respect to Hardenberg's attitude toward the Schmalz affair in 1815/1816 (cf. above, p. 120).

[23] Boyen, *Erinnerungen*, III, 75–76; cf. also Meinecke, *Boyen*, I, 297.

[24] Cf. above, p. 172.

maintain that the pressure of conservative opinion on Frederick William III was at least a considerable factor in the situation. So far as the king is concerned, even apart from the nocturnal festivities mentioned by Boyen, it would be entirely consonant with his past and future actions to suppose that he was uneasy about the Landsturm. As regards Hardenberg, we have dating from this period two conflicting utterances of his, both contained in directives to Wittgenstein. In one, the chancellor urged the minister of police to keep a close watch on signs of revolutionary agitation; in the other, he described as unnecessary measures suggested by Wittgenstein for maintaining order in the event that the Landsturm attempted to take the law into its own hands.[25]

Evidently we can do no more than speculate about the problem on the basis of actual information available on the attitude of the king and of Hardenberg. But a truer perspective can be gained by ceasing to treat the Landsturm as an isolated phenomenon and by putting it instead in its proper place in the reform movement as a whole. The Landsturm of 1813 was not different in kind but only in degree from the Landwehr and from universal service, and all three were consistent products of the general principles of reform for which Stein and Scharnhorst and Boyen stood. Similarly, the opposition also operated on coherent principles, and the protests against the Landsturm from both the upper and middle classes were connected with the protests against the Landwehr and universal service and against the reformers generally. Many of the same personalities who attacked the Landsturm had participated and were later to participate in the resistance to other reform measures. The fundamental question, as Boyen's great biographer pointed out long ago, was not whether the Landsturm was a good or a bad, a useful or a useless institution but whether "the reform party which had brought about the [Landsturm] law represented revolutionary tendencies dangerous to the continued existence of the monarchy." [26] The

[25] Hardenberg's directives in Blumenthal, *Der preussische Landsturm,* pp. 53, 134–135.

[26] Meinecke, *Boyen,* I, 291.

circumstance that the attacks on the Landsturm were almost instantaneously successful, whereas attacks on other reform measures either failed or had to be sustained over much longer periods, is indicative not only of the peculiar shortcomings which the Prussian Landsturm undoubtedly had and which Scharnweber criticized but also of its greater vulnerability to imputations of revolutionary tendencies, as the most extreme embodiment of egalitarian principles yet experienced in Prussia, of which Lecocq, Knesebeck, Wittgenstein, and others took advantage.[27]

As a matter of fact, not only were the "aristocratic party" not content to leave the Landsturm alone even after the amending decree of July 17, but throughout the spring and summer of 1813 the Landwehr, itself only just established, was also already under attack.[28] Even Marwitz, who welcomed the Landsturm and complained that the government was stifling spontaneous risings by imposing too many rules—"apparently they do not want free men, but mere machines"—declared that it was essential to retain strict discipline and chains of command. As the Landwehr commissioner of his district, Marwitz insisted on his unlimited authority: "Our objective will not be attained if any fool feels free to play tricks on me instead of attending to his own business!"[29] Marwitz would, of course, have denied the suggestion that he himself preferred machines to free men as his subordinates.

[27] Meinecke (*ibid.*, I, 287–288) makes the point that the Landwehr had "historic connections" while the Landsturm was rootless; while this distinction is no doubt historically valid, I would think that it was not one which was relevant to actual contemporary opinion about the two institutions and therefore would not help to explain the ease with which the Landsturm was dislodged.

[28] See Boyen, *Erinnerungen*, III, 49; Schön, *Papiere*, VI, 536–540. Cf. the curious document (Knesebeck to Quast, Sept. 30, 1813) *ibid.*, VI, 545. For continued attacks on the Landsturm, see Dohna to Schön, March 24, 1814, *ibid.*, VI, 292; Voss to Wittgenstein, Sept. 19, 1813, in Haake, "Verfassungsfrage," XXVI, 543.

[29] Marwitz to Burgsdorff, Feb. 11, 1813, in Kayser, *Marwitz*, p. 258, and *ibid.*, p. 266. For Marwitz on the Landsturm, see above, p. 171, n. 4.

Universal Service and the Landwehr, 1814–1818

The Landsturm by its very nature had been a temporary phenomenon. There was doubtless some significance in the ease with which it was diverted into harmless (and useless) channels; but sooner or later it would have been abandoned in any event. The real struggle over military reform centered on the same two issues which had been paramount during the years of peace before 1813: the abolition of exemptions in conscripting for the army (universal military service) and the organization of a trained reserve whose members normally pursued civilian careers. These two causes were the personal concern of Hermann von Boyen perhaps even more than they had been those of Scharnhorst, his mentor. Boyen infused them with spiritual and cultural meaning; in this respect he stands perhaps closer than any of the rest of the reformers to Baron Stein. Precisely because he saw the interrelationship of superficially isolated issues, Boyen fought for them with determination—or merely with stubbornness, according to the observer's leanings.[30]

Boyen, a native Prussian, was appointed minister of war, on the suggestion of Hardenberg, in the late spring of 1814, after the entry of the allied sovereigns into Paris had signalized the end of hostilities against Napoleonic France.[31] Just a few days before his appointment, the king had ordered reinstatement of the old exemptions from military service which had been suspended for the duration of the war by the decree of February 9, 1813.[32] This decree conveniently symbolizes the fact that Boyen was faced from the beginning with the long-range problems of organizing a peacetime army, not with the ephemeral ones of mobilizing for war.

[30] See, for example, Ernst Rudolf Huber, *Heer und Staat in der deutschen Geschichte* (2nd ed., Hamburg, 1943, first pub. 1938), p. 158, who attributes Boyen's devotion to the Landwehr to "doctrinaire obstinacy."

[31] For the circumstances of Boyen's appointment, see Meinecke, *Boyen*, I, 385–386.

[32] Decree of May 27, 1814, *Gesetz-Sammlung* for 1814, p. 62; cf. Meinecke, *Boyen*, I, 395–398.

Within a few months Boyen evolved a plan which formed the basic military law of his tenure of office.[33] This law, although it also included provisions concerning the formation of a new Landwehr, was chiefly concerned with re-establishing universal military service: "Every native is obliged to defend his fatherland on completing his twentieth year." But in order not to interfere unduly with the peacetime pursuit of learning and trade, Boyen divided the army into four distinct grades: the regular army, a first and second reserve army (the Landwehr), and the Landsturm. The regular army was to consist of volunteers supplemented by men between twenty and twenty-five conscripted by lot for three years.[34] An exception was made, however, for "young men from the educated classes who can provide their own clothing and weapons," who had the privilege of serving for one year only, in special rifle corps, if they so wished. These so-called *Einjährigen* later had first call, other things being equal, on officer positions in the Landwehr.[35]

The first reserve army (*Landwehr des ersten Aufgebots*) was to serve with the regular army in the event of war but in peacetime was demobilized except for drill and exercises. It was to be selected from men between twenty and twenty-five not

---

[33] "Gesetz über die Verpflichtung zum Kriegsdienste," Sept. 3, 1814, *Gesetz-Sammlung* for 1814, pp. 79–82; cf. Meinecke, *Boyen*, I, 401–403.

[34] After the completion of their three years, such conscripts were furloughed home for an additional two years, rather than discharged, and were available as replacements in the regular army in event of war.

[35] There seems to be considerable theoretical justice in the complaint sometimes made that this system of *Einjährigen* itself constituted the first breach in, and therefore a compromise of, the principle of universal service to which Boyen professed himself dedicated (see, e.g., Huber, *Heer und Staat*, pp. 151–152). It should be remembered, on the other hand, that societies more democratic and equalitarian than nineteenth-century Prussia have often similarly indulged wealth or education. Cf. also the feelings of an ardent military reformer like Gneisenau on the subject of his own son's service: "I cannot relieve him of the obligation to devote a few years of his life to the liberation of his country. . . . But I shall see to it that he fulfills this obligation in an easier way, and in one more congenial to his habits and upbringing" (Gneisenau to his wife, Feb. 27, 1813, Griewank, ed., *Gneisenau*, p. 210).

conscripted into the regular army and from all men between twenty-six and thirty-two. The second reserve army (*Landwehr des zweiten Aufgebots*) would, in wartime, perform garrison duty and provide reinforcements for the regular army; it was to be selected from veterans of the regular army and of the first reserve and all others under forty. Finally, the Landsturm, to be mobilized only on the king's orders in the event of invasion, was to include all men between seventeen and fifty not serving in any of the other military units.

What is perhaps most surprising about this law is not any of its provisions but rather the ease with which it was adopted. Boyen's proposals were, if anything, more radical in their effect on the whole social structure of Prussia than Scharnhorst's prewar plans had been; and certainly Boyen's mental kinship with Stein might have been expected to evoke the antireform forces in full cry. Particularly effective resistance could be looked for from within the government, where ministers like Bülow, Schuckmann, Kircheisen, and Wittgenstein, were consistent opponents of the reform principle of civil equality and had been in the forefront of the attack on the Landsturm during the previous year. But in fact the opposition to Boyen's proposals was minor. Boyen's biographer, Friedrich Meinecke, was puzzled by this phenomenon and attempted, with partial success, to explain it.[36] His explanation fell into three parts. First, he held, Boyen and his associates used great care and intelligence in presenting the law. For instance, although the Landsturm was mentioned in the draft of the law, in an accompanying memorandum to the king (which was also circulated among the ministers) Boyen played down this part of his plan, saying that not too much should be attempted at one time.[37] Boyen and his aides took the principle of universal service tacitly for granted and depicted the one-year term for the educated wealthy class as a privilege instead of a burden. They also, and this constitutes the second element in Meinecke's explanation, urged on the king the

[36] Cf. Meinecke, *Boyen*, I, 403–411.

[37] Memorandum of Boyen and Grolman to the king, Aug. 24, 1814, *ibid.*, I, 417–422.

advantages of having the law on the books before the conferences at Vienna, where the military aspects of the new German Confederation would be under discussion. In this way, little time was allowed for intrigue or for second thoughts.

Less plausible than these two is the third element in the explanation. It was simply "the general change in mood resulting from the War of Liberation, the fresh atmosphere in which people were living." This element had certainly been present during the Landsturm controversy of 1813, but Wittgenstein, Kircheisen, Ancillon, and others had seemed little affected by it. The problem, in view of the political structure of Prussia, was surely not whether Boyen's law was acceptable to the masses but rather why no objections were raised against it by the small circle of influential men habitually opposed to measures inspired by similar principles and why, in peacetime, conscription on the basis of universal service could pass easily in 1814 when it had been rejected throughout the years 1807 to 1812. Much more fruitful, it would appear, than this third suggestion in Meinecke's early biography of Boyen is his later allusion to foreign affairs as a likely influence on the matter under discussion. We need not invoke Ranke's "primacy of foreign policy" to tell us that throughout the reform period internal developments in Prussia were guided, at times even dictated, by events and decisions beyond her borders. In the matter under discussion, Meinecke acutely points out that in 1814 Prussia, and specifically the king, was freed from considerations of foreign policy that had previously inhibited the development of a national as opposed to a class army, from the fear that such a body would appear to Napoleon as a sign of aggressive intent.[38] A possible additional factor of significance for the easy passage of Boyen's law might be found in the actual operation of universal service and the Landwehr during the year of war with considerable military success and without

---

[38] See above, p. 160, n. 39, and accompanying text. Further corroboration might be found in the reported efforts of foreign powers to have the Landwehr abolished in 1817: see Gneisenau to Clausewitz, Dec. 23, 1817, Griewank, ed., *Gneisenau*, p. 355.

much evidence to substantiate the gloomy predictions of revolution.

Whatever the explanation for the absence of opposition, Boyen's law of September 3, 1814, was undeniably a measure of the greatest importance, comparable in stature to the Emancipation Edict of 1807. But unfortunately both laws were more conspicuous for their brevity than for their clarity. They were long on resounding general principles and short on particulars which would make those principles meaningful. Hence both laws were in immediate need of supplementary legislation elucidating their meaning and defining their application. For instance (to take only the most important example), Boyen's law bespoke its author's conviction of the inseparable connection between the principle of universal military service and the idea of a reserve army independent, in peacetime, from the regular army, instead of one based on a furlough system. But obviously such a connection remained, in practice, impalpable so long as the bare skeleton of Landwehr organization contained in the decree was not filled out with concrete details of administration. These details were not immediately forthcoming. In the spring of 1815 Boyen drafted a separate law designed to fill the need which was accepted by the king, but its final completion was interrupted by the renewed war following Napoleon's return from Elba.[39]

Meanwhile the principle of universal service itself was already coming under attack, and the remobilization demanded by the fresh period of belligerence served only to bring the issue more sharply into focus. Objections came from many sources and took many forms.[40] The moribund provisional national assembly urged on Hardenberg the dangers of indiscriminate conscription of essential workers and demanded assurances that agriculture and trade would continue to receive due attention. Similar petitions were received from

---

[39] Meinecke, *Boyen*, II, 173–174.

[40] For the following manifestations of dissatisfaction, see *ibid.*, II, 143–149; for the protest of the university of Breslau, see also in more detail Helfritz, *Geschichte der preussischen Heeresverwaltung*, pp. 369–374.

groups of merchants and factory owners who demanded exemption for some of their workers. But, in general, economic arguments against universal service were not so numerous as objections on social grounds on the part of the former privileged classes. For example, one nobleman declared that three of his sons had served during the war, that many of his employees had volunteered, but that he himself was exempt, by virtue of ancient customs and family rights, from compulsory service. A group of East Prussian nobles and free farmers objected to a system which made no distinction between "the fathers and brothers of the brave volunteers of 1813" and the lowliest servant. But it was not only the landed aristocracy whose privileges were at stake. The middle-class citizens of Berlin and Breslau were equally anxious for the restoration of exemptions. They went so far as to assert that the government was not constitutionally empowered to remove the exemptions. Even institutions of learning took part in the assault: the University of Breslau attacked what was referred to as the militarization of all citizens and especially the equalization of masters and servants, educated and uneducated, cultured and uncultured, which resulted in destroying individuality and substituting "an indistinct . . . , undifferentiated mass."

Such attacks on universal service were usually ignored, sometimes angrily rejected. It was a principle which had come to stay in Prussia. Its advantages as a method of recruiting over the old canton system were too obvious to the king and to Hardenberg to be obscured by such palpably selfish objections. But a different situation obtained with respect to the Landwehr, despite the close relationship between the two ideas. The decree containing detailed provisions for the organization of the Landwehr was finally enacted on November 11, 1815.[41] The technical provisions, though important in the aggregate in that they made the institution practicable, need not detain us individually. The most noteworthy feature of the law from a general point of view was the reiteration and implementation of Boyen's favorite idea concerning the relationship of the Landwehr to everyday civilian life, with the

[41] *Gesetz-Sammlung* for 1816, pp. 79–91.

object of making the Landwehr an ordinary and respected part
of that life instead of a self-sufficient and strictly military institution.[42] Accordingly, every Landwehr regiment was assigned
a district, varying in size with the density of the population.
From this district the regiment drew its replacements, and in
it were located its headquarters and arms and supply depots.
The Landwehr in each locality was a local institution.

An effort was made, furthermore, to secure for the Landwehr all possible autonomy from the regular army. Paid (i.e.,
regular) administrative personnel were kept to a minimum; at
the highest level, however, the Landwehr of an entire province was under the supervision of an inspector on the staff
of the commanding general of the province, and this inspector was responsible, in addition, for the flow of recruits into
the regular army. The smaller Landwehr units were led by
reserve officers. Replacements for retiring officers were to be
chosen by the corps of officers from among three candidates
nominated by the civilian authorities of the district in which
the retiring officer lived.[43]

Connected with the regular army only loosely, officered for
the most part by its own locally selected men, and locally
administered, Boyen's Landwehr did indeed in no small measure achieve its author's aim of creating a reserve army indigenous to the districts which it served. But precisely to the
extent that Boyen separated the Landwehr (in peacetime)
from the regular army and to the extent that his actions mili-
tated against a vertical organization of society by imposing a
horizontally unifying, indigenous force, he excited the wrath
of many adherents of the old military and social order. High-
ranking officers like August, the royal prince, and Borstell,
Scharnhorst's enemy of 1807, doubted the usefulness, from a
military standpoint, of a Landwehr such as Boyen had organized
it. They cited numerous complaints by Landwehr inspectors

[42] Cf. Meinecke, *Boyen*, II, 174.

[43] Certain limitations were imposed upon the local authorities in their
selection. The candidates were required to be either former regular army
officers, former volunteer riflemen with good records, noncommissioned
officers who were landowners, or owners of 10,000 thalers capital.

about incompetent or inexperienced officers, and they produced arguments designed to refute analogies with the successful wartime Landwehr.[44] Prince August, in particular, advocated a return to the old furlough system of maintaining a
reserve. He declared that the separation of the Landwehr from
the regular army in peacetime would have bad effects on their
co-operation in wartime and that training in the Landwehr
was generally inadequate under Boyen's system.[45]

As in the controversy over the Landsturm, there was some
justification in these technical objections made by military
men to Boyen's Landwehr. During these first years of its existence the Landwehr tended, for example, to contain too many
officers who had held temporary commissions during the war
and had then failed the easy examination for a permanent
commission in the regular army. In the provinces just acquired by Prussia at the Congress of Vienna, some officers had
no experience at all. But these defects of a fledgling organization were already beginning to disappear, and in 1818 denial of
Landwehr commissions to inexperienced men was ordered.
After that time officer replacements were drawn mainly from
the *Einjährigen*.[46] It was therefore unreasonable to subject the
whole concept of the Landwehr to attack because of such early
mistakes. A far saner attitude was displayed by none other than
Marwitz. Hardenberg's old adversary defended the Landwehr
as indispensable to national defense but attacked specific parts
of the Landwehr law of November 21, 1815, as being too
speculative and theoretical. He objected, like the other military
men, to the separation between the Landwehr and the regular
army, but unlike many of them he also objected to the exceptions made for the educated classes. At any rate, he had
the grace to call Boyen honest, industrious, and well-meaning.[47]

[44] Meinecke, *Boyen*, II, 203–205.

[45] Max Lehmann, ed., "Denkschrift des Prinzen August von Preussen
über die Landwehr," *Militär-Wochenblatt*, 1897, No. 50, pp. 1428–1434.

[46] Meinecke, *Boyen*, II, 205–206.

[47] Marwitz to the crown prince, September 1816, Meusel, ed., *Marwitz*,
II[2], 498–499; and *ibid.*, I, 605–607. To be sure, four years later Marwitz had
changed his mind: "This Boyen, who loved only the common rabble . . ."
(*ibid.*, I, 640).

To the attacks on the Landwehr on military grounds were added prolific social and political arguments. Just as Boyen saw the Landwehr as an instrument for arousing the nation's enthusiasm and for teaching it participation in public affairs, so, conversely, the Landwehr presented itself as a target for attack to anyone, with or without military knowledge, who was hostile to the process of social leveling initiated by Stein in 1807. Soon a vicious circle developed: the more the egalitarian tendencies of the Landwehr were attacked, the more Boyen distrusted the attackers and insisted on the maintenance of his system.[48]

This social and political opposition to the Landwehr came from three different quarters. In the first place, there was the now familiar objection of the large cities to being subject to any form of military service at all. Breslau and Berlin were again the main sources of this sentiment. In Breslau a small revolt in the summer of 1817 took the form of widespread refusals to take the Landwehr oath, but this movement was easily suppressed and turned out to have been fomented by foreign agents.[49] In Berlin the resistance was genuine and stronger, mainly on the grounds of financial loss incurred during absence on maneuvers. Despite some concessions on Boyen's part, the Landwehr could not be maintained in Berlin. The municipal administration and the minister of the interior, Schuckmann, supported the rich ruling class which formed the nucleus of the resistance, and Boyen was powerless against this array.[50]

While the distinguished townspeople of Berlin objected to having to serve in the Landwehr themselves, no such idea was in the minds of the landed nobles. What they resisted was not their own but their employees' service in the new egalitarian force. The "old patriarchal conditions," complained the Committee of the East Prussian–Lithuanian Estates, were destroyed by the Landwehr, which interfered with church services, ab-

---

[48] For further elaboration on the social implications of the Landwehr, see Meinecke, *Boyen*, II, Book VI, chaps. ii and iv, *passim*, and especially p. 213.

[49] Cf. above, n. 38.

[50] For this paragraph, see Meinecke, *Boyen*, II, 263–268.

sorbed employees' time on many Saturdays and Mondays as
well as on Sundays, and undermined, by sending its members
around the countryside and encouraging them to gather socially,
"that quiet simplicity which is the main source of the peasant's
integrity and industry"—in other words, his docility. The
committee, being headed by Dohna, could hardly forbear to
refer to the East Prussian Landwehr of 1813, where officers
from field grade up had been nominated by the local Estates,
and to complain that the Estates were not assigned a sufficiently
important role in the Landwehr; the Estates should, for example, rule on requests for exemptions on grounds of economic
hardship.[51] A more sharply political issue was raised by Prince
August: Landwehr men, even the officers, were more civilians
than soldiers and were, therefore, like the French National
Guard during the Revolution, unreliable in the event of internal unrest.[52] In another quarter the Landwehr was actually
called "an instrument of revolution." [53]

The third source of opposition to the Landwehr was located in the opposite political quarter: namely, on the Left.
Far from attacking the Landwehr for disrupting established
social relationships, representatives of this school of thought
denounced Boyen's creation as halfhearted and stunted by
compromise. The leader of this group was Theodor von Schön,
now president (governor) of the province of East Prussia. "Our
Landwehr law," wrote Schön to Dohna, "is a perfect monster,
with excrescences at all the corners but with no head." He
pointed, and with justification, at the absurdities resulting from

[51] *Ibid.,* II, 257–263.

[52] Lehmann, ed., "Denkschrift des Prinzen August," *Militär-Wochenblatt,*
1897, No. 51, pp. 1449–1456.

[53] Beyme, as reported by Gneisenau to Clausewitz, Dec. 23, 1817, Griewank, ed., *Gneisenau,* p. 355. In one sense, this description was partially
justified. There was a faction of radicals which did regard the Landwehr as
an instrument for revolution, precisely because they regarded the regular
army as the instrument of despotism; therefore they encouraged any strengthening of the Landwehr and any weakening of the regular army. But this
faction was important only in southern Germany, not in Prussia, and
certainly had no connections with Boyen. See the statement of Rotteck, in
Reinhard Höhn, *Verfassungskampf und Heereseid: Der Kampf des Bürgertums um das Heer (1815–1850)* (Leipzig, 1938), pp. 19–27.

the system of recruiting established by Boyen, under which thousands of young men between twenty and twenty-five were serving neither in the regular army nor in the Landwehr, while many over twenty-five on whom the choice had fallen for service in the regular army were bound later to serve in the Landwehr as well until the age of forty. "There is much good will in the war ministry but little reflection, and they are trying to achieve their aims by stealth instead of by forthright means," Schön scolded.[54]

Far more important than any of these manifestations of opposition to the Landwehr among the public, and in the end decisive, was the intrigue against it at court, which finally won over the king. As Boyen had been aware throughout, the emulation by Frederick William III of certain of the least mature character traits of his ancestor, Frederick William I, inclined him to view with little enthusiasm any military formation which did not exhibit the traditional military virtues of discipline and glitter. This predilection was assiduously fostered by such bureaucrats as Bülow and Schuckmann, who had no understanding for Boyen's ideas about giving the army strong roots in the nation, and by such military men as Knesebeck and the king's brother-in-law, Duke Charles of Mecklenburg. This group was provided with an important new talking point by the Wartburg festival: the cry of "demagogues in the army" was strengthened and this time directed particularly at the Landwehr. In a memorandum for the king written in the winter of 1817, Duke Charles described the Landwehr as "a close approach to a dangerous arming of the people" which might easily slip out of the government's control. He asserted that the Landwehr, far from attaching the people to the army, was in fact alienating them by providing a rival. The local Landwehr armories would be dangerous nuclei of resistance in the event of a popular revolt. Moreover—and again considerations of foreign policy enter the picture—the duke thought that

---

[54] Schön to Dohna, March 7, 1816, and July 27, 1818, Schön, *Papiere*, VI, 378–379, 438–439; cf. Meinecke, *Boyen*, II, 319–321. Note that Schön confided his views to Dohna, whose objections to the Landwehr were of quite a different nature.

the large number of Landwehr regiments made an unneces-
sarily offensive impression abroad.[55] His proposed solution was
the total reintegration of the Landwehr into the regular army.[56]
Prince Metternich, who was far from enamored of the idea
of a national army in Prussia, took a similar line, warning
Hardenberg of the "civilian party" in Prussia which wanted
to substitute "a senseless system of mere popular forces" for a
proper army.[57]

The opposition to the Landwehr on the part of some of
Boyen's colleagues within the government received an eminently practical expression when the minister of finance,
Bülow, proposed to cut down the military budget for 1817
by reducing the personnel of the Landwehr and by restoring
the pre-Jena furlough system. Such a step would have completely undermined Boyen's system, in that it would have re-
established all the social relationships bound up with the old
army, including the aristocratic officer corps. Probably universal service itself would not long have survived this blow. But
Boyen was able to ward off this threat by offering his resignation, which the king, out of a sense of fairness, refused.[58]

By way of an epilogue, Bülow's administration of his own
department was shortly afterwards subjected to such unfavorable comment by a government commission headed by Hum-

[55] Cf. above, p. 184. It should be remembered that before Bismarck's time
domestic conservatism in Prussia was often accompanied by a cautious
foreign policy.

[56] Duke Charles' memorandum as summarized in the rebuttal of Witzleben, the king's adjutant, Wilhelm Dorow, ed., *Job von Witzleben: Mittheilungen desselben und seiner Freunde zur Beurtheilung preussischer Zustände
und wichtiger Zeitfragen* (Leipzig, 1842), pp. 102–110; cf. Meinecke, *Boyen,*
II, 357–358. Cf. the unaccountable approval of Duke Charles expressed by
Schön in his *Papiere,* III, 61.

[57] From Metternich's essay "Ueber die Lage der preussischen Staaten,"
November 1818, *Aus Metternich's Papieren,* III, 175. The main purpose
of this essay was to dissuade Frederick William III and Hardenberg from
creating a national assembly (cf. above, p. 138); but, as always, opposition
to constitutional and to military reform were intimately related. On pressure from Vienna against the Landwehr, cf. also Clausewitz to Gröben, Dec.
26, 1819, in Kessel, "Zu Boyens Entlassung," p. 52.

[58] For this episode, see Meinecke, *Boyen,* II, 300–307.

boldt that Bülow, although he was Hardenberg's brother-in-law, was transferred to another position.[59] This development foreshadowed the events of 1819, when Humboldt was to find himself ranged with Boyen against most of the other ministers, although this time against Hardenberg as well. But Humboldt's affinity with the war minister was a spiritual as well as a historical one; they did not always agree on matters of detail, but they stood on common ground on the big questions—especially on the biggest question of all, whether Prussia should develop according to the concepts of freedom which Stein had suggested or according to the concepts of tutelage, aristocratic or bureaucratic, advocated by Wittgenstein, Metternich, and Ancillon. Upon the answer to this question depended, ultimately, not only the fate of Boyen's Landwehr but also, and even more important, the fate of the constitution, which early in 1819 was entrusted into the hands of Humboldt. Thus Boyen and Humboldt stood, in 1819, for the same principle, and when at the end of that year they were both dismissed, that event was to mark the end of the reform era.

[59] Gebhardt, *Humboldt,* II, 235 ff., and cf. above, p. 130.

PART FOUR

The End of an Era

CHAPTER XI

The Year 1819:

The Triumph of Reaction

WILHELM VON HUMBOLDT, who had been in the second rank of the reformers ever since the advent of Stein, rose in the year 1819 to the front rank, and thereby became perhaps the chief symbol of the reform movement at the hour of its death. It is not a gratuitous gibe, but a necessary part of the historical record, to state that Humboldt probably preferred the function of principal pall-bearer to that of a subordinate patron. Humboldt is sometimes mentioned as one of those rare combinations of intellectual eminence with political power which afford some people the hope that the age of the philosopher king may yet come to pass; but in Humboldt the consciousness of intellectual superiority triumphed in the end over his political ambitions.

The Recall of Humboldt

Humboldt's sincerity as a reformer, however, is not to be impugned. He had thought long and deeply on political questions and was as profoundly convinced as Stein, and certainly more profoundly convinced than Hardenberg, that the Prussian state stood in urgent need of reform. But Humboldt was also, and above all, a self-conscious intellectual. He was a member of the neohumanist movement, which flourished in Germany at the end of the eighteenth century. Neohumanism, refining Renaissance humanism with the rationalist heritage of the

197

Enlightenment and absorbing some of the cosmopolitanism of the eighteenth century, produced through Goethe a high ideal of world culture which demanded the self-development and unsparing self-devotion of every gifted individual. In his old age Goethe, in *Faust,* came to regard it as a higher wisdom to labor modestly at humble tasks; but Humboldt never renounced the aristocratic individualism of his neohumanist youth. The development of his own personality appeared to him to be the lifework to which he should dedicate himself, not indeed for his own sake but for the sake of humanity. In an early political work Humboldt had applied these individualist precepts to problems of government and had arrived at an orthodox liberal position placing very narrow limits on the scope of state interference in the life of a society. Later, following the Prussian collapse before Napoleon, Humboldt had acknowledged that Prussia could not rise to her feet without severe measures imposed from above and had even abandoned a diplomatic sinecure at the Vatican amid the cultural treasures of Rome to return, at the suggestion of Stein, to the barracks atmosphere of Berlin to head the newly established division of education and religion in the ministry of the interior. In that position he had accomplished a revolution in the Prussian system of education before he became involved with his superiors in the controversy about the establishment of a council of state. Subsequently he had returned to diplomatic activities as ambassador to Austria and later as Hardenberg's aide at the Congress of Vienna. When finally the council of state was formed in 1817, Hardenberg had offered Humboldt a ministry without portfolio and a seat on the council, but the latter had declined to serve in the same government with Bülow and Schuckmann and had returned once more to ambassadorial duties, this time in London.[1]

[1] The most balanced general treatment of Humboldt is that of Kaehler, *Wilhelm von Humboldt und der Staat;* on political questions Gebhardt, *Wilhelm von Humboldt als Staatsmann* is still necessary, though deficient and in some respects obsolete; for the educational reforms, see Eduard Spranger, *Wilhelm von Humboldt und die Reform des Bildungswesens*

Although originally pleased with his new assignment, Humboldt before long became worried about his wife, who had been prevented by poor health from accompanying her husband into the English climate. As early as the spring of 1818 Humboldt began to request his recall from the London post. He explicitly disavowed, in a letter sent to Hardenberg for transmittal to the king, any desire for another position but declared himself willing to attend sessions of the council of state if the king so wished.[2] There is no evidence to doubt that his wife's illness was his chief reason for desiring to return to Germany; on the other hand, he admitted to her that he was tired of working in peripheral positions and that he was determined to decline all offers of another assignment except for a seat on the council of state unless certain ministers were first dismissed.[3]

Hardenberg, however, did not pass on to the king Humboldt's request for recall. Instead he wrote to the latter offering him diplomatic posts at Frankfurt or in Italy; he had been "profoundly shocked" by Humboldt's request and wished to do everything possible to keep his talents in the service of the state, but since Humboldt had earlier stipulated unacceptable conditions for entering the Berlin government, he hoped that one of these positions might serve as a compromise.[4] Humboldt interpreted this letter as unwillingness on Hardenberg's part to have him in Berlin, coupled with reluctance to have it said

(Berlin, 1910); for neohumanism, *id., Wilhelm von Humboldt und die Humanitätsidee* (Berlin, 1908), also Schnabel, *Deutsche Geschichte*, I, 204–234. For Humboldt's very significant relationship with Hardenberg before the clash of 1818–19, see the very fine, though somewhat repetitious analysis of Kaehler, *op. cit.*, pp. 281–324, 334–351, 357–365.

[2] Humboldt to the king, April 4, 1818, and covering letter to Hardenberg, Humboldt, *Gesammelte Schriften*, XVII, 220–225.

[3] Letter of May 5, 1818, Anna v. Sydow, ed., *Wilhelm und Caroline von Humboldt in ihren Briefen* (Berlin, 1906–16), VI, 186 (hereafter Sydow, ed., *Briefe*).

[4] Hardenberg to Humboldt, May 8, 1816, *ibid.*, VI, 196–197. The stipulation referred to was the dismissal of Bülow and Schuckmann; cf. also above, p. 129.

that he had retired; [5] and he forthwith replied to Hardenberg persisting in his request for recall from London and declaring (somewhat disingenuously) that he really did offer his services on the council of state, that he was therefore not rejecting the idea of another position, but that on the other hand he did not wish to appear to be demanding one. He repeated that the seat on the council of state was the only post which he deemed appropriate, that another ambassadorial assignment would be little better than exile, and that a ministerial post was unacceptable not only because of some of the incumbent ministers but also because the ministers as such were not endowed with sufficient responsibility.[6] This latter reason alluded to the chancellor's own position, superior to the ministers, with the right of interference in the affairs of any ministry, and with the exclusive right of regular audiences with the king. Humboldt had already expressed his views on this position in unmistakable terms to Hardenberg himself: "I do not believe that Your Highness' . . . present status is the correct one. . . . In my opinion the only fitting position for a state chancellor is that of president of the ministry and of the council of state." [7] This constitutional stand of Humboldt's was to become crucial in his fight for reform and for his own political destiny.

Hardenberg, presumably not much pleased with Humboldt's attitude, persisted in his refusal to pass on to the king the latter's request for recall but instead now suggested to Humboldt that he substitute a request for a temporary leave of absence, during which he could discuss his future activities personally in Berlin.[8] Humboldt, in turn, was becoming exasperated with Hardenberg's behavior and was determined not to let the matter rest until the king had seen his original

[5] Humboldt to Caroline, May 19, 1818, *ibid.,* VI, 197. Humboldt's interpretation is supported by his biographer (Gebhardt, *Humboldt,* II, 300), who declared that Hardenberg had "put Humboldt on ice" in London and did not welcome the prospect of his return. Cf. also the subsequent text.

[6] Humboldt to Hardenberg, May 29, 1818, Humboldt, *Gesammelte Schriften,* XVII, 230–233.

[7] Memorandum for Hardenberg, dated July 14, 1817, *ibid.,* XII¹, 199.

[8] Hardenberg to Humboldt, Sept. 4, 1818, Sydow, ed., *Briefe,* VI, 298–299.

request for recall.[9] Once again he urged the chancellor to present his letter to the king without further delay. He reiterated
his earlier arguments and rejected the idea of asking for leave;
but as a compromise, if Hardenberg really felt he could not
recall Humboldt to Berlin, he suggested the stratagem of
accomplishing his return to Germany by assigning him to execute in Frankfurt certain negotiations between Prussia and
the Confederation.[10] Hardenberg seized on this suggestion,
Humboldt returned to Germany, had audiences with the king
and the chancellor, and was assured that he would not be sent
back to London. But still he mistrusted Hardenberg: "He
is afraid that I will head an opposition faction." Nothing, he
protested to his wife, was farther from his intentions; but at
the same time he regretted that the Frankfurt negotiations
would prevent him from attending the winter sessions of the
council of state, and he betrayed the real bent of his thoughts
when he commented on a rumor that Hardenberg was shortly
going to produce a constitution for Prussia: "I would be more
afraid of that than of ten years without any constitution. Such
haste after so much delay, and this secret drafting by one man,
and at *his* age!" [11] It was because he was sure that the constitution
would be under discussion that he was so anxious to attend the
meetings of the council of state, and conversely he felt that
for the same reason Hardenberg wished to prevent him from
attending them: because he wanted to grant the constitution in
solitary and munificent glory.

In mid-January 1819 Humboldt received in Frankfurt a
Cabinet Order appointing him to a new ministry consisting
of five departments detached from the ministry of the interior,
chief among them being those concerned with constitutional
matters and negotiations with the Estates (*die ständischen
Angelegenheiten und Verhandlungen mit den Landständen*).
He was to have seniority as of his first ministerial appointment

[9] Humboldt to Caroline, Sept. 11, 1818, *ibid.*, VI, 300.

[10] Humboldt to Hardenberg, Sept. 14, 1818, Humboldt, *Gesammelte
Schriften*, XVII, 243.

[11] Cabinet Order to Humboldt, Oct. 19, 1818, Sydow, ed., *Briefe*, VI, 353–
354; Humboldt to Caroline, Nov. 4, 13, 17, *ibid.*, VI, 364–370, 375–376, 381.

and a seat on the council of state; but his repeatedly stated condition for entering the government, the removal of Schuckmann and Bülow, was not met. Even more significantly, Humboldt's suspicions concerning Hardenberg were confirmed in the latter's casual postscript to the covering letter, containing the information that he was personally working on the constitution which the king wished speedily to promulgate.[12]

With complete consistency, Humboldt declined to accept the appointment. He now regarded Hardenberg himself as the chief obstacle. The chancellor's work on a constitution, Humboldt wrote privately, in itself represented interference in the ministry offered to him and was a further token of the peculiarly irresponsible nature of the chancellorship, which placed the ministers in the position of hirelings. The test which Humboldt established for ministerial responsibility was the right of private audience with the king, and this right, he felt, was incompatible with the existing constitutional position of the chancellor.[13] Determined not to abandon the principles on which he had settled, Humboldt wrote to the king asking permission to postpone his decision on accepting the offered post until his return to Berlin, when its exact scope could be defined. His own definition he gave as follows:

I am appointed to be the organ in the ministry of state through which proposals as to the contemplated representative [ständischen] constitution will reach Your Royal Majesty, and I am to be responsible . . . for putting it into effect.[14]

Simultaneously he wrote to Hardenberg:

I had thought that the draft for a constitution would emanate from my department, and I cannot deny that I would find it difficult to conduct such an important matter according to the ideas of others [i.e., Hardenberg's]. Besides, I cannot conceive how one man alone can work out a constitution, or even work out its basic principles.

[12] Cabinet Order and Hardenberg's covering letter to Humboldt, Jan. 11 and 16, 1819, *ibid.*, VI, 439–441.

[13] Humboldt to Caroline, Dec. 21, 1818, and Jan. 22, 1819, *ibid.*, VI, 413, 442.

[14] Humboldt to the king, Jan. 24, 1819, Humboldt, *Gesammelte Schriften*, XVII, 276–277.

He proposed reactivation of the constitutional commission which had been created in 1817 as an organ of the council of state, to which he, Humboldt, would submit his plans.[15]

Humboldt's attitude, however justified it may have been from his point of view, certainly appeared extremely arrogant, and his surprise at receiving what he termed an "ungracious" reply testified to an inability to gauge the impression of his own actions on others. This reply was in the form of a Cabinet Order, which he had no doubt was the work of Hardenberg, disapproving his request for postponement, inviting him to accept at once, and concluding:

Moreover, there is no mention in my Cabinet Order of the 11th inst. of your being the organ of the ministry of state through which the *proposals* for the contemplated representative constitution are to reach me. I have already in part determined its principles and shall myself determine others in due course, as well as the means whereby before its promulgation it shall be carefully examined and considered.[16]

Still Humboldt did not give up. In his rejoinder to the king he asserted that his assumptions concerning his functions were based on normal ministerial procedure—i.e., that the minister responsible for a given department should make all proposals and dispositions relevant to it. He had felt it necessary to seek clarification as to whether he would have sufficient independence to discharge the responsibilities of his office. The whole tenor of Humboldt's letter conveyed hostility to the chancellorship and to its incumbent, and his premises were those applicable to a system of responsible government on the British model, which was incompatible not only with the chancellorship but with the Prussian type of monarchy as well.[17]

Hardenberg, of course, saw this document and understood clearly the challenge it contained to his own political existence. Determined to maintain himself in his high position, not

[15] Humboldt to Hardenberg, Jan. 24, 1819, *ibid.*, XVII, 275.

[16] Cabinet Order to Humboldt, Jan. 31, 1819, Sydow, ed., *Briefe,* VI, 465–466. Humboldt's comments are in Humboldt to Caroline, Feb. 8, 1819, *ibid.*, VI, 464; cf. Gebhardt, *Humboldt,* II, 337.

[17] Humboldt to the king, Feb. 9, 1819, Sydow, ed., *Briefe,* VI, 470–479.

merely as a first minister but as a superminister, he appended numerous critical marginal notes to Humboldt's letter. The most significant of these concerned Humboldt's demand for independence in his ministry:

What kind of independence does he want? He is to have as much as all the other ministers. It is only me that he is attacking. Let the king decide whether I am dispensable or not. If I am not considered necessary, I will gladly retire without further ado. But so long as His Majesty deems my services useful, I shall maintain my authority.

His concluding verdict was that Humboldt must decide at once whether to accept the post as offered.[18]

By his threat of resignation, Hardenberg forced the king to decide between himself and Humboldt, between the chancellorship and a responsible ministry, and it was not in the king's nature not to decide for the former. In a curt Cabinet Order, with the air of an ultimatum, the king confronted Humboldt with a demand to accept or reject the offered position. Reluctantly Humboldt yielded to the argument of a friend that rejection would play into Hardenberg's hands, made his submission, and accepted.[19] But to the king only, and not to Hardenberg, had he capitulated; it was to be expected that his feud with the chancellor would be fought to a finish once he assumed his duties. Hardenberg was too jealous of the special prerogatives of his position, and Humboldt too intolerant of them, to afford much hope of harmonious co-operation. Over one issue or another, the two were almost bound to clash. Ironically enough, the question of a representative constitution for Prussia was not likely to be that issue, for Hardenberg's and Humboldt's ideas were not far enough apart here to cause serious difficulties in the absence of other sources of friction. The establishment of representative government in Prussia went by default in 1819 because the two men most anxious

[18] Hardenberg's marginal comments in Gebhardt, *Humboldt,* II, 340–345.
[19] Cabinet Order to Humboldt, Feb. 17; Witzleben to Humboldt, Feb. 19; Humboldt to Caroline, Feb. 26, 1819, Sydow, ed., *Briefe,* VI, 493–495. Humboldt to the king, Feb. 27, 1819, Humboldt, *Gesammelte Schriften,* XVII, 285–286. For an analysis of the crisis of January–February 1819, see Kaehler, *Humboldt,* pp. 395–419.

to promote it were personally incompatible and divergent in their political background and heritage.

Humboldt's ideas for a Prussian constitution are contained in a famous draft completed in February 1819, just before he had accepted the ministry for constitutional affairs.[20] In a formal sense, this lengthy document, exploring profound questions of political theory, is hardly comparable with the brief skeleton of a draft constitution submitted to the king by Hardenberg.[21] Nevertheless, the two plans reveal a significant area of agreement in point of content. Both men believed that the national constitution should be based on local and provincial ones, with provincial assemblies limited in their competence to provincial matters. Both insisted that representation be given to social classes and not to individuals and that a deputy must be a member of the class he represented; both planned a bicameral assembly with a veto power on legislation but reserved for the government the right of initiating laws. Perhaps the most important difference concerned the manner of election of the deputies. Humboldt wished to institute direct election by the populace, while Hardenberg preferred election of the national deputies by the members of the provincial assemblies; but even this did not constitute a fundamental disagreement. In general, both drafts can be characterized as tending toward a moderate form of representative government within the undisputed framework of monarchy and as avoiding all radical political ideas.

If Hardenberg did not differ fundamentally from Humboldt

[20] Humboldt's "Denkschrift über Preussens ständische Verfassung," Humboldt, *Gesammelte Schriften*, XII¹, 225–296. Cf. Gebhardt, *Humboldt*, II, 307–332; Siegfried Kähler, *Beiträge zur Würdigung von Wilhelm v. Humboldt's Entwurf einer ständischen Verfassung für Preussen im Jahre 1819* (Freiburg, 1914), pp. 47–56; Paul Lenel, "Wilhelm von Humboldt und die Anfänge der preussischen Verfassung," *Deutschrechtliche Beiträge*, IX (1913), 93–119.

[21] The body of the draft in Alfred Stern, *Geschichte Europas seit den Verträgen von 1815 bis zum Frankfurter Frieden von 1871* (Berlin, 1894–1924), I, 649–653; the introduction and Hardenberg's commentary for the king in Haake, "Verfassungsfrage," XXX, 344–345; cf. Gebhardt, *Humboldt*, II, 355–358.

in his ideas on a representative constitution, neither did he lag behind the latter in the zeal with which he urged on the king the need for prompt consummation of the matter, first on May 3, 1819, in a covering letter to his draft constitution and then again a month later. This time Frederick William III was moved to action. He summoned a conference with General Witzleben, his adjutant; Wittgenstein, the lord chamberlain; Ancillon, the crown prince's tutor; Count Bernstorff, the foreign minister; and Daniel Ludwig Albrecht, the cabinet secretary. The chancellor was not invited; Humboldt was still in Frankfurt. At this conference it was decided to form a small subcommittee of the constitutional commission of 1817, under the presidency of Humboldt, with the task of reporting on plans for a constitution, including Hardenberg's plan, to the full commission. The motivation behind this decision varied among the various participants. Most of them apparently wished to cultivate Humboldt as a counterweight to Hardenberg; Witzleben and perhaps Albrecht were interested in the constitution itself and considered Humboldt a better agent in its behalf than the aging chancellor. To the latter, however, these differences mattered little; he had hoped to make his own draft constitution the sole basis for discussion and presumably to confront Humboldt on his arrival with a *fait accompli*. Moreover, the mere holding of such a conference in his absence represented a severe blow to his prestige and would have been unthinkable five years earlier. It cannot, indeed, be denied that the formation of a new "kitchen cabinet" indicated by this conference was an undesirable political phenomenon; it suggested a revival of the cabinet system of the era before 1807, which had been attacked by both Stein and Hardenberg as the major obstacle to political reform in Prussia.[22]

This lengthy account of what were only the preliminaries to the final climax of the Prussian reform movement has been necessary in order to show why that climax turned into an anticlimax and why Hardenberg and Humboldt, both striving

---

[22] For the developments related in this paragraph, see Haake, "Verfassungsfrage," XXIX, 368–369, XXX, 349–352, 361–363; Gebhardt, *Humboldt*, II, 358–360.

to equip Prussia with a moderate representative constitution, were destined to pull in opposite directions because of their personal and political antipathies, secretly encouraged by third parties. These latter intrigues, designed to employ Humboldt as an unwitting tool with which to undermine Hardenberg's position, attained their greatest momentum only after Humboldt's arrival in Berlin early in August 1819. But in the meantime other events, not related to the Hardenberg-Humboldt feud, had taken place which further diminished the chances of a constitution for Prussia. These events formed the culmination of the affair of the "demagogues" which had been building up ever since the tragicomedy on the Wartburg in October 1817, and they led to the triumph of Metternich's policy of reaction in Prussia and in all of Germany.

Mannheim, Teplitz, Carlsbad, and Vienna:
the Triumph of Metternich

In 1817 the Wartburg incident had occurred in an atmosphere rendered hostile to "popular" or "constitutional" movements by the preceding troubles over a constitution in Württemberg.[23] Similarly, the renewed demagogue scare of 1819 followed in the wake of political clashes in the other south German states, Baden and Bavaria, where representative assemblies had recently been introduced.[24] But the development in southern Germany that held most significance for Prussia and her constitution was the assassination of Kotzebue in Mannheim.[25] Those who believed in the existence of a widespread seditious conspiracy found powerful confirmation in this event. Here, they asserted, was evidence that the time was far from propitious for giving the people a chance to participate in government by granting a representative constitution; on the contrary, measures must be taken to suppress popular un-

[23] See above, pp. 125–126.
[24] On Baden, see Schnabel, *Deutsche Geschichte*, II, 226–234; on Bavaria, Treitschke, "Verfassungskampf," pp. 416–419, also Eugen Franz, *Bayerische Verfassungskämpfe: Von der Ständekammer zum Landtag* (Munich, 1926), chaps. ii–iv; cf. Stägemann to Varnhagen, March 6, 1819, Varnhagen, *Aus dem Nachlass*, p. 85.
[25] Cf. above, p. 139.

rest which was giving rise, not merely to acts of disrespect toward the monarchy and the established order like those on the Wartburg, but now to bloodshed as well. Kotzebue's assassin, the unfortunate Karl Sand, a gentle theological student who had been seized by an unreasoning hatred for his victim, became for some a martyr in the cause of freedom but for others a detestable symbol of revolution.[26]

The movement to make political capital out of the assassination in Prussia was led by Metternich's henchman, Prince Wittgenstein. It was evident, he declared, that there were societies in existence dedicated to the purpose of

changing the present public constitution both of Germany as a whole and of the several states of the German Confederation, partly by means of spreading demagogic principles and religious fanaticism among the youth and the people, partly by violent means, and substituting a new constitution based on unity, liberty, and popular national traditions [*Volkstümlichkeit*].

He advocated strict investigation and punishment of all those involved in such activities.[27] Hardenberg accepted this pro-

[26] For an excellent, succinct description of the psychological effects of the assassination, see Varnhagen, *Denkwürdigkeiten*, V, 65–66. A significant measure of its impact was the attitude of Gneisenau, himself accused in 1815 of being a Jacobin and in 1819 still under suspicion. In justification of the Carlsbad Decrees which resulted from the agitation about Sand, Gneisenau wrote: "In view of the gravity of the danger the ministers cannot be blamed for them, since the investigations seem to show that there has really been talk of one indivisible German Republic, of this end justifying all means, even the most bloody. . . . Every unprejudiced person must be struck by the frequency with which otherwise respectable people have defended Kotzebue's assassination" (Gneisenau to Princess Radziwill, Nov. 20, 1819, Griewank, ed., *Gneisenau*, pp. 365–366; cf. Gneisenau to Clausewitz, Dec. 23, 1817, *ibid.*, p. 354).

[27] Wittgenstein's memorandum of June 24, 1819, in Ernst Müsebeck, "Siegmund Peter Martin und Hans Rudolph von Plehwe, zwei Vertreter des deutschen Einheitsgedankens von 1806–1820," *Quellen und Darstellungen zur Geschichte der deutschen Burschenschaft und der deutschen Einheitsbewegung*, II (Heidelberg, 1911), 187–188. Cf. also the report of Wittgenstein's assistant Kamptz, dated July 14, 1819, in Adolf Stölzel, *Brandenburg-Preussens Rechtsverwaltung und Rechtsverfassung dargestellt im Wirken seiner Landesfürsten und obersten Justizbeamten* (Berlin, 1888), II, 460.

posal and persuaded the king to issue a Cabinet Order tablishing a commission of investigation.[28] The chancellor cou.. not or would not understand that the desire of Wittgenstein and his cohorts to suppress the "demagogues" was merely a facet of a comprehensive plan to steer Prussia away from the path of constitutionalism. Hardenberg thought it possible to press for a constitution with one hand while strengthening the political power of its sworn opponents with the other, and he saw nothing incongruous in urging haste on the king in the matter of the constitution on the ground that Wittgenstein's plans for prosecuting seditious groups would be useless "if it was not demonstrated at the same time that the legitimate desires of the people are heeded." [29] To be sure, Hardenberg was confronted with a dilemma. He felt much less secure than formerly in his relations with the king, and it was still possible that Wittgenstein would discover Hardenberg's own association with the secret societies in 1815. In order, therefore, to avoid antagonizing Wittgenstein and to give no grounds for suspicion concerning his own sympathies, he considered it expedient to support the persecutions. Hardenberg was still anxious to crown his career by giving Prussia a constitution, but the means he employed were dubious. From Wittgenstein it was only a step to Metternich, in whose arms Hardenberg's constitutional ideas received the kiss of death.

From the point of view of the Hofburg, Prussia, being Austria's chief rival in Germany, had at all costs to be prevented from espousing a liberal political philosophy and a liberal form of government, lest she become the focus of all liberal hopes in Germany. In the course of the year 1819 Austrian interference in internal Prussian affairs, hitherto confined principally to prodding Prussia toward a firmer stand against the secret societies and the "demagogues," became overt intervention in the constitutional struggle. The opportunity for such action was provided by a holiday trip of Frederick William III, accompanied by Wittgenstein and Bernstorff, to the Bohemian resort town of Teplitz in July 1819. Metternich

[28] M. Lenz, *Geschichte der Universität Berlin*, II[1], 59.
[29] Haake, "Verfassungsfrage," XXX, 349.

interrupted his own vacation in nearby Carlsbad long enough
to visit the Prussian king's headquarters and to dispel whatever holiday atmosphere may have prevailed in Teplitz. He
submitted to Frederick William III a memorandum declaring
that a representative constitution was incompatible with
monarchy; that the only acceptable kind of representative assemblies were provincial Estates of the traditional type; and
that if nevertheless some sort of national assembly were deemed
necessary, its members must be chosen by the provincial deputies from among their own number and its convocation retained
exclusively by the king.[30]

The weak monarch fell under Metternich's spell and begged
the Austrian to help him to solve his problems. Metternich
replied: "If Your Majesty is determined to avoid introducing
any popular representation in your state . . . , help is possible. Otherwise, there is no remedy." Thereupon Frederick
William asked Metternich to confer with Hardenberg, who
was being summoned to Teplitz. Metternich agreed but asked
that Bernstorff and Wittgenstein also attend his meetings with
the chancellor. Frederick William was delighted and enjoined
the Austrian: "Try to bind them in writing; you can rely
completely on Prince Wittgenstein." Of this latter fact nobody was better aware than Metternich, and he despised the
king who plotted with the foreigner against his own chief
minister: "Where such words are spoken, there is scarcely any
government," he wrote to his imperial master. But of course
he welcomed this weakness which virtually delivered Hardenberg into his hands. Hardenberg, seeking to gain time in order
to recover the ascendancy over his monarch which he had lost
to Metternich, showed the latter a radically expurgated version
of his constitutional draft for Prussia, in which the national
assembly consisted of only one small chamber chosen both by
and from the provincial deputies; all mention of the assem-

---

[30] P. Bailleu, ed., "Metternich's Teplitzer Denkschrift," *Historische Zeitschrift,* L (1883), 190–192; cf. *Aus Metternich's Papieren,* III, 265. On the
development of the so-called "monarchical principle," see Heinrich O.
Meisner, *Die Lehre vom monarchischen Prinzip im Zeitalter der Restauration und des Deutschen Bundes* (Breslau, 1913), and cf. below, p. 213.

bly's competence and periodicity was omitted, as was the
miniature "bill of rights" with which he had concluded the
original draft. Hardenberg signed a formal undertaking not
to introduce in Prussia "any general [i.e., national] popular
representation incompatible with her geographical and internal situation," in other words to confine himself to a central
committee of the provincial assemblies, suggested by Metternich as the very most that could be granted. He undertook also
to take appropriate steps against the "demagogues," especially
by curbing freedom of speech and by removing seditious writers and teachers from their posts. The whole protocol constituted a declaration of Austro-Prussian solidarity with respect to the internal affairs of Germany. Metternich rejoiced
that "the systematic efforts which I have made . . . for years
to frighten the king away from that step whose inescapable and
direct consequence would be the final overthrow of all existing institutions," i.e., a constitution, had at Teplitz been
crowned with final success.[31]

But even greater victories were to be Metternich's. Having
secured the assent of Prussia, he was ready to make the whole
German Confederation follow Austrian policy. The next step
in the accomplishment of this program was taken at Carlsbad.
There, during the month of August 1819, the representatives
of the nine largest German states assembled, partly, no doubt,
to restore their own health by taking the waters, but chiefly to
restore, as they believed, the health of Germany by drawing
up the Carlsbad Decrees.[32] These were the notorious laws

[31] For the general narrative of the events at Teplitz we are dependent on
Metternich's own reports to his emperor of July 30 and Aug. 1, 1819, *Aus
Metternich's Papieren*, III, 258–264. No doubt these reports were calculated
to reflect as favorably as possible on the success of their author's activity,
but in the main their accuracy is borne out by the other evidence: Hardenberg's expurgated draft constitution is documented by Gebhardt, *Humboldt*, II, 367–368; Hardenberg's so-called "Teplitz Protocol" is quoted by
Heinrich von Treitschke, *Deutsche Geschichte im neunzehnten Jahrhundert*
(Leipzig, 1879–1885), II, 632–634; cf. also *ibid.*, II, 550–552, III, 757–758;
id., "Verfassungskampf," p. 420; for a friendlier view, see Haake, "Verfassungsfrage," XXX, 358–359.
[32] On the Carlsbad conferences and decrees, see Treitschke, *Deutsche*

which established machinery under the control of the Confederation—that is to say under Austrian control—to investigate and suppress the demagogues by curtailing freedom of speech and publication.

From this subject the delegates turned to a more general discussion of the political affairs of the German states, and particularly of their constitutions. The basis for discussion was a lengthy exegesis by Friedrich von Gentz, Metternich's private secretary, on Article 13 of the Act of Confederation of 1815. This famous article stated simply: "A *landständische* constitution will be introduced in all the states of the confederation," and was regarded in some quarters as placing the authority of the confederation behind the movement for constitutional government. But the word *landständisch* was ambiguous, and Gentz's interpretation was designed to show, in the interests of Austrian policy, that the adoption of a *landständische* constitution not only did not imply, but indeed precluded, the establishment of representative government. Truly *landständische* constitutions, wrote Gentz,

are based on the natural foundation of a well-ordered civil society where the peculiar positions of the various classes and corporations [this term, of course, is used in its medieval sense] have given rise to special class [*ständische*] relations and rights, which have in the course of time been legally modified without infringing the essential prerogatives of the sovereign.

In such constitutions, only "representatives or deputies of corporations existing of their own right [*durch sich selbst bestehender*] may participate in legislation," in contrast to "representative" constitutions, under which not the rights and interests of individual classes, but the whole people, are represented.[33] "Representative" constitutions

---

Geschichte, II, 555–566; and the protocol and documents in Johann Ludwig Klüber, *Wichtige Urkunden für den Rechtszustand der deutschen Nation* .(ed. C. Welcker; 2nd ed., Mannheim, 1845).

[33] Gentz's analysis obviously leans heavily on that of Adam Müller and through him on Burke. Cf. Adam Müller on corporations and "moral persons," above, p. 73.

are always based, in the last analysis, on the erroneous conception of the supreme sovereignty of the people. . . . [They] have a persistent tendency to substitute the phantom of so-called popular liberty (for which read popular tyranny [*Wilkühr*]) for civil order and respect for authority and the delusion of a general equality of rights (or, what amounts to the same thing, general equality before the law) for the indestructible, divinely ordained differences in social standing and privileges.

Expressed in terms of political institutions, an assembly of Estates (like those of some of the Prussian provinces) was permissible, according to Gentz, but not the "representative" assemblies of the states of the Confederation of the Rhine or those launched in Nassau, Weimar, and southern Germany since 1814.[34] The representative system involved ministerial responsibility, publicity of debate, freedom of the press, unlimited right of petition—all institutions, according to Gentz, incompatible with the monarchical form of government. In summary, Gentz's argument, based on a feudal or aristocratic conception of society, was to equate "representative" constitutions with popular sovereignty and "landständische" constitutions with monarchical sovereignty, with the corollary that only the latter were permissible under Article 13.[35]

[34] Note how closely Gentz's argument paralleled that of the Prussian conservatives who held that if there was to be a Prussian constitution, it must be modelled on the provincial constitutions. Cf. above, pp. 127–128.

[35] Gentz's memorandum in Klüber, *Wichtige Urkunden*, pp. 213–223. For background on the discussions of Article 13, see Meisner, *Die Lehre vom monarchischen Prinzip*, pp. 175–183. For incisive comment on the memorandum, see *ibid.*, pp. 183–194, especially the following passages: "Regard for Austrian conditions . . . combined with a sincere fear, on the part of the diplomats of the Hofburg, of the allegedly impending revolution in Germany, made it possible for Gentz, who usually thought so acutely and logically, to produce . . . a piece whose contents induce equal astonishment at its sophistical untruths and at its lack of political realism" (pp. 183–184); "he [Gentz] is defending not the monarchical principle but the absolutist principle, and . . . inequality of subjects before the law" (p. 192). Gentz made quite explicit the connection between his discussion of constitutions and the matter of the demagogues: "The popular election, which is an intrinsic part of the representative system, . . . is always . . . the last step toward demagoguery."

Despite Metternich's efforts, Gentz's interpretation of Article 13 failed of adoption at Carlsbad.[36] But the whole question of constitutions was raised again in the Diet of the Confederation at sessions continuing far into the year 1820 and interspersed with frequent conferences between ministers of the leading member states. It was not until June 8, 1820, that the Final Act, an amendment to the Act of Confederation of 1815, was accepted by the Diet. Article 57 stated:

All power in the state [must] remain in the hands of the sovereign, and the sovereign can be obliged by a *landständische* constitution to permit participation of the Estates in government only to the extent that the latter may exercise certain specified rights.[37]

Although this article did not incorporate Gentz's principles as explicitly as Gentz and Metternich might have wished, it clearly contemplated as potential representative bodies only the traditional Estates of the Realm and further contemplated that even they could be restricted to such activities as the sovereign might assign to them.

Throughout the negotiations at Carlsbad and Vienna, Austrian policy had received consistent support from the Prussian delegate, Count Bernstorff;[38] and it was Hardenberg himself, in the "Teplitz Protocol," who had set in motion the whole process of suppressing both freedom of speech and liberal constitutions throughout Germany. The final success of Metter-

[36] See Treitschke, *Deutsche Geschichte*, II, 558–559.

[37] The Final Act is printed in Karl Zeumer, ed., *Quellensammlung zur Geschichte der deutschen Reichsverfassung in Mittelalter und Neuzeit* (Leipzig, 1904), pp. 474–480.

[38] To the despair of friends of the constitution in Prussia; see e.g., Stägemann to Benzenberg, Nov. 9, 1819, Rühl, ed., *Briefe und Aktenstücke*, III, 8; cf. Gentz to Adam Müller, Dec. 15, 1819, *Briefwechsel zwischen Friedrich Gentz und Adam Heinrich Müller* (Stuttgart, 1857), pp. 308–309. For a sample of Bernstorff's activities, see his memorandum at Carlsbad, Klüber, *Wichtige Urkunden*, pp. 255–256. It is symptomatic of the complete change in Prussian policy that Bernstorff's actions in 1819 contrast sharply with the efforts of Hardenberg and Humboldt on behalf of representative constitutions in Germany at the Congress of Vienna in 1814–1815: cf. Meisner, *Die Lehre vom monarchischen Prinzip*, pp. 168–172, and the material there cited.

nich's German policy therefore owed not a little to Hardenberg
and to his official representative. But even his detractors are
agreed that the chancellor's purpose in these maneuvers was
to gain time through deception. He was not really anxious
to suppress free speech, but rather, by pacifying both Metternich and his own king, whom the former had beguiled into
his camp, Hardenberg hoped to strengthen his own position
(and, above all, to avoid suspicion himself) so that in due course
he could, after all, impose his constitutional ideas on Prussia.
The success or failure of this tortuous policy can be measured
only in terms of subsequent developments in the constitutional
struggle in Prussia.

The Dismissal of Humboldt, Boyen, and Beyme

It was not long after the Teplitz conferences that signs began to appear indicating the fate of the Prussian constitutional
movement. Hardenberg, having abandoned his constitutional
draft for Metternich's benefit at Teplitz, could not find the
courage to return to it afterwards and instead drew up still a
third draft, different both from his original plan and from the
one which he had shown to Metternich. It is instructive to
compare this latest sketch with his first one to ascertain the
extent to which in the intervening three months Hardenberg
had adopted Metternichian ideas.[39] Much remained unchanged,
especially the form; in content, the arrangements for local and
provincial elections and assemblies and what Humboldt called
the "Chinese-boxes" system of pyramidal local-to-national elections were common to both drafts, even the wording being
identical in some places. But with respect to the national
assembly there were important differences. In the new draft,
the deputies were to be elected from among, as well as by, the
members of the provincial assemblies, as Metternich had insisted, with the result of establishing a closer link between

[39] For the purposes of this comparison, see the old draft of May 3, 1819,
in Stern, *Geschichte Europas*, I, 649–653, and cf. above, p. 205; the new
draft of August 11, in Treitschke, *Deutsche Geschichte*, II, 635–637; commentary *ibid.*, II, 589–591, *id.*, "Verfassungskampf," pp. 425–430; and Lenel,
"Humboldt und die Anfänge der deutschen Verfassung," p. 103.

the national and provincial assemblies. The national assembly, moreover, was reduced in size and therefore in stature, and one chamber was suggested as preferable to two in that it would be easier to manipulate. Where in the first draft annual meetings had been proposed, in the later one this question was left open, likewise the manner of voting, which in the earlier plan had been prescribed as by head and not by class; [40] the question of ministerial responsibility to the assembly was now also left undecided. Perhaps the most significant commitment from which Hardenberg withdrew was the decision that a bill rejected by the assembly was to be tabled pending possible reintroduction at the following year's session, a decision which conceded at least a suspensive veto power to the assembly. In leaving this question open in his later draft, Hardenberg left room for the possibility that a bill rejected by the assembly might be decreed into law nevertheless. On the other side of the ledger, the new constitutional sketch also left undecided the question whether the assembly might initiate legislation, a power reserved exclusively to the government in the earlier plan. Finally, the declaration of individual rights guaranteed by the constitution was substantially repeated but was followed by a closing reference to the maintenance of the monarchical principle.

On balance, the conclusion appears unavoidable that Hardenberg had not indeed capitulated to Metternich entirely but had made significant concessions to Austrian wishes regarding constitutions to be granted in the German states. But even a compromise was enough to condemn, on pragmatic grounds, Hardenberg's policy of deception at Teplitz, for ultimately he was deceiving no one more than himself if he believed that by formal concessions and diplomatic maneuvering he was actually gaining a free hand in the matter of the constitution. In fact, his hands were tied more than ever. Furthermore, if his thought was to strengthen his position within Prussia, he was likewise mistaken, for there arose in Prussia a powerful group opposed to the very policy of making concessions to the

[40] For the possible significance of this difference, cf., of course, the French Estates General of 1789.

Metternich-Wittgenstein faction. Directed originally at Hardenberg's accommodation to Austrian wishes in the treatment of the "demagogues," this opposition soon expanded into an attack on the whole "Carlsbad policy" of following the Austrian lead in Germany. Since this was a policy to which Hardenberg had committed himself, such an attack constituted a direct threat to his political position. In defending himself against this attack, Hardenberg sacrificed the constitution. Once again, and this time conclusively, it was demonstrated that a policy of systematically closing avenues for the expression of public opinion was incompatible with a policy of giving that same public opinion a voice in government through representation in a national assembly.

The first important sign of political opposition to Hardenberg's handling of the alleged revolutionary conspiracy (i.e., of the "demagogues") was in the form of a memorandum to the king from the entire ministry, including such opponents of reform as Schuckmann, Kircheisen, and Lottum.[41] Significantly, the ministers were concerned not so much with the merits of a policy of suppressing civil liberties as with its political effects. They protested that the activities of the police were carried on behind their backs; it was not proper that ministers should be obliged to seek information of this nature in the newspapers. They proposed to transfer the whole matter out of the hands of the police to a judicial commission for orderly legal investigation. This document represented a clear, if indirect, attack on Hardenberg's single-handed approach to the question of civil liberties and an attempt to vindicate the ministers' right to official information and their duty of bearing joint responsibility for official action. In view of Humboldt's imminent arrival in Berlin, it was highly significant that the other ministers should in this way have reached a posi-

[41] Memorandum dated July 16, 1819, Gebhardt, *Humboldt*, II, 396–397. Gebhardt reports that only Bernstorff was absent and failed to sign the document, but in fact Wittgenstein (who still held ministerial rank as lord chamberlain) was, of course, also in Teplitz at this time. For Wittgenstein's movements, cf. M. Lenz, *Geschichte der Universität Berlin*, II¹, 60, 63, 65. Schuckmann had a special interest in the petition since, as minister of the interior, he would normally control the police.

tion with respect to Hardenberg's prerogatives as chancellor identical with the one that Humboldt had adopted some months earlier.

The ministers' move met with little success. The king rejected their request as currently impossible of fulfillment. He assured them that there was no danger of the police exceeding their powers, since Hardenberg had been expressly directed to prevent any such development. A judicial commission such as the ministers desired would be established once the facts had been ascertained. This reply was obviously totally unsatisfactory to the ministers, who repeated their representations to Hardenberg. The latter likewise turned them down in a reply drafted by Kamptz, Wittgenstein's chief aide in the demagogue hunt.[42]

Meanwhile Humboldt had finally arrived in Berlin and made common cause with the other ministers in their attempt to remove Hardenberg from his chancellor's pedestal. He drafted a new memorandum to the king, on which he obtained the signatures of most of the ministers, substantially repeating his arguments of the previous winter. The chancellor was to become a prime minister, *primus inter pares,* with each minister in full control of, and accountable for, the policies and activities of his department. The ministers together would form a cabinet with joint responsibility for matters transcending the competence of a single minister. The cabinet was to meet regularly and a copy of its proceedings was to be sent to the king. As for the specific issue of seditious activities, the ministers repudiated the spirit of persecution behind the current police practices. No repressive action, they declared, should be taken secretly or extralegally.[43]

[42] Cabinet Order of July 23; ministers' memorandum of July 30, signed by Beyme, Kircheisen, Bülow, Boyen, and Lottum, but not by Schuckmann; Hardenberg's reply of Aug. 22, 1819, Gebhardt, *Humboldt,* II, 397–398.

[43] Ministers' memorandum of Aug. 26, 1819, *ibid.,* II, 371–383. Those not signing included Wittgenstein, for obvious reasons; Bülow, presumably because of his feud with Humboldt in 1817; and Bernstorff and Klewiz, who were absent. It is interesting to note that Humboldt himself believed in the existence of agitators among the people and viewed them with distaste (cf. Humboldt to Caroline, Jan. 23, 1818, Sydow, ed., *Briefe,* VI, 110).

Hardenberg defended himself against this attack on his political position by his familiar means of making marginal comments for the king's benefit. He pleaded his age and deafness as an excuse for not acting as a prime minister by presiding at ministerial conferences. Although conceding the justice of some of the ministers' ideas, he did not yield on the two main issues. He rejected the idea of becoming a *primus inter pares,* and he defended the necessity of the existing police powers by referring to the excesses of the *Zeitgeist* and, with approval, to the Carlsbad Decrees. As in the earlier controversy with Humboldt, Hardenberg appealed to the king's sentiments by offering his resignation if the king considered him no longer useful.[44] Finally, in response to still another rejoinder from the ministers, Hardenberg persuaded the king to issue a Cabinet Order to the ministers expressing royal displeasure at their deportment and at their lack of confidence in his assurances and rejecting once again the charges of arbitrariness on the part of the police. At the same time the chancellor acceded to the ministers' request to see the records of the police investigations of the alleged revolutionaries and augmented the police investigating commission by three legal specialists, the whole to be presided over by the ministers of justice and the interior, Kircheisen and Schuckmann.[45]

By yielding on the specific issue of the police investigations and to the two ministers most directly concerned, Hardenberg scored a limited political success. It was a success because Humboldt's support suddenly dwindled, but it was limited in the sense that it was achieved at the ultimate expense of the Prussian constitution. Humboldt drew up a new memorandum in which he dismissed the matter of the police investigations as of small importance compared to the tremendous significance of the "Carlsbad policy" of submission to Austria's inter-

[44] Hardenberg's marginal comments quoted and summarized in Gebhardt, *Humboldt,* II, 371–383.

[45] Ministers' rejoinder of Sept. 8, signed by the previous signers plus Bülow and Klewiz, but without Schuckmann, who as minister of the interior was preparing a separate memorandum; Cabinet Order of Sept. 16, 1819, *ibid.,* II, 398–400.

ference, both directly and through her control of the Diet of the Confederation, in Prussian internal affairs. Humboldt linked this question to the issue of ministerial responsibility by insisting that the foreign minister must consult his colleagues before entering into agreements, such as those concluded at Carlsbad, which had domestic repercussions.[46] But when Humboldt submitted this document to the other ministers, he was unable to obtain a united front. They decided instead to submit individual views of Humboldt's memorandum. The result was that only two ministers, Boyen and Beyme, now supported Humboldt, compared to the six or seven who had previously sided with him.[47] Suddenly, from a majority movement among the ministers, the attack on the chancellor's prerogatives had turned into factious sniping: Boyen, Beyme, and Humboldt appeared in the light of rebels. Moreover, they were rebels not only against Hardenberg but against the king himself, since the Carlsbad policy was the king's at least as much as it was the chancellor's.[48] As for the question of ministerial responsibility, Frederick William III had little understanding and even less liking for such ideas.

One among the three rebels, Boyen, incurred the king's disfavor on still another issue. Frederick William III had evolved a plan for curtailing the independence of the Landwehr, for which he had never been able to develop much enthusiasm. But a Landwehr independent of the regular army was essential to Boyen's whole program, and, guided by the principle that a minister could not permit in his department the execution of policies of which he disapproved, Boyen submitted his

[46] Humboldt's memorandum of Oct. 5, 1819, Humboldt, *Gesammelte Schriften*, XII², 364–374; cf. Humboldt to Boyen, Sept. 17, 1819, in Meinecke, *Boyen*, II, 376: "Now a federal fortress [Mainz] is converted into a punitive institution! Contempt for Prussia has indeed gone far."

[47] For the reaction of the various ministers, see Gebhardt, *Humboldt*, II, 407–412. Altenstein's position, which was intermediate, is quoted in greater detail by Müsebeck, *Kultusministerium*, pp. 276–279, cf. comment p. 224.

[48] Cf. Schnabel, *Deutsche Geschichte*, II, 284–285; and Meinecke, *Boyen*, II, 381. Humboldt denied that this issue had anything to do with his dismissal, but here he was surely mistaken (Humboldt to Stein, March 22, 1820, Botzenhart, ed., *Stein*, V, 618).

resignation when the king insisted on his plan. After unsuccessfully urging him to reconsider, Frederick William III accepted Boyen's resignation on Christmas Day.[49] The significance of this event far transcended problems of military organization; the Landwehr was still a political as well as a military issue, and Boyen represented, in the eyes of Prussian conservatives, the entire cause of reform and radicalism in the tradition of Stein.[50] Humboldt, although disagreeing with some of Boyen's military ideas, had early understood that the war minister was an ally in the struggle to make Prussia over into a constitutional monarchy and had supported Boyen's stand on the Landwehr.[51]

Following Boyen's resignation, Hardenberg wrote in his diary: "The minister of war has gone; this is a big step, but to no avail if Beyme and Humboldt stay together. B. and H. must be dismissed." The chancellor was determined to kill the movement toward ministerial responsibility. Forthwith he confronted the king with the choice between himself and the two ministers: "I am more convinced hourly . . . that there is no other solution but either firmly to maintain the present administration, at whose head Your Royal Majesty's high con-

[49] For Boyen's dismissal, see Meinecke, *Boyen*, II, 380–388; Boyen, *Erinnerungen*, III, pp. viii–ix. It appears that Hardenberg, although he subsequently rejoiced at it, had no hand in this decision (Clausewitz to Gröben, Dec. 26, 1819, in Kessel, "Zu Boyens Entlassung," p. 54)—further evidence, incidentally, of Hardenberg's growing political isolation except when he made special efforts to make himself felt. Cf. also *ibid.*, pp. 52–53, for Clausewitz' analysis of and reaction to the dismissal.

[50] Cf. Huber, *Heer und Staat*, p. 167: "Whoever opposed the people's state was bound to reject the people's army. . . . It is no accident that Boyen was removed by the forces which opposed a new political constitution as well as the existing organization of the people's army. Externally, to be sure, Boyen's resignation grew out of differences of opinion concerning the organization of the Landwehr, but in fact it represented a victory for reaction in the constitutional controversy. . . . His dismissal stands at a turning point in Prussian history; it is witness to the abandonment of attempts to construct a political constitution to correspond to the military constitution."

[51] Cf. Humboldt to Schön, Dec. 26, 1819, Humboldt, *Gesammelte Schriften*, XVII, 344.

fidence has placed me, or else to yield to those men and to dismiss me." The outcome was a foregone conclusion, and on the last day of the year 1819 the government severed its remaining connection with the reform movement.[52] Prussia returned to the authoritarian tradition, moving toward the failure of 1848 and the triumph of authoritarianism in the unification of Germany under Bismarck.

It would be facile to assert that these later "turning points" in German history (to revert to Meinecke's terminology) could have been avoided simply by allowing Humboldt to remain in office. But certainly a constitution would have represented a major step away from authoritarianism, and there were signs that Humboldt, if given time, could have introduced the representative constitution which both he and Hardenberg, broadly speaking, desired. Before his dismissal Humboldt had begun to make progress in this direction.[53]

Since Humboldt, then, apparently afforded the best hope of attaining a constitution, the chancellor's plotting against the minister may be fairly described as frustrating his own designs.[54] This plotting is intelligible only against the background of personal hostility between the two men that had been smoldering at least since Humboldt's request for recall from London. Since both had contributed to the growth of this antagonism, posterity, in attempting to assess responsibility for the failure of the constitutional movement, might well say, "A

[52] Hardenberg's diary, in Treitschke, *Deutsche Geschichte,* II, 368; Hardenberg to the king, Dec. 28, Cabinet Order of Dec. 31, 1819, in Gebhardt, *Humboldt,* II, 413, n. 1, 414.

[53] On Humboldt's efforts toward a constitution in the autumn of 1819, see Treitschke, "Verfassungskampf," pp. 430–431; Haake, "Verfassungsfrage," XXXII, 109–110; cf. Humboldt, *Gesammelte Schriften,* XII², 381–455. On the "turning points," cf. Chap. I, above.

[54] Some may doubt that Hardenberg still sincerely wanted a constitution and a national assembly, but his continuing devotion to this aim is documented in Treitschke, "Verfassungskampf," pp. 317, 431–432, and Paul Bailleu, "Kronprinz Friedrich Wilhelm im Ständekampf 1820," *Historische Zeitschrift,* LXXXVII (1901), 67. See also Humboldt's own testimony to the king's support of Hardenberg's constitutional goal, Humboldt to Niebuhr, Sept. 22, 1819, and Humboldt to Boyen, Nov. 21, 1819, Humboldt, *Gesammelte Schriften,* XVII, 332, 341–342.

plague on both their houses." But further examinations shows
such a judgment to be inadequate. While it is true that Humboldt was as intransigent as Hardenberg when their ideas
clashed, his motivation was not the same. To Humboldt the
question of ministerial responsibility, which was the chief
bone of contention, was not merely a matter of pride or of predilection. It was, on the contrary, intimately connected in his
thinking with the national assembly which he was entrusted
with forming. His attacks were directed at the office of chancellor, not at its occupant. He took the position that any constitution, any national assembly, was scarcely worth while so long
as a nonresponsible chancellor hovered above the ministers
and the assembly alike. To Humboldt a national assembly was
meaningful only if all the ministers were made responsible to
it; Hardenberg, on the other hand, would not hear of abolishing the office of chancellor which he occupied, even if it was an
anomaly in a new constitution. While both men by their actions contributed to the sacrificing of the constitution, Humboldt sacrificed it for an idea, whereas Hardenberg sacrificed
it, ultimately, to maintain his personal power.[55]

But even this goal proved to be an illusion. After 1819 Hardenberg found himself at the head of a government which
fundamentally was operating against his will. He occupied
the empty shell of an exalted office from which most of the
furniture of actual power had disappeared. Many vital decisions no longer depended on him but were made behind his
back with the connivance of some of his subordinates. The
constitution, which he had determined to make the crowning
achievement of his career, now eluded him altogether.
Whereas Humboldt had begun to secure the co-operation of
the Prussian nobility, Hardenberg had long since forfeited the

---

[55] But cf. the remarks of Kaehler, *Humboldt*, pp. 419–421, as a corrective
to Gebhardt's completely one-sided portrayal in Humboldt's favor and to
Treitschke's extravagant denigrations of Hardenberg (e.g., "Verfassungs-
kampf," pp. 432–433). See also Humboldt's own reflections on his dismissal,
Humboldt to Stein, March 22, 1820, Botzenhart, ed., *Stein*, V, 618; and cf.
Stägemann to Benzenberg, Jan. 15, 1820, Rühl, ed., *Briefe und Aktenstücke*,
III, 17–18.

respect of many of their leaders. When, therefore, the chancellor attempted, after Humboldt had gone, to continue working toward a constitution, these nobles' aversion to him and to all his works caused them to cluster around the crown prince, under whose guidance the *coup de grâce* was administered to the idea of a national assembly.[56] The chancellor lived on another three years, clinging grimly to the outward trappings of political power.

Seeking to defend his constitutional position as chancellor against incursions from below, Hardenberg had succeeded only in placing himself in an isolation far more impotent than splendid. Was he the hero of a *Schicksalstragödie,* the prey of a cruel fate which snatched victory from him when it was almost within his grasp, or the hero of a classical tragedy, the victim of his own weaknesses and mistakes?

The verdict of posterity has tended to the latter answer, first authoritatively advanced by Treitschke and later formulated by Meinecke in his masterly phrase: "Eine liberale Politik mit illiberalen Mitteln war eine innere Unmöglichkeit" (a liberal policy carried out by illiberal means was an intrinsic impossibility).[57] By this he meant that Hardenberg could have defended liberal institutions in Prussia only by resolute opposition to Metternich and to his influence over Frederick William III, not by vying with Metternich for leadership of the movement toward reaction in order to strengthen his own position. Once caught in the machinery of reaction and repres-

[56] On the friendliness of the nobility toward Humboldt, see Dohna to Humboldt, Dec. 23, 1819, in Gebhardt, *Humboldt,* II, 354; Meusel, ed., *Marwitz,* I, 626–627, II², 263–265; documents in Müsebeck, "Die märkische Ritterschaft," pp. 354–356, 358–364, 367, but cf. *id.,* "Die ursprünglichen Grundlagen des Liberalismus und Konservatismus in Deutschland," *Korrespondenzblatt* des Gesamtvereins der deutschen Geschichts- und Altertumsvereine, LXIII (1915), 22; see also Ancillon to the crown prince, in Haake, *Ancillon,* p. 126. On the change in the nobles' attitude toward the constitution after Humboldt's departure, see Müsebeck, "Die märkische Ritterschaft," pp. 368–369, 375–376; on the crown prince and his activities, Bailleu, "Kronprinz Friedrich Wilhelm," pp. 67–73; Treitschke, "Verfassungskampf," pp. 446 ff.

[57] Meinecke, *Boyen,* II, 370.

sion of which the "demagogues" were the most obvious tar so runs this argument, Hardenberg could not escape. Only perseverance, not pliability, could have saved the constitution. "We do not dare to assert," wrote Meinecke, "that a stronger character could have succeeded [in winning the king over], but if anyone could have succeeded it would have had to be a strong personality." [58]

Some of the writers of this persuasion (though not Meinecke), taking the argument further, have tended to regard the chancellor in his later years as anxious above all else simply to remain in power, no longer much concerned with the constitution or, for that matter, with any other political program or principle.[59] But Hardenberg even in his old age was surely more than a mere timeserver. He still wanted a constitution, but he insisted on having it on his own terms, and these included his own retention of the chancellorship. Like many politicians and political parties who cling to office, he did so, in part at least, because he believed himself capable of better government than his rivals; and further, like almost all politicians, he found himself abandoning parts of his scheme for better government in order to secure the rest. The difference was that Hardenberg insensibly abandoned so much that finally he had given up more than remained intact. He abandoned freedom of speech, he abandoned Prussia's position of parity with Austria in Germany, and finally he abandoned Humboldt and with him the constitution itself—these, indeed, were "illiberal means" for carrying out a liberal policy. In this action personal motives were, no doubt, involved, first in his fear of exposure by Wittgenstein of his dealings with Gruner and the secret societies in 1815, later in his fear of eclipse by Humboldt. But it is chiefly the means, and not the ends, of his policy that are vulnerable.

Some more recent historians, emphasizing that Hardenberg's chief problem in trying to give Prussia a constitution was to conciliate his monarch and admitting that his way

[58] *Ibid.*, II, 361.

[59] See K. A. v. Müller, *Görres in Strassburg*, p. 21; also Schnabel, *Deutsche Geschichte*, II, 277–278, 287.

of approaching this problem was the way of subterfuge and deception, have tried to show that this approach was basically the correct one. Nothing, they argue, could have been accomplished by Hardenberg's insisting inflexibly on liberal principles of government; "only very gradually could Hardenberg hope to free the king" from the views insinuated to him by the Wittgensteins and Knesebecks.[60] To retain the friendship of his enemy Wittgenstein and hence the confidence of the king was the only way to secure the constitution.

This argument fails to convince me.[61] Without pressing too hard the obvious objection that the events themselves proved Hardenberg and his defenders wrong, I would suggest that the policy of concluding temporary alliances in order to gain a later advantage over one's allies is a practice which may, unfortunately, be ineradicable in the field of international relations but which need not be extended to domestic politics as well; [62] and this not only on ethical grounds but on practical ones. Instead of compacting with Schuckmann and Kircheisen, the chancellor would have better attained his ends by throwing his influence on the side of Humboldt and Boyen; in his personal contact with Frederick William III he could have used the medium of Boyen's friend Witzleben, the king's adjutant, instead of that of Wittgenstein. It is difficult, furthermore, to find for Hardenberg's tactics in 1819 any practical justification such as has been offered for his policy in 1811.[63] There was a fundamental difference between the situations of those two years. In 1811 large sections of the population were up in arms against the chancellor's policy (or at least this was the impression that the conservatives contrived to make) in sincere defense of legally established institutions; in 1819 the

[60] Haake, "Verfassungsfrage," XXIX, 327. Cf. *ibid.*, XXIX, 332, 338, XXX, 326–329; also Müsebeck, "Die märkische Ritterschaft," p. 181, Huber, *Heer und Staat,* p. 167, G. P. Gooch, *Studies in German History* (London, New York, and Toronto, 1948), p. 18.

[61] Cf. also the very apt criticism of Haake in the review of his *Verfassungskampf* by F. Hartung, *Historische Zeitschrift,* 125 (1922), 314–316.

[62] It is, perhaps, relevant to recall that Hardenberg's favorite sphere of activity was international diplomacy.

[63] See above, pp. 85–86, 95–96.

opposition derived its strength from the intrigue at court of egotists and dissemblers, some of them in the service of a foreign power. The potential appeal of the opposition to the king's instinctive sentiments was much stronger in 1811 than in 1819; Hardenberg could have undertaken in 1819, therefore, to dispel the subtle influence of Metternich with more hope of success than he had in 1811 to dissuade the king from his well-founded belief that his own privileges might be connected with those of the nobility. Where in 1811 the chancellor, by being persistent, might have placed himself in the position of an interloper between the king and his faithful nobles, in 1819 he had merely to be an interloper between the king and Metternich, and he could have rallied much support for such a stand had he chosen to take it.

Despite the justice of such an indictment against Hardenberg, the king himself must bear some of the blame for the debacle of 1819; but I do not think that the primary responsibility can be shifted to him. No doubt the king, as the symbol of the absolute state, was supreme; his will was law. But in the particular instance of Frederick William III this situation meant that his will had to be shaped. He had, certainly, some innate prejudices; he had been seized by a very real fear of revolutionary upheavals and therefore sincerely believed the Austrian fairy tales about the "demagogues." At times he exhibited streaks of obstinacy, especially in military matters. But on the whole, his was a malleable nature; Stein, Scharnhorst, Boyen, even Hardenberg himself, had found ways to persuade him of the necessity of courses of action to which he was instinctively averse, and his power as the symbol of absolute monarchy was used throughout his long reign for extremely divergent ends. Conversely, Hardenberg had also had ample opportunity to learn the consequences of acquiescing in the king's indecision and of humoring his moodiness.[64] If Wittgenstein and Metternich gained ascendancy over the

[64] Cf. for Hardenberg's early experiences with Frederick William III, Karl Griewank, "Hardenberg und die preussische Politik 1804–1806," *Forschungen zur brandenburgischen und preussischen Geschichte,* XLVII (1935), *passim,* especially pp. 257, 279–280.

king's mind after 1815, it was because Hardenberg neglected
to maintain his influence on it. Frederick William III as an absolute monarch was a constant, a datum, with which everybody
else had to reckon, rather than a decisive causal agent.

There was, no doubt, a general trend toward conservatism
after 1815. Its basis was partly economic—a desire for order
and stability in which to revive an economy devastated by
years of war and of the Continental System—and partly ideo-
logical and political, a reaction against the principles of the
French Revolution. This trend had its effect not only on the
king but also on the public opinion which had just begun to
develop during the War of Liberation, so that it was more difficult to gain support for liberal movements in 1819 than in
1813.[65] The year 1819 itself saw the departure from the universities and from the influential *Burschenschaften* of the academic generation of 1815, which had been fired by enthusiasm
in the war. But one has to be a believer in the potency of a
Zeitgeist to be convinced that those in power, especially in
an absolute monarchy, can do nothing but be swept along by
such vague currents of feeling and opinion. It is a new the-
ology of history to declare that a certain course of events was
determined by a *Zeitgeist*. There are always opportunities to
be taken or missed. If this were denied, "the writing of history
would become the demonstration of an antecedent theorem." [66]

[65] Cf. for example Schön's analysis of the difference in atmosphere before
and after 1815, in Mayer, "Politische Erfahrungen und Gedanken," pp.
434–435. Nevertheless it is to be noted that the year 1818 saw the introduction of the Prussian Customs Law which was the first step toward the
Zollverein of 1834. This was decidedly a reform measure carried out by
men close to Stein, Humboldt, and the reform movement, and its success is
further evidence that Frederick William III had no firmly established political principles.

[66] The phrase is taken from the anonymous review of A. J. P. Taylor,
The Habsburg Monarchy, in the London *Times Literary Supplement*,
Feb. 26, 1949. Cf. even Lenin: "There is no situation from which there is
absolutely no way out."

CHAPTER XII

Conclusion

IN SUMMARIZING and assessing the various factors in the failure of the Prussian reform movement, I should like first to clarify one element in the situation which has repeatedly appeared in this account: namely, the relationship of nationalism to the reform movement. This problem has in the past received little attention because of the assumption, current among historians until quite recently, that nationalism and liberalism were everywhere natural and inseparable allies in the early nineteenth century. The evidence, however, does not support this generalization in the case of Germany. The political structure of Germany forbade such a straightforward alignment: like Italy merely a "geographical expression," and with its component parts themselves often artificially constituted, Germany presented to its inhabitants a highly diffuse target at which to aim their patriotic loyalty.[1] The result was that there were various manifestations of that loyalty. Liberals were not more nationalistic than conservatives, but they were nationalistic in a different way. Before 1815 the Prussian re-

[1] For the unique and complex problems of Germany in this respect, see also above, p. 15. For more detailed investigation and for documentation of the generalizations and conclusions here presented, see my article "Variations in Nationalism during the Great Reform Movement in Prussia"; most recently also, for Stein, see Wilhelm Mommsen, *Stein, Ranke, Bismarck: Ein Beitrag zur politischen und sozialen Bewegung des 19. Jahrhunderts* (Munich, 1954), pp. 21–23.

formers, generally speaking, directed their patriotism at the ideal of a united Germany and not so much at the existing Prussian state. After 1815 the positions were reversed. With the formation at the Congress of Vienna of a German Confederation subservient to the policies of the conservative Metternich, Prussian conservatives now transferred their loyalty to this new superstate, while the liberals sought to resist its invasion of the sovereign rights of Prussia. In addition, there persisted throughout the period a widespread sentimental allegiance among conservatives toward the historic provinces of Prussia; while the romantic movement, with its ambivalent political implications, still further beclouded the issue.

All this is not to deny that there was a fundamental and very real affinity between nationalism and liberalism even in Germany; on the contrary, this affinity is exemplified in the thought of men like Humboldt, Fichte, and Stein himself. But the peculiar complexity of the German political scene meant that the natural connection between the two movements was drowned in a welter of conflicting loyalties instead of being allowed to come to fruition. In the long run, some liberals countered the alliance of Confederation "nationalism" and territorial absolutism by developing the *kleindeutsch* concept; but this, as 1848 was to show, represented a conjunction of interests too artificial to offer a permanent solution to the "German question." Here also we return to 1819 as the essential prelude to 1848.[2]

In the short run, the reform movement was weakened by the failure of liberals and German nationalists to reach a working alliance in Prussia, especially after 1815. In the light of the advantages that liberalism derived from such an alliance elsewhere in Europe—for example in Italy or in Belgium— the uniqueness of the German situation which prevented a similar alignment there may well be regarded as an important factor in the decline of liberalism in Prussia. One may conjecture that the reformers might have been able to survive the period of reaction against the French Revolution and to press the reform movement to a successful conclusion had they

[2] Cf. Meinecke's centenary article referred to in Chap. I above.

been bolstered by a strong and homogeneous nationalist movement.

Yet, clearly, the fluid state of nationalist sentiment in Prussia was only one of many factors which combined to weaken the reformers and to strengthen their opponents. Seen in a larger framework, possibly the most important was the collapse of the European balance of power before Napoleon, which rendered the Prussian government, and particularly the timid Frederick William III, vulnerable to pressure from abroad. When order was at length restored in Europe, the most conspicuous beneficiary was Metternich. Taking advantage of Prussia's diplomatic ineptitude during the settlements of 1814 and 1815 and capitalizing on the degeneration of the French Revolution into the Terror and regicide, Metternich was able to foster in Prussia the idea of a connection between the German liberal movement and Jacobinism, a connection which did serious damage to the cause of reform.

But Napoleon's own influence during the period of his ascendancy had been equally significant. Having suffered a catastrophic military defeat and with Russia virtually powerless to help her, Prussia was completely at the emperor's mercy, and his authority, when he chose to exercise it, was directed most frequently against popular or liberal reforms.[3] His effect on Scharnhorst's military plans was direct, and the consequences of his insistence on Stein's dismissal after discovering the latter's secret plot can hardly be overrated. Indirectly, Napoleon's influence extended even further. His exaction of an indemnity, under threat of reoccupation, produced a financial crisis in Prussia. In some respects, to be sure, this crisis was favorable to the reform movement: it impressed on many government officials the necessity of an efficient and broadly based administration; it brought about the convocation in 1808 of the East

[3] Haake, "Verfassungsfrage," XXVI, 527–528, asserts that Napoleon actually said that public opinion in Prussia must not be given the opportunity of manifesting its anti-French tendencies. According to Haake's language this remark should be contained in Prince Wilhelm's dispatch to the king from Paris dated Feb. 26, 1808, in Hassel, *Geschichte der preussischen Politik*, I, 450–451, but I cannot find it there or anywhere else. Still, it is certainly plausible enough.

Prussian assembly at which the income tax was introduced; and it was the immediate cause of the collapse of the ineffectual Altenstein-Dohna government and of Hardenberg's return to power in 1810. But on balance, the crisis affected the reform movement adversely. Important sections of the population became alienated from the government because of its attempt to levy high taxes and to control their collection. This type of sentiment found expression in the first instance in the provincial assemblies in 1809 and 1810, but its most significant manifestation occurred during the constitutional crisis of 1811. Hardenberg, having assumed power with a program of raising new revenues with which to pay the French indemnity, encountered the opposition of large sections of the nobility in attempting to execute this program; and this opposition extended beyond the matter of taxation to the larger issue of Hardenberg's own constitutional position relative to the traditional rights of the aristocracy. A direct chain of cause and effect thus linked the constitutional crisis of 1811 to Napoleon's financial pressure. It is not unlikely, however, that open hostility between Hardenberg and the landed gentry would have developed anyway, if not on this question then on some other. Marwitz, the leader of the opposition faction, felt a personal grudge against the chancellor which the latter fully reciprocated.

There were, indeed, a number of such personal antagonisms which adversely affected the progress of the reform movement: Scharnweber's dispute with Hippel and with Gneisenau which contributed to the modification of the Landsturm; an intramural private feud within the liberal ranks between Gneisenau and Humboldt which cost the latter Gneisenau's support in the constitutional struggle of 1819;[4] most important, Humboldt's estrangement from Hardenberg which the latter, at least, regarded as personal. More generally, Stein and Scharnhorst, especially the latter because of his bourgeois origins, evoked personal jealousies and resentments which inevitably had political repercussions.

Still, it would be a serious mistake to regard the resistance

[4] See Gebhardt, *Humboldt,* II, 289.

to the reform movement as a product only of personal pique, narrow prejudice, and calculated malevolence. The reformers were faced with an opposition which was often intelligent as well as courageous. The body of conservative political and social thought current in Prussia in the early nineteenth century was of just as high an intellectual order as the body of liberal thought prompting the reforms, and any adversary of reform who took his stand honestly on this ground deserves the respectful attention of posterity. But even more indicative of the intellectual integrity of some, at least, of the leaders of the opposition was their unwillingness to follow theory blindly. For example, some of the conservatives refused to swallow whole the orthodox conservative doctrine of Adam Müller. It is of great interest to note that one does not encounter the same names in all phases of the opposition to the reforms. Some men who were normally conservatives supported one or more aspects of the reform movement, following their own independent line of thinking; conversely, also, others who regarded themselves as in general sympathy with reform ideals would on occasion join the ranks of the opposition on issues where their personal convictions conflicted with those of the reformers.

Numerous examples of both kinds of independent thought can be cited. Marwitz, that bitter opponent of agrarian and constitutional reform and of military reform in peacetime, was an enthusiastic supporter of the Landwehr and even of the Landsturm in wartime.[5] Marwitz and the conservative political philosopher Friedrich von Savigny both opposed the persecution of the "demagogues," which was an instrument in the hands of the conservative courtier Wittgenstein. Hippel, though in general opposed to agrarian and constitutional reform, was the author of the Landsturm law of 1813.[6] On the other side, Schön, the ghost writer of Stein's "Political Testament," in general opposed, on the ground of economic liberalism, gov-

[5] It should also be noted that Marwitz had on his own initiative planned to emancipate the serfs on his private lands before the October Edict of 1807 (see Kayser, *Marwitz,* p. 37).

[6] See Bach, *Hippel,* pp. 234–235, 239.

ernment interference in the economic relations of noble landowners and free peasants.[7] Marshal Blücher, the alleged Jacobin of 1815, endorsed conscription, regulated his peasants,
and urged speedy adoption of a constitution, but advocated
the retention of patrimonial justice and, despite the new penal
regulations, as late as 1815 inflicted corporal punishment on
insubordinate soldiers.[8] Vincke, the admirer of British parliamentary government who favored its imitation in Prussia,
opposed peacetime conscription. But the most conspicuous
instance of an entirely individual approach to the problems of
the Prussian reform period is provided by Count Dohna.
Clearly he regarded himself as a reformer, since he dated from
his own dismissal the beginning of Prussia's departure from the
principles of Stein.[9] But even at that time, apart from his luke-
warm pursuit of reform during his ministry, he opposed the
creation of a national assembly, while after his retirement from
office he became the leader of the Committee of the East
Prussian–Lithuanian Estates, which in 1811 played a prominent role in the opposition to his former chief, Hardenberg.
On the military scene, Dohna rejected conscription in 1810,
founded the East Prussian Landwehr and was a defender of
the Landsturm in 1813, and after 1815 opposed Boyen's Landwehr on the ground that it interfered too much with normal
country life. In his personal relations, he was a close friend of
Schön, liked Boyen, and despised Schuckmann, Bülow, and
the instigators of the secret police but had no respect for
Humboldt, whom he regarded as weak and too intellectual.[10]
A recent writer has summed up Dohna as "a colorless idealist
who harbored a few liberal dreams and a great many aristocratic prejudices." [11]

In the light of all these individual divergencies, it would be
quite misleading to classify all the prominent persons of the

[7] Cf. also Mayer, *Retablissement Ost- und Westpreussens*, pp. 84–85.

[8] See Unger, *Blücher*, II, 348, and Friedrich C. Sell, *Die Tragödie des
deutschen Liberalismus* (Stuttgart, 1953), p. 59.

[9] Dohna to the crown prince, Feb. 28, 1822, Bezzenberger, ed., *Aktenstücke*, p. 1, n. 2.

[10] Schön, *Papiere*, VI, 361.

[11] Görlitz, *Stein*, p. 283.

reform period as either proreform or antireform *tout court*. The urge so to classify probably derives in part from the importance of political parties in our own society; but in the Prussia of the reform period, political parties would have been an incomprehensible concept to all but the most educated. Politics was still a matter of private initiative, and the politicians were still individualists. Their fastidiousness in insisting on working conditions of their own choosing proved in some instances to be an obstacle in the path of reform. Thus Humboldt resigned in 1810 rather than continue in a subordinate position which he felt did not do justice to his talents, and later he declined for two years to re-enter the ministry lest he be polluted by contact with Bülow and Schuckmann. Niebuhr and Schön also voluntarily left government service in self-righteous disgust. If Schön, for example, had been as persistent as Wittgenstein, he might have been able to counteract the latter's machinations.

Hardenberg, by contrast, erred on the side of catholicity in his choice of collaborators. It is true that even under Stein, and increasingly during the Altenstein-Dohna ministry, the government had not presented a homogeneous front, but this phenomenon became much more pronounced after Hardenberg assumed the chancellorship. He placed obstacles in his own way by "packing" the Assembly of Notables, and to a lesser extent the provisional national assembly, with nobles. The three government agents sent out on tour in 1817 and the men who composed the constitutional commission of 1819 seemed to be chosen deliberately so as to represent widely divergent opinions. Such measures are not necessarily unwise, but they were unwise for Hardenberg, since in the end he meant to have his own way after all. Believing that he was being tactful by allowing all sides equal opportunity, he in fact merely stored up trouble for himself by asking questions to which he would accept only one answer. When other answers were given, the difficulties were far greater than if the questions had never been asked.

This self-defeating tactic was, furthermore, only one aspect of Hardenberg's haphazard pursuit of reform. He always preferred devious to direct means of attaining his ends. He was slow to delegate authority, and when he did so he did it either carelessly or perversely; a conspicuous case in point was his abandonment of Raumer's ideas on agrarian reform in favor of the more accommodating ones of Scharnweber, followed later by his abandonment of Scharnweber as well, after having stated that his draft was in all important respects inviolable. Hardenberg adopted no consistent policy toward the opposition in 1811 and finally capitulated in the laws of September of that year. From 1815 on, while pressing for adoption of a constitution, he modified Stägemann's draft of the decree of May 22, and then finally, having compromised himself by endorsing Gruner's secret society, he retreated before Metternich and was provoked by Humboldt into deserting the constitutional cause altogether. In military reform, Hardenberg did not lift a finger either to preserve the Landsturm in 1813 or to support Boyen in 1819 in his struggle to retain the Landwehr as an independent institution. The record resulting from this capricious conduct of affairs is formidable. In every phase of reform and at every stage of his career as chancellor, Hardenberg achieved less than he set out to achieve, and finally, by resisting the demand for ministerial responsibility on grounds of personal prestige and convenience, he put an end to the reform movement altogether. Fundamentally, despite good intentions, he had accomplished nothing except to replace a weakening royal absolutism with a weakening ministerial absolutism. Indeed, except for the admixture of liberal economics, Hardenberg's career would have belonged in western Europe in the seventeenth and not in the nineteenth century.

But having said that, one must add at once that his circumstances, after all, resembled those of Cardinal Richelieu more than those of the Duc de Richelieu. By the same token that political parties were still beyond the horizon of German development, so it was evident in other respects also that Germany was many decades behind her western neighbors in her social and political history,[12] and there were limits to the

[12] For an excellent survey of the comparative situation, see Clapham, *Economic Development of France and Germany*, pp. 82–92.

rapidity with which the gap could be closed. The most striking element in the backwardness of Germany was the virtual
absence of a politically influential middle class.[13] Since it was
the middle class that had prompted political progress and reform in western Europe, this was a fact of profound importance for Germany. Even a numerically small middle class
could have provided leadership for the masses, but there was
no alternative source of that leadership. The churches, for
example, which traditionally offered guidance to the masses,
were officially indifferent to the reform movement; even the
Protestant church reform which culminated in the unification
of the Lutheran and Calvinist denominations in Prussia had
no connection with the secular currents in society.[14] Individually, the active membership of both the Catholic and Protestant churches ranged from one political extreme to the
other (from Adam Müller, let us say, to Görres, and from
Bishop Eylert to Friedrich Daniel Schleiermacher), although
one may hazard the guess that the principal dignitaries of
both hierarchies were inclined to conservatism. Hardenberg's
secularization of church land in Silesia must have cost him
the good will of many Catholics.

Görres and Schleiermacher, as a matter of fact, were almost
alone in attempting to arouse any interest in political and
social reform among the general populace in Prussia. It was
not so much a question of influencing public opinion as of
creating public opinion. Görres, with his *Rheinische Merkur,*
was perhaps the only first-rate publicist of the period; Schleiermacher supplemented his less ambitious journalistic activities
from the pulpit.[15] Otherwise, the periodical and pamphlet

[13] On this point, see particularly Aris, *History of Political Thought in
Germany,* p. 31; also pp. 35–48, 361–362, 375, 379–380.

[14] Cf. Schnabel, *Deutsche Geschichte,* IV, 341–342.

[15] On Görres, cf. above, pp. 130–131, also Czygan, *Zur Geschichte der Ta-
gesliteratur,* III, 319–371; the bibliography in Aris, *History of Political
Thought in Germany,* is far more useful than the chapter that precedes it.
On Schleiermacher's activities on behalf of reform, see Wilhelm Dilthey,
"Schleiermachers politische Gesinnung und Wirksamkeit," in his *Gesam-
melte Schriften* (Leipzig and Berlin, 1914–36), XII, 22–25; Günther Holstein,
Die Staatsphilosophie Schleiermachers (Bonn and Leipzig, 1923), pp. 2,

literature is remarkably barren of propaganda for reform.[16] So profoundly political a thinker as Hegel did not even have any knowledge of the reform movement in Prussia as late as 1809.[17] But the most devastating proof of the unwillingness or incapacity of middle-class intellectuals to mold public opinion is provided by the example of Fichte. Fichte's dream, expressed in the *Reden an die deutsche Nation* and elsewhere, of educating the people to patriotism and to a capacity for active participation in public affairs exactly corresponded to the basic premises underlying Stein's projects for reform. Fichte dealt more in terms of spiritual independence and self-reliance, while Stein always subordinated abstract to practical purposes, but the fundamental affinity of the two men is undeniable. Yet Fichte himself never showed any awareness of this fact. The *Reden* themselves were academic lectures with no appreciable effect on affairs of state; Fichte explicitly stated that education in the formal sense was the only field in which the state could, in the circumstances of 1806–1807, exercise any useful function.[18] And while it is possible to attribute some intellectual influence on certain individuals to Fichte,[19] he never made any

---

95–99, 197–201; Czygan, *Zur Geschichte der Tagesliteratur,* II, 134–146. Incidentally, Hardenberg's acquiescence in the suppression of the *Rheinische Merkur,* which had enjoyed his special protection, is further proof of his weakness in the cause of reform.

[16] See Czygan, *Zur Geschichte der Tagesliteratur,* and Karl Hagen, "Ueber die öffentliche Meinung in Deutschland von den Freiheitskriegen bis zu den Karlsbader Beschlüssen," *Historisches Taschenbuch,* Neue Folge VII (1846), 599–700, VIII (1847), 493–666. To be sure, the evidence is limited, and furthermore censorship restricted journalists.

[17] Franz Rosenzweig, *Hegel und der Staat* (Munich and Berlin, 1920), II, 62.

[18] Fichte, "Reden an die deutsche Nation," in his *Sämmtliche Werke* (ed. J. H. Fichte; Berlin, 1846), VII, 432. On the ineffectiveness of the lectures, see H. C. Engelbrecht, *Johann Gottlieb Fichte: A Study of His Political Writings with Special Reference to his Nationalism* (New York and London, 1933), pp. 128–132, and Rudolf Körner, "Die Wirkung der Reden Fichtes," *Forschungen zur brandenburgischen und preussischen Geschichte,* XL (1927), 65–87.

[19] Particularly on Altenstein: see Eduard Spranger, "Altensteins Denkschrift von 1807 und ihre Beziehungen zur Philosophie," *Forschungen zur brandenburgischen und preussischen Geschichte,* XVIII (1905), 471–517;

effort to make his views count politically. In his private letters he betrayed not the slightest interest in the reform movement, not even in the progress of the reforms in the system of education under the aegis of Humboldt.[20] Indeed, it was only this educational phase of the reform movement which was substantially completed, and in the absence of means to the practical application of the new principles of self-reliance and co-operation introduced in the schools, the educational reforms too were socially frustrating rather than, as Stein had intended, socially productive.

Since the poverty of this record must be laid partly at the door of Fichte and of those others who sympathized with the purposes of the reformers without coming to their aid, the responsibility of Hardenberg for the failure of the reform movement is to that extent reduced. It was out of the question to assimilate Prussia without further ado to the political pattern of Britain, France, or the Netherlands without the social basis present in those countries. Moreover, it was inevitable that if reform was to come in Prussia at all it would have to come in the first instance from above; self-government, paradoxically, had to be introduced by command.[21] But even after

---

and Ernst Müsebeck, "Fragmentarische Aufzeichnungen Altensteins über die auswärtige Politik Preussens vom 28./29. Dezember 1805," *loc. cit.,* XXVIII (1915), 167–173.

[20] J. G. Fichte, *Briefwechsel* (ed. Hans Schulz; Leipzig, 1925). There is even a slighting reference to Humboldt: Fichte to Altenstein, June 10, 1809, *ibid.,* II, 533.

[21] I cannot agree with Carl E. Schorske, who in a review (*Journal of Modern History,* XXIV [1952], 308–309) of the new edition of Fritz Hartung's constitutional history of Germany chides the author for believing that "the way of renovation" was "to draw the people into the state, not to subordinate the state to the people" and for engaging in "national mythmaking" in which "the state was an end, liberalism and constitutional reform a means, a way of strengthening the state." It is unrealistic and unhistorical now, and would have been so then, to demand of Prussia in 1819 to turn itself forthwith into a liberal state on the western model. On the contrary: Hardenberg's application of western economic liberalism to Prussian agriculture miscarried, and importation of unadulterated western political liberalism would likewise have miscarried. Surely we are beginning to learn that liberalism and democracy make demands on people to which they cannot respond without education and experience.

making these allowances, we must still charge Hardenberg with considerable responsibility for the loss of impetus in the reform movement. He failed to use the instrument of reform from above, which was in his hands, to foster the paradox of self-government by command. Stein had surmounted the paradox by the force of his ethical principles, which demanded the development of civic spirit, and by his realization that the reform of Prussian society was a long-range proposition whose later stages must be prepared in the beginning, however anomalous the temporary consequences. Hardenberg's task was not to achieve self-government but to establish the possibility of, and a tendency toward, self-government; and this he did not do. Instead, he established a precedent for the ministerial absolutism of Bismarck. It would not, indeed, have been possible for Prussia in 1819 to duplicate British or French politics and society, but it would have been possible for Prussia in 1819 to have turned her back definitely on the authoritarian principle in her political structure and on the feudal principle in her social structure. It was the survival of both that led Prussia on to the later "turning points" of 1848 and 1866; and their survival meant nothing less than the failure of the reform movement. That failure represented the accumulated interest on twelve years' investment in vacillation and compromise.

Bibliography

IN VIEW of the very large number of works consulted which proved to be of relatively little value for the present subject, I have divided this bibliography into two general parts. In the first part, all bibliographical and primary material and the more important secondary material are given under topical headings with explanatory comments. In the second part, works of minor value for this study are listed in alphabetical order. Works consulted but not used are omitted.

PART I

A. *Bibliographies*

The general and indispensable bibliography for German history is the *Dahlmann-Waitz Quellenkunde der deutschen Geschichte* (9th ed., ed. Hermann Haering; 2 vols., Leipzig, 1931–32). Also useful are Friedrich M. Kircheisen, *Bibliographie des napoleonischen Zeitalters einschliesslich der Vereinigten Staaten von Nordamerika* (2 vols., Berlin, 1908), and Ernst Wermke, *Bibliographie der Geschichte von Ost- und Westpreussen* (Königsberg, 1933).

B. *Primary Sources*

Under this heading are listed only those publications containing exclusively primary material, save for editorial elucidation. Much primary material, of course, is to be found in secondary works as well.

The basic collection of laws and decrees is the *Gesetz-Sammlung für die königlich preussische Staaten,* first published in Berlin for the years 1810 and 1811, and thereafter annually. A supplement for the earlier years was later published under the title *Sammlung der für die königlichen preussischen Staaten erschienenen Gesetze und Verordnungen von 1806 bis zum 27sten Oktober 1810* (Berlin, 1822). Some few laws are more readily accessible in Wilhelm Altmann, ed., *Ausgewählte Urkunden zur brandenburg-preussischen Verfassungs- und Verwaltungsgeschichte* (2 vols., Berlin, 1897).

Collections of printed sources are made on a number of different organizing principles, the most important being temporal, topical, and personal. By far the most valuable in the first group is the first volume of a projected large-scale source collection which may now never be completed: Preussisches Staatsarchiv, *Die Reorganisation des preussischen Staates unter Stein und Hardenberg*, Part I, Allgemeine Verwaltungs- und Behördenreform (ed. Georg Winter, Vol. I: *Vom Beginn des Kampfes gegen die Kabinettsregierung bis zum Wiedereintritt des Ministers vom Stein*, Leipzig, 1931). An earlier and less pertinent volume taken from the Prussian state archives, and overlapping slightly in point of time, is Herman Granier, ed., *Berichte aus der Berliner Franzosenzeit 1807–1809: Nach den Akten des Berliner Geheimen Staatsarchivs und des Pariser Kriegsarchivs* (Vol. LXXXVIII of the series *Publikationen aus den K. Preussischen Staatsarchiven*, Leipzig, 1913). On a much smaller scale, but quite useful, is R. Röpell, ed., "Zur inneren Geschichte Preussens in den Jahren 1811–12," *Uebersicht der Arbeiten und Veränderungen der schlesischen Gesellschaft für vaterländische Kultur im Jahre 1847* (Breslau, 1848), pp. 339–360. Likewise restricted geographically is Adalbert Bezzenberger, ed., *Aktenstücke des Provinzial-Archivs in Königsberg aus den Jahren 1786–1820 betreffend die Verwaltung und Verfassung Ostpreussens* (Königsberg, 1898), one of the most valuable collections of miscellaneous documents. Also to be mentioned here is F. de Martens, *Recueil des traités et conventions conclus par la Russie avec les puissances étrangères* (Vol. VII, St. Petersburg, 1885).

Considerable source material on the military history of the period has been printed. The most important collection is in the archival series *Die Reorganisation des preussischen Staates unter Stein und Hardenberg* already mentioned: Part II, Das preussische Heer vom Tilsiter Frieden bis zur Befreiung 1807–1814 (Vol. I, ed. Rudolf Vaupel; Leipzig, 1938), which reaches the year 1808. Max Lehmann is responsible for four small but significant publications: "Preussen und die allgemeine Wehrpflicht im Jahre 1809," *Historische Zeitschrift*, LXI (1889), 97–109; "Preussen und die allgemeine Wehrpflicht im Jahre 1810," *Historische Zeitschrift,* LXIX (1892), 431–461; "Vier Denkschriften Scharnhorst's aus dem Jahre 1810," *Historische Zeitschrift,* LVIII (1887), 55–105; and "Denkschrift des Prinzen August von Preussen über die Landwehr," *Militär-Wochenblatt,* 1897, No. 50, pp. 1428–1434, No. 51, pp. 1449–1456. Friedrich Meusel published two fragments from the writings of Marwitz on military subjects which are of only minor interest: "Marwitz' Schilderung der altpreussischen Armee," *Preussische Jahrbücher,* 131 (1908), 460–484; and "Die Neuformation der preussischen Armee nach dem Tilsiter Frieden (1807–08) von Generalleutnant Friedrich August Ludwig von der Marwitz," *Jahrbücher für die deutsche Armee und Marine,* July–Dec. 1808, pp. 169–176.

There are a number of publications of sources in connection with the East Prussian assembly of February 1813 and the Landwehr there created. These include, in chronological order of appearance: "Errichtung der Landwehr und des Landsturms in Ostpreussen, Westpreussen am rechten Weichsel-Ufer und Litthauen im Jahre 1813," *Beihefte zum Militair-Wochenblatt,* Jan.–Oct. 1846, used by all subsequent editors but considerably supplemented by them; Robert Müller, ed., "Urkunden zur Geschichte der ständischen Versammlungen zu Königsberg im Januar und Februar 1813 betreffend die Errichtung der Landwehr," *Altpreussische Monatsschrift,* Neue Folge XIII (1876), 324–342, 436–465, 600–642, XIV (1877), 101–161, 318–339, well edited, useful, though unfortunately left incomplete; "Der 24. Januar 1813 in Königsberg: nach den Papieren des Ministers Theodor von Schön und dem Tagebuch des Landhofmeisters v. Auerswald," *Altpreussische Monatsschrift,* Neue Folge XIV (1877), 297–317, and "Von der 'Landesverrätherei' des ostpreussischen Adels im Jahre 1813," *Altpreussische Monatsschrift,* Neue Folge XVIII (1881), 385–397, contain little of value here; Adalbert Bezzenberger, ed., *Urkunden des Provinzial-Archivs in Königsberg und des gräflich Dohnaschen Majorats-Archivs in Schlobitten betreffend die Erhebung Ostpreussens im Jahre 1813 und die Errichtung der Landwehr* (Königsberg, 1894), gives the crucial information on the origin of the permission of substitutes in the Landwehr; Maximilian Schultze, *Königsberg und Ostpreussen zu Anfang 1813: Ein Tagebuch vom 1. Januar bis 25. Februar 1813* (Berlin, 1901), prints the diary of an opponent of the Landwehr.

An important source collection on a different aspect of the reform movement is W. v. Eisenhart Rothe and A. Ritthaler, eds., *Vorgeschichte und Begründung des deutschen Zollvereins 1815–1834:*

Akten der Staaten des deutschen Bundes und der europäischen Mächte (3 vols., Berlin, 1934), which has an excellent brief introduction by Hermann Oncken.

Among the source collections organized around an individual, the outstanding one is Freiherr vom Stein, *Briefwechsel, Denkschriften und Aufzeichnungen* (ed. Erich Botzenhart; 7 vols., Berlin, n.d. [1930's]), the most complete printed collection of material for the reform period thus far available. A larger collection, but one much concerned with literary as well as political writings, is the *Gesammelte Schriften* of Wilhelm von Humboldt (ed. Albert Leitzmann, Bruno Gebhardt, and Wilhelm Richter for the Preussische Akademie der Wissenschaften; 17 vols. in 20, Berlin, 1903–36). Theodor von Schön's papers, anonymously edited by his son: *Aus den Papieren des Ministers und Burggrafen von Marienburg Theodor von Schön* (6 vols., Halle, 1875–83), supplemented by: *Weitere Beiträge und Nachträge zu den Papieren des Ministers und Burggrafen von Marienburg Theodor von Schön* (Berlin, 1881), contain scattered useful material, especially concerning Count Dohna. Franz Rühl, ed., *Briefe und Aktenstücke zur Geschichte Preussens unter Friedrich Wilhelm III. vorzugsweise aus dem Nachlass von F. A. von Stägemann* (3 vols., Leipzig, 1899–1902), supplemented by: *Aus der Franzosenzeit: Ergänzungen zu den Briefen und Aktenstücken zur Geschichte Preussens unter Friedrich Wilhelm III. vorzugsweise aus dem Nachlass von F. A. von Stägemann* (Leipzig, 1904), contains miscellaneous material, much of it trivial, but some of it important. This collection is inadequately edited and therefore difficult to use. Fürst Richard Metternich-Winneburg, ed., *Aus Metternich's nachgelassenen Papieren* (8 vols. in 7, Vienna, 1880–84), supplies in Vol. III much valuable material on Metternich's schemes for frustrating the constitutional movement in Prussia. [Wilhelm] Dorow, ed., *Job von Witzleben . . . : Mittheilungen desselben und seiner Freunde zur Beurtheilung preussischer Zustände und wichtiger Zeitfragen* (Leipzig, 1842), is a straggly book useful as the only source of information on the Duke of Mecklenburg's opposition to the Landwehr.

Of considerably less importance are the following: Georg Küntzel and Martin Hass, eds., *Die politischen Testamente der Hohenzollern nebst ergänzenden Aktenstücken* (2 vols., Leipzig and Berlin, 1911), containing some early writings of Frederick William III on affairs of state; B. G. Niebuhr, *Nachgelassene Schriften nichtphilologischen Inhalts* (Hamburg, 1842); Carl von Clausewitz, *Politische Schriften und Briefe* (ed. Hans Rothfels; Munich, 1922); Friedrich von Gentz,

Staatsschriften und Briefe (ed. Hans von Eckardt; 2 vols., Munich, 1921) and *Tagebücher* (4 vols. in 2, Leipzig, 1873–74), a miserably edited jumble of names.

In a class by themselves are Johann Gottlieb Fichte's "Reden an die deutsche Nation," in Vol. VII of his *Sämmtliche Werke* (ed. J. H. Fichte; Berlin, 1846), pp. 257–499, and his "Der Patriotismus und sein Gegentheil: Patriotische Dialogen vom Jahre 1807," in Vol. III of his *Nachgelassene Werke* (ed. J. H. Fichte; Bonn, 1835), pp. 221–274.

As distinguished from collections concerned with writings of a general nature, there are several important publications of letters. Of great interest is Anna v. Sydow, ed., *Wilhelm und Caroline von Humboldt in ihren Briefen* (7 vols., Berlin, 1906–16), which contains indispensable material on Humboldt, since he wrote to his wife at great length about everything; these letters are particularly important for the development of his relationship with Hardenberg. Karl Linnebach began to edit *Scharnhorsts Briefe,* but only Vol. I (Munich and Leipzig, 1914) was published. Karl Griewank, ed., *Gneisenau: Ein Leben in Briefen* (Leipzig, 1939), contains considerable new material, as does Dietrich Gerhard and William Norvin, eds., *Die Briefe Barthold Georg Niebuhrs* (2 vols., Berlin, 1926–29). Varnhagen von Ense's *Aus dem Nachlass: Briefe von Stägemann, Metternich, Heine und Bettina von Arnim etc.* (Leipzig, 1865), is useful chiefly for Stägemann's wry comments.

Of secondary interest in the category of letters are the following: Karl Griewank, ed., *Briefwechsel der Königin Luise mit ihrem Gemahl Friedrich Wilhelm III. 1793–1810* (Leipzig, n.d. [1929]), which has a good introduction by the editor; Paul Bailleu, ed., *Briefwechsel König Friedrich Wilhelm's III. und der Königin Luise mit Kaiser Alexander I.* (Vol. LVII of the series *Publicationen aus den K. Preussischen Staatsarchiven;* Leipzig, 1900); J. G. Fichte, *Briefwechsel* (ed. Hans Schulz; 2 vols., Leipzig, 1925); Julius Heyderhoff, ed., "Benzenberg der Rheinländer und Preusse 1815–1823: Politische Briefe aus den Anfängen der preussischen Verfassungsfrage," *Rheinisches Archiv,* No. 7 (Bonn, 1928); *Lebensnachrichten über Barthold Georg Niebuhr aus Briefen desselben und aus Erinnerungen einiger seiner nächsten Freunde* (3 vols., Hamburg, 1838–39); Franz Rühl, ed., *Briefwechsel des Ministers und Burggrafen von Marienburg Theodor von Schön mit G. H. Pertz und J. G. Droysen* (Leipzig, 1896); W. v. Unger, ed., *Blüchers Briefe* (Stuttgart and Berlin, 1913); Wolfgang Windelband, ed., "Friedrich Eichhorns Briefe an Gneisenau (1809–1818)," *Deutsche Revue*, XLIV (1919), 50–61, 135–154, 264–281; Friedrich Carl Wittichen, ed., *Briefe von und an Friedrich von Gentz* (3 vols. in 4, Munich and Berlin, 1909–13), which should be used in conjunction with *Briefwechsel zwischen Friedrich Gentz und Adam Heinrich Müller* (Stuttgart, 1857). H. Kochendörffer, ed., *Briefwechsel zwischen Stein und Vincke* (Münster, 1930), and Wilhelm Steffens, ed., *Briefwechsel Sacks mit Stein und Gneisenau (1807/17)* (Stettin, 1931), are largely superseded by Botzenhart's complete edition of Stein's papers.

There are several important works setting forth the conservative political philosophy of the period. Pride of place should probably go to G. W. F. Hegel's *Philosophy of Right* (trans. S. W. Dyde; London, 1896), although other works were actually more influential at the time. For example, Friedrich Ancillon's *Ueber Souveränität und Staats-Verfassungen: Ein Versuch zur Berichtigung einiger politischen Grundbegriffe* (2nd ed., Berlin, 1816, first pub. 1815) is a very clearly written and concise statement of the conservative position and was widely read; it should be supplemented, for an understanding of the author's opinions, by Max Lehmann, ed., "Ancillon's Denkschrift vom 4. Februar 1813," *Historische Zeitschrift*, LXVIII (1892), 275–300. (A later and longer work of Ancillon's is *Ueber den Geist der Staatsverfassungen und dessen Einfluss auf die Gesetzgebung* [Berlin, 1825]; likewise in part too late for the period under consideration, and further handicapped by its monumental proportions, was the famous work of Carl Ludwig von Haller, *Restauration der Staats-Wissenschaft oder Theorie des natürlich-geselligen Zustands der Chimäre des künstlich-bürgerlichen entgegengesetzt* [2nd ed., 6 vols., Winterthur, 1820–34; first pub. 1816–25].) Adam H. Müller's *Die Elemente der Staatskunst* (3 vols., Berlin, 1809), a German version of the conservative theories of Edmund Burke, is a lucid exposition; also of interest is Müller's *Vermischte Schriften über Staat, Philosophie und Kunst* (2 vols. in 1, Vienna, 1817). Johann Ludwig Klüber, *Wichtige Urkunden für den Rechtszustand der deutschen Nation* (ed. C. Welcker; 2nd ed., Mannheim, 1845), prints the protocols of the meetings at which the Carlsbad Decrees were drawn up, including particularly Friedrich Gentz's essay on the constitution of the German Confederation. Friedrich Otto von Diericke's *Ein Wort über den preussischen Adel* (Berlin, 1817) may be considered as typical of the views of the rank-and-file, non-intellectual conservative.

In marked contrast to the latter work stands that of the Junker and intellectual *malgré lui,* Ludwig von der Marwitz, who is the subject of the most comprehensive source collection dealing with a practical, as opposed to a theoretical, conservative of the reform period: Friedrich Meusel, ed., *Friedrich August Ludwig von der Marwitz: Ein märkischer Edelmann im Zeitalter der Befreiungs-kriege* (2 vols. in 3, Berlin, 1908–13). A planned third volume was never published because of the editor's death in World War I, but the work is nevertheless substantial and valuable. The editor also published some documents separately (apart from those on entirely military subjects already mentioned): "Aus Marwitz' Memoiren: der Zusammenbruch des preussischen Staates 1806," *Deutsche Rundschau,* 162 (1915), 426–450, and 163 (1915), 242–281, 357–396; "Ein Aufsatz des Grafen von Finckenstein über Hardenbergs Finanzreform von 1810 (mit einigen Briefen von Finckenstein und Marwitz im Anhang)," *Forschungen zur brandenburgischen und preussischen Geschichte,* XIX (1906), 522–532; "Eine Denkschrift des Grafen von Finckenstein 'Über die Freiheiten der Ritterschaft' (1811)," *Historische Zeitschrift,* 101 (1908), pp. 337–349.

Of great interest are some of the polemical pamphlets connected with the so-called *Demagogenverfolgungen.* The first shot was fired by [Theodor Anton Heinrich] Schmalz in a broadside which became one of the manuals of the witch-hunters of the period: *Berichtigung einer Stelle in der Bredow-Venturinischen Chronik für das Jahr 1808: Über politische Vereine, und ein Wort über Scharnhorsts und meine Verhältnisse zu ihnen* (Berlin, 1815). Schmalz followed up with *Ueber des Herrn B. G. Niebuhrs Schrift wider die meinige, politische Vereine betreffend* (Berlin, 1815) and *Letztes Wort über politische Vereine* (Berlin, 1816). An important pamphlet in support of Schmalz was the anonymous *Die deutschen Roth- und Schwarz-Mäntler: Eine Seiten-Patrouille zu den französischen schwarzen und weissen Jakobinern* (Neubrandenburg, n.d.). In opposition to Schmalz, the lead was taken by B. G. Niebuhr with his *Ueber geheime Verbindungen im preussischen Staat, und deren Denunciation* (Berlin, 1815); support was given by F. Schleiermacher, *An den Herrn Geheimrath Schmalz: Auch eine Recension* (Berlin, 1815), and by the anonymous pamphlet *Die neuen Obscuranten im Jahre 1815: Dem Herrn Geheimrath Schmalz in Berlin und dessen Genossen gewidmet* (Leipzig and Altenburg, 1815). Of a different nature, but also contributing to the persecution of the liberal elements, was a memorandum for Tsar Alexander I by his minister, Pozzo di Borgo, printed in Comte Charles Pozzo di Borgo, ed., *Correspon-*

dance diplomatique du comte Pozzo di Borgo ambassadeur de Russie en France et du comte de Nesselrode, etc. (2 vols., Paris, 1890–97).

A miscellaneous source collection of minor importance is [Wilhelm Dorow, ed.,] *Denkschriften und Briefe zur Charakteristik der Welt und Litteratur* (5 vols. in 3, Berlin, 1838–41), dilettantishly edited.

C. General Works

The best general history of Germany in the nineteenth century is the still unfinished work of Franz Schnabel, *Deutsche Geschichte im neunzehnten Jahrhundert* (2nd ed., 4 vols., Freiburg, 1948–51). The older classic of the same name by Heinrich von Treitschke (3 vols., Leipzig, 1879–85), though in some respects obsolete, contains some vital documentary material. Also useful in the latter respect is Vol. I of Alfred Stern, *Geschichte Europas seit den Verträgen von 1815 bis zum Frankfurter Frieden von 1871* (10 vols., Berlin, 1894–1924). The same author's *Abhandlungen und Aktenstücke zur Geschichte der preussischen Reformzeit 1807–1815* (Leipzig, 1885) likewise contains documents incorporated into essays on various aspects of the period. Good for background in their two fields are Guido de Ruggiero,*The History of European Liberalism* (trans. R. G. Collingwood; Oxford and London, 1927), and A. Sartorius von Waltershausen, *Deutsche Wirtschaftsgeschichte 1815–1914* (Jena, 1920).

Friedrich Meinecke's *Das Zeitalter der deutschen Erhebung 1795–1815* (Bielefeld and Leipzig, 1906) is a masterly and literate summary of the period for the general reader from which the student can learn much. The same author's *1848: Eine Säkularbetrachtung* (Berlin, 1948) interprets the reform period in the light of later developments in Germany. Only one volume appeared of Paul Hassel, *Geschichte der preussischen Politik 1807 bis 1815* (Vol. VI of the series *Publicationen aus den K. Preussischen Staatsarchiven;* Leipzig, 1881), covering the years 1807–8, the period also dealt with by Hans Haussherr, *Erfüllung und Befreiung: Der Kampf um die Durchführung des Tilsiter Friedens 1807/1808* (Hamburg, 1935). The only general treatment of the reform period in English is the useful book by Guy Stanton Ford, *Stein and the Era of Reform in Prussia, 1807–1815* (Princeton, London, and Oxford, 1922).

An indispensable work on the background of the reform period is Otto Hintze's essay "Preussische Reformbestrebungen vor 1806," in his *Historische und politische Aufsätze* (Vol. III; Berlin, n.d.), 29–59, more recently supplemented by Gerhard Ritter, "Die preussischen Staatsmänner der Reformzeit und die Polenfrage," in Albert

Brackmann, ed., *Deutschland und Polen: Beiträge zu ihren geschichtlichen Beziehungen* (Munich and Berlin, 1933), pp. 207–219. On the political theory of the conservatives, Sigmund Neumann's *Die Stufen des preussischen Konservatismus: Ein Beitrag zum Staats- und Gesellschaftsbild Deutschlands im 19. Jahrhundert* (Berlin, 1930) is an excellent summary; Heinrich O. Meisner's *Die Lehre vom monarchischen Prinzip im Zeitalter der Restauration und des Deutschen Bundes* (Breslau, 1913) is an investigation of a particular aspect of conservatism which makes some useful distinctions. Friedrich Lenz, *Agrarlehre und Agrarpolitik der deutschen Romantik* (Berlin, 1912), concentrates heavily on Adam Müller. Ernst Müsebeck, "Die ursprünglichen Grundlagen des Liberalismus und Konservatismus in Deutschland," *Korrespondenzblatt* des Gesamtvereins der deutschen Geschichts- und Altertumsvereine, LXIII (1915), 1–26, provides a brief but quite profound analysis.

D. *Memoirs*

Easily the outstanding set of memoirs is that of Boyen: Friedrich Nippold, ed., *Erinnerungen aus dem Leben des General-Feldmarschalls Hermann von Boyen* (3 vols., Leipzig, 1889–90), a fine and reliable source. Also dependable, but naturally of less stature, is Boyen's *Beiträge zur Kenntnis des General von Scharnhorst und seiner amtlichen Thätigkeit in den Jahren 1808 bis 1813, etc.* (Berlin, 1833). A very disappointing set for my purposes is Leopold von Ranke, ed., *Denkwürdigkeiten des Staatskanzlers Fürsten von Hardenberg* (5 vols., Leipzig, 1877), concerned predominantly with foreign affairs. K. A. Varnhagen von Ense's *Denkwürdigkeiten des eigenen Lebens* (3rd ed., 6 vols., Leipzig, 1871) contains more gossip than history but is informative on public opinion. Friedrich von Raumer's *Lebenserinnerungen und Briefwechsel* (2 vols. in 1, Leipzig, 1861) is delightfully written but rather reticent on public affairs. Wilhelm Dorow, *Erlebtes aus den Jahren 1790–1827* (4 vols. in 2, Leipzig, 1843–45), has some information. More eyewitness history than memoirs are the two related works of the civil servant Magnus Friedrich von Bassewitz: *Die Kurmark Brandenburg im Zusammenhang mit den Schicksalen des Gesammtstaats Preussen während der Zeit vom 22. Oktober 1806 bis zu Ende des Jahres 1808* (pub. anonymously; 2 vols., Leipzig, 1851–52) and *Die Kurmark Brandenburg im Zusammenhange mit den Schicksalen des Gesammtstaats Preussen währen der Jahre 1809 und 1810* (ed. Karl von Reinhard; Leipzig, 1860).

E. *Biographies*

(Note: works whose emphasis is on a topic rather than on a person are included under subsequent topical headings, even when the person's name appears in the title.)

Gerhard Ritter's *Stein: Eine politische Biographie* (2 vols., Stuttgart and Berlin, 1931) comes close to being the perfect biography; but it has by no means completely superseded the earlier and larger work of Max Lehmann, *Freiherr vom Stein* (3 vols., Leipzig, 1902–5), which contains considerable unique material; judgments tend to be harsh. Franz Schnabel's *Freiherr vom Stein* (Leipzig and Berlin, 1931) does not claim to be in the same class, being merely a summary, but is very literate and suggestive. The pioneer work of G. H. Pertz, *Das Leben des Ministers Freiherrn vom Stein* (7 vols., Berlin, 1850–55), is largely superseded. No comparable work on Hardenberg exists: Carl Ludwig Klose's *Leben Karl August's, Fürsten von Hardenberg, königlich preussischen Staatskanzlers* (Halle, 1851) was no more than a worthy first attempt. Wilhelm Steffens' *Hardenberg und die ständische Opposition 1810/1811* (Leipzig, 1907) is a thorough but not completely satisfactory examination of Hardenberg's concessions during the crisis of 1811 which rightly stresses his achievement as well. Hans Haussherr, *Die Stunde Hardenbergs* (Hamburg, 1943), is likewise concerned only with the first years of the chancellorship and, though using a considerable amount of unpublished material, the work is vitiated by a violent prejudice against Hardenberg induced by adherence to National Socialist values. A competent biography of Hardenberg is the most conspicuous desideratum in the literature of the reform period.

Max Lehmann's earlier biography, *Scharnhorst* (2 vols., Leipzig, 1886–87), while not as successful as his *Stein,* is a reliable guide to the general's activities and views. It leaves the prior work of Georg Heinrich Klippel, *Das Leben des Generals von Scharnhorst* (3 vols. in 1, Leipzig, 1869–71), largely outdated. Rudolf Stadelmann's "Scharnhorst und die Revolution seiner Zeit," *Das innere Reich,* V^1 (April–Sept. 1938), 44–65, is a perceptive essay distinguishing Scharnhorst's achievement and personality from those of the other reformers. The same author's *Scharnhorst: Schicksal und geistige Welt, ein Fragment* (Wiesbaden, 1952) was unfortunately left incomplete by his death. G. H. Pertz and Hans Delbrück, *Das Leben des Feldmarschalls Grafen Neithardt von Gneisenau* (5 vols., Berlin, 1864–80), provide a large quantity of documentary material on the question of the demagogues but the book is somewhat disappointing on military matters. Delbrück later published a digest of the work under the same title, in a revised edition of which he added some new material (2nd revised ed., 2 vols., Berlin, 1894; first pub. 1882). Friedrich Meinecke's *Das Leben des Generalfeldmarschalls Hermann von Boyen* (2 vols., Stuttgart, 1896–99) is a fine book in every way and a first-rate source. Some sidelights are offered by Eberhard Kessel, "Zu Boyens Entlassung," *Historische Zeitschrift,* 175 (1953), 41–54.

Bruno Gebhardt, *Wilhelm von Humboldt als Staatsmann* (2 vols., Stuttgart, 1896–99), provides much valuable material, especially on the crisis of 1819, but the work is uneven and stops short of any real answers to the pressing questions; it is not always adequately documented and is exceedingly hostile to Hardenberg. Holding a fairer balance is S. A. Kaehler, *Wilhelm von Humboldt und der Staat: Ein Beitrag zur Geschichte deutscher Lebensgestaltung um 1800* (Munich and Berlin, 1927), who offers fewer documents but more mature judgments; Kaehler is inclined to condemn Humboldt as an idealist.

The solution to the long-raging controversy over Schön is given by M. Baumann's *Theodor von Schön: Seine Geschichtsschreibung und seine Glaubwürdigkeit* (Berlin, 1910), which cuts through the confusion with honesty and clarity, supplemented by the early pages of Hans Rothfels' *Theodor von Schön, Friedrich Wilhelm IV. und die Revolution von 1848* (Halle, 1937). Two contributions by Eduard Wilhelm Mayer, *Das Retablissement Ost- und Westpreussens unter der Mitwirkung und Leitung Theodors von Schön* (Jena, 1916) and "Politische Erfahrungen und Gedanken Theodors von Schön nach 1815," *Historische Zeitschrift,* 117 (1917), 432–464, make some good points. Schön's friend, the enigmatic Count Dohna, was accorded a worshipful biography by Johannes Voigt: *Das Leben des königlich preussischen Staatsministers Friederich Ferdinand Alexander Reichs-Burggrafen und Grafen zu Dohna-Schlobitten* (Leipzig, 1833), which is of limited value. Günther Holstein's *Die Staatsphilosophie Schleiermachers* (Bonn and Leipzig, 1923), though poorly organized and obscurely written, is useful for distilling the political content of Schleiermacher's sermons; in this respect it supplements the far more profound essay of Wilhelm Dilthey, "Schleiermachers politische Gesinnung und Wirksamkeit," in his *Gesammelte Schriften* (12 vols., Leipzig and Berlin, 1914–36), XII, 1–36.

Turning to the conservatives, Franz Rosenzweig, *Hegel und der Staat* (2 vols., Munich and Berlin, 1920), is unusually successful in setting political theory against the background of events; the book reveals Hegel's ignorance of the nature of the reform movement in Prussia. Jakob Baxa's *Adam Müller: Ein Lebensbild aus den Befreiungskriegen und aus der deutschen Restauration* (Jena, 1930) is a good biography but rather diffuse. Paul Haake's *Johann Peter Friedrich Ancillon und Kronprinz Friedrich Wilhelm IV. von Preussen* (Munich and Berlin, 1920) consists mostly of very full quotations from correspondence; it is a dull, shapeless, but valuable book. Of far greater literary merit is Reinhold Steig's *Heinrich von Kleist's Berliner Kämpfe* (Berlin and Stuttgart, 1901); on a member of Kleist's circle, Herma Becker's *Achim von Arnim in den wissenschaftlichen und politischen Strömungen seiner Zeit* (Berlin and Leipzig, 1912) is a rather amateurish but occasionally useful essay.

Only two of the more active conservatives have been given substantial biographies. Joh. Gust. Droysen's *Das Leben des Feldmarschalls Grafen York von Wartenburg* (4th ed., 2 vols. in 1, Leipzig, 1863) is an old-fashioned but penetrating account useful chiefly for the period of Stein's ministry. Walther Kayser's *Marwitz: Ein Schicksalsbericht aus dem Zeitalter der unvollendeten preussisch-deutschen Erhebung* (Hamburg, 1936) is an apologia tainted with National Socialist ideology and full of hortatory phrases; it offers some material not contained in Meusel's Marwitz collection. Kayser's article, "Marwitz und die unvollendete preussisch-deutsche Erhebung," *Nationalsozialistische Monatshefte*, VII (1936), 113–120, gives an even more outspokenly National Socialist interpretation. Gerhard Ramlow's *Ludwig von der Marwitz und die Anfänge konservativer Politik und Staatsanschauung in Preussen* (Berlin, 1930) is a capable analysis, leaning heavily on Meusel and concentrating on political theory. Friedrich Schinkel, ed., *Preussischer Adel: Aus den nachgelassenen Schriften Friedrich August Ludwigs von der Marwitz* (Breslau, 1932), is useful only for a sympathetic and intelligent introduction; the text is excerpted from Meusel's edition. Willy Andreas' "Marwitz und der Staat Friedrichs des Grossen," *Historische Zeitschrift*, 122 (1920), 44–82, is a well-fashioned, mildly critical, but not very original analysis, based on Meusel.

The fine biography of Metternich, Heinrich Ritter von Srbik, *Metternich: Der Staatsmann und der Mensch* (2 vols., Munich, 1925), fails to clarify completely the connection of his subject with Prussian events between 1815 and 1819.

F. *Agrarian Reform*

Georg Friedrich Knapp's *Die Bauern-Befreiung und der Ursprung der Landarbeiter in den älteren Theilen Preussens* (2 vols., Leipzig, 1887) is unique in this field. It contains large numbers of valuable documents, though inadequately correlated. The narrative is often too brief. His *Die Landarbeiter in Knechtschaft und Freiheit* (Leipzig, 1891) and *Grundherrschaft und Rittergut* (Leipzig, 1897) are briefer treatments of the same theme, with some new material used. Georg Winter, "Zur Entstehungsgeschichte des Oktoberedikts und der Verordnung vom 14. Februar 1808," *Forschungen zur brandenburgischen und preussischen Geschichte*, XL (1927), 1–33, is good for the period covered. Three provinces have received individual treatment: for Silesia, Johannes Ziekursch, *Hundert Jahre schlesischer Agrargeschichte: Vom Hubertusburger Frieden bis zum Abschluss der Bauernbefreiung* (Breslau, 1915), covers too much ground to give enough detail; for Brandenburg and Pomerania, Hans Goldschmidt, *Die Grundbesitzverteilung in der Mark Brandenburg und in Hinterpommern vom Beginn des dreissigjährigen Krieges bis zur Gegenwart* (Berlin, 1910), offers some interesting statistics. A general reference work useful as a guide through the maze of technical terms is Ludwig Elster, ed., *Wörterbuch der Volkswirtschaft* (2 vols., Jena, 1906–7).

G. *Constitutional Reform*

The standard work on German constitutional history in general is that of Fritz Hartung, *Deutsche Verfassungsgeschichte vom 15. Jahrhundert bis zur Gegenwart* (5th ed., Stuttgart, 1950), a very sound book indeed. More specifically on the constitutional problems of the Prussian reform period, the most thorough treatments are the essay of Heinrich von Treitschke, "Der erste Verfassungskampf in Preussen. (1815–1823.)," *Preussische Jahrbücher*, XXIX (1872), 313–360, 409–473, and the series of articles by Paul Haake, "König Friedrich Wilhelm III., Hardenberg und die preussische Verfassungsfrage," *Forschungen zur brandenburgischen und preussischen Geschichte*, XXVI (1913), 523–573, XXVIII (1915), 175–220, XXIX (1916), 305–369, XXX (1918), 317–365, XXXII (1920), 109–180, the latter being summarized very turgidly in the author's *Der preussische Verfassungskampf vor hundert Jahren* (Munich and Berlin, 1921). Haake seeks to shift the blame for the failure of the constitutional effort from Hardenberg's shoulders, where Treitschke and intervening writers had placed it, to the king's, with not altogether convincing results. Treitschke's essay, inadequately documented, was a valiant first inroad into the field, boldly executed under the banner of *kleindeutsch* unity. Haake supplies much new material but is still often forced to interpolate doubtful conclusions on it to maintain his thesis. The articles are not well organized, have long digressions, and are humorlessly written. Ernst Meier's *Die Reform der Verwaltungs-Organisation unter Stein und Hardenberg* (Leipzig, 1881) is the best background text.

On individual phases of the constitutional struggle, the most successful work is by Ernst Walter Zeeden, *Hardenberg und der Gedanke einer Volksvertretung in Preussen 1807–1812* (Berlin, 1940), which contains much valuable new archival material but is poorly organized. The only detailed examination of the Altenstein-Dohna ministry is the partial reprint of the dissertation of Rudolf Lobethal, *Verwaltung und Finanzpolitik in Preussen während der Jahre 1808–1810 (Von der Entlassung Steins bis zum Antritt Hardenbergs.)* (Berlin, 1914), a well-documented and well-written work. Paul Haake, "Die Errichtung des preussischen Staatsrats im März 1817," *Forschungen zur brandenburgischen und preussischen Geschichte,* XXVII (1914), 247–265, shows how Hardenberg was forced to yield on that issue; supplementary material on the same question is to be found in Hans Schneider's "Die Entstehung des preussischen Staatsrats 1806–1817: Ein Beitrag zur Verfassungsreform Preussens nach dem Zusammenbruch," *Zeitschrift für die gesamte Staatswissenschaft,* 102 (1942), 480–529 (now substantially incorporated in the author's *Der preussische Staatsrat 1817–1918: Ein Beitrag zur Verfassungs- und Rechtsgeschichte Preussens* [Munich and Berlin, 1952]). Edmund Richter's *Friedrich August von Staegemann und das königliche Verfassungsversprechen vom 22ten Mai 1815* (Schweidnitz, 1913) is a routine and very padded textual examination of the decree's origin. Alfred Stern, "Die preussische Verfassungsfrage im Jahre 1817 und die Rundreise von Altenstein, Klewiz, Beyme," *Deutsche Zeitschrift für Geschichtswissenschaft,* IX (1893), 62–99, presents some good material in rather confusing fashion. There are two interesting short treatments of Humboldt's connection with the constitutional question in 1819: Paul Lenel's "Wilhelm von Humboldt und die Anfänge der preussischen Verfassung," *Deutschrechtliche Beiträge,* IX (1913), 93–119, and Siegfried Kähler's *Beiträge zur Würdigung von Wilhelm v. Humboldts Entwurf einer ständischen Verfassung für Preussen vom Jahre 1819* (Freiburg,

1914). Material for an epilogue is given by Paul Bailleu, "Kronprinz Friedrich Wilhelm im Ständekampf 1820," *Historische Zeitschrift,* LXXXVII (1901), 67–73.

Two very useful essays are confined to Brandenburg: Otto Schönbeck's "Der kurmärkische Landtag vom Frühjahr 1809," *Forschungen zur brandenburgischen und preussischen Geschichte,* XX (1907), 1–103, rather breathless; and Ernst Müsebeck's "Die märkische Ritterschaft und die preussische Verfassungsfrage von 1814 bis 1820," *Deutsche Rundschau,* 174 (1918), 158–182, 354–376, a mature analysis based on considerable new material.

H. *Fiscal Reform*

The best treatment of the fiscal problem during the early years of the reform period is Karl Mamroth's *Geschichte der preussischen Staats-Besteuerung 1806–1816,* of which only one volume was published, reaching the year 1812 (Leipzig, 1890). Much less satisfactory on the remaining period, though supplying some important documents, is Carl Dieterici, *Zur Geschichte der Steuer-Reform in Preussen von 1810 bis 1820* (Berlin, 1875). On single aspects of the question, Conrad Bornhak, "Die preussische Finanzreform von 1810," *Forschungen zur brandenburgischen und preussischen Geschichte,* III (1890), 555–608, is useful, though not completely reliable; Otto Schönbeck's "Die Einkommensteuer unter den Nachfolgern Steins: Ein Beitrag zur Geschichte des Ministeriums Altenstein-Dohna," *Forschungen zur brandenburgischen und preussischen Geschichte,* XXV (1913), 117–177, is unwieldy but valuable.

On the abolition of guilds and economic monopolies, the standard work is Kurt von Rohrscheidt's *Vom Zunftzwange zur Gewerbefreiheit* (Berlin, 1898), which combines good documentation with the broadest kind of generalizations. On the Customs Law of 1818, W. O. Henderson, *The Zollverein* (Cambridge, 1939), is very brief. The most comprehensive work in German is Gustav Schmoller's *Das preussische Handels- und Zollgesetz vom 26. Mai 1818 im Zusammenhang mit der Geschichte der Zeit, ihrer Kämpfe und Ideen* (Berlin, 1898). Also helpful is Hermann Freymark, *Die Reform der preussischen Handels- und Zollpolitik von 1800–1821 und ihre Bedeutung* (Jena, 1898).

I. *The "Demagogues"*

There is no comprehensive treatment of this subject. Two volumes of the *Geschichte der deutschen Burschenschaft,* Vol. I by Paul

Wentzcke (Heidelberg, 1919), Vol. II by Georg Heer (Heidelberg, 1927) (Vols. VI and X respectively of the series *Quellen und Darstellungen zur Geschichte der Burschenschaft und der deutschen Einheitsbewegung*, ed. Herman Haupt), provide the best approach. In Vol. I of the same series (Heidelberg, 1910), pp. 4–17, appears an article by Friedrich Meinecke, "Zur Geschichte des Hoffmannschen Bundes," which is supplementary to his earlier book, *Die Deutschen Gesellschaften und der Hoffmannsche Bund: Ein Beitrag zur Geschichte der politischen Bewegungen in Deutschland im Zeitalter der Befreiungskriege* (Stuttgart, 1891). More useful than either of these, on the same subject, is Justus von Gruner's "Justus Gruner und der Hoffmannsche Bund," *Forschungen zur brandenburgischen und preussischen Geschichte*, XIX (1906), 485–507, which proves Hardenberg's involvement in the secret movement for German unification. The same writer's article in Vol. XXII (1909) of the same periodical, pp. 169–182, is a labored and speculative attempt to describe how Schmalz got his medal: "Die Ordensverleihung an den Geheimen Rat Professor Schmalz 1815." On a related problem, H. Ulmann, "Die Anklage des Jakobinismus in Preussen im Jahre 1815," *Historische Zeitschrift*, XCV (1905), pp. 435–446, is useful. On the *Tugendbund*, the three treatments in decreasing order of merit are: Paul Stettiner's *Der Tugendbund* (Königsberg, 1904); August Fournier's "Zur Geschichte des Tugendbundes," in his *Historische Studien und Skizzen* (Prague and Leipzig, 1885), pp. 301–330; and August Lehmann's *Der Tugendbund* (Berlin, 1867).

Valuable new material on Altenstein and Arndt respectively was provided by two contributions of Ernst Müsebeck: *Das preussische Kultusministerium vor hundert Jahren* (Stuttgart and Berlin, 1918) and "Die Einleitung des Verfahrens gegen E. M. Arndt: Eine Untersuchung zur Geschichte der Reaktion in Preussen nach 1815," *Historische Zeitschrift*, 105 (1910), 517–563. Scattered useful sidelights are thrown by Max Lenz, *Geschichte der königlichen Friedrich-Wilhelms-Universität zu Berlin* (4 vols. in 5, Halle, 1910–18). Walter Obenaus, *Die Entwicklung der preussischen Sicherheitspolizei bis zum Ende der Reaktionszeit* (Berlin, 1940), examines the persecutors rather than the victims; he hints disapproval of the National Socialist police state. P. Bailleu, ed., "Metternich's Teplitzer Denkschrift," *Historische Zeitschrift*, L (1883), 190–192, fills a gap in the documentation.

J. Military Reform

William O. Shanahan, *Prussian Military Reforms 1786–1813* (New York, 1945), covers most of the period briefly. An excellent new treatment is that of Gerhard Ritter, *Staatskunst und Kriegshandwerk: Das Problem des "Militarismus" in Deutschland* (Vol. I, Munich, 1954).

Two articles discuss the king's relation to military reform: Friedrich Thimme, "König Friedrich Wilhelm III., sein Anteil an der Konvention von Tauroggen und an der Reform von 1807–1812," *Forschungen zur brandenburgischen und preussischen Geschichte,* XVIII (1905), 1–59, depicts him as a reformer; a more subtle and better-written reply came from Alfred Herrmann, "Friedrich Wilhelm III. und sein Anteil an der Heeresreform bis 1813," *Historische Vierteljahrschrift,* XI (1908), 484–516. Two interesting articles are concerned with Borstell: Max Lehmann's "General Borstell und der Ausbruch des Krieges von 1813," *Historische Zeitschrift,* XXXVII (1877), 55–76, and Rudolf Stadelmann's "Das Duell zwischen Scharnhorst und Borstell im Dezember 1807," *Historische Zeitschrift,* 161 (1940), 263–276.

The controversy over Schön's role in military reform features Max Lehmann's attack, *Knesebeck und Schön: Beiträge zur Geschichte der Freiheitskriege* (Leipzig, 1875), which contains some good material on the Landwehr of 1813; the anonymous rebuttal was entitled *Zu Schutz und Trutz am Grabe Schön's: Bilder aus der Zeit der Schmach und der Erhebung Preussens (von einem Ostpreussen)* (Berlin, 1876), a labyrinthine volume.

On the East Prussian assembly of 1813, August Witt's "Der preussische Landtag im Februar 1813," *Historisches Taschenbuch,* Dritte Folge, VIII (1857), 533–615, is partly obsolete and must be used with caution but is in general a good narrative. On the Landsturm, Maximilian Blumenthal, *Der preussische Landsturm von 1813* (Berlin, 1900), is pedestrian but useful, giving much documentary material, though often in paraphrase rather than directly.

K. Nationalism

The literature on the subject of German nationalism is enormous. This list is therefore highly selective and contains only those works most pertinent to its effect on the progress of reform in Prussia. In addition, many works listed under previous headings are also relevant.

The fundamental book in the field is Friedrich Meinecke's *Welt-bürgertum und Nationalstaat: Studien zur Genesis des deutschen Nationalstaates* (6th ed., Munich and Berlin, 1922; first pub. 1907). Supplementary material by the same author is to be found in some of the essays in *Preussen und Deutschland im 19. und 20. Jahrhundert: Historische und politische Aufsätze* (Munich and Berlin, 1918) and *Preussisch-deutsche Gestalten und Probleme* (Leipzig, 1940). The other large-scale work on the problem of German nationalism is Heinrich Ritter von Srbik's *Deutsche Einheit: Idee und Wirklichkeit vom Heiligen Reich bis Königgrätz* (4 vols., Munich, 1935–42), a prolonged funeral oration from the Austrian and *grossdeutsch* point of view on the demise of Germany as a nation in the nineteenth century, rather overwritten but offering some original insights and synthesizing a vast mass of diffuse material. Also of interest is Paul Kluckhohn's *Persönlichkeit und Gemeinschaft: Studien zur Staatsauffassung der deutschen Romantik* (Halle, 1925).

The periodical literature is vast. Arnold Berney, "Reichstradition und Nationalstaatsgedanke (1789–1815)," *Historische Zeitschrift*, 140 (1929), 57–86, is particularly good on Stein, and on Humboldt Ernst Schaumkell, "Wilhelm von Humboldt und der preussische Staatsgedanke," *Forschungen zur brandenburgischen und preussischen Geschichte*, XLVII (1935), 309–335, offers some new material. While we await Hans Kohn's sequel to his *Idea of Nationalism*, we have three valuable recent articles of his: "The Eve of German Nationalism (1789–1812)," *Journal of the History of Ideas*, XII (1951), 256–284; "Romanticism and the Rise of German Nationalism," *Review of Politics*, XII (1950), 443–472; and "Father Jahn's Nationalism," *Review of Politics*, XI (1949), 419–432. My article, "Variations in Nationalism during the Great Reform Movement in Prussia," appeared in the *American Historical Review*, LIX (1953–54), 305–321.

PART II

Anderson, Eugene Newton, *Nationalism and the Cultural Crisis in Prussia, 1806–1815* (New York, 1939).

Aris, Reinhold, *History of Political Thought in Germany from 1789 to 1815* (London, 1936).

Arndt, F., *Hardenberg's Leben und Wirken* (Berlin, 1864).

Bach, Theodor, *Theodor Gottlieb von Hippel, der Verfasser des Aufrufs: "An mein Volk."* (Breslau, 1863).

Blumenthal, Max, "Preussische Communal-Gesetzgebung in der

Reformperiode," *Sammlung gemeinverständlicher wissenschaftlicher Vorträge,* Series II, Vol. XV (1900), 151–237.

Bodelschwingh, E. von, *Leben des Ober-Präsidenten Freiherrn von Vincke* (Vol. I, Berlin, 1853; no more published).

Borcke-Stargordt, Henning Graf von, "Zur preussischen Agrargesetzgebung der Reformzeit," *Mensch und Staat in Recht und Geschichte, Festschrift für Herbert Kraus* (Kitzingen/Main, 1954), pp. 307–327.

Bornhak, Conrad, *Geschichte des preussischen Verwaltungsrechts* (3 vols., Berlin, 1884–86).

Brinkmann, Carl, "Der Nationalismus und die deutschen Universitäten im Zeitalter der deutschen Erhebung," *Sitzungsberichte der Heidelberger Akademie der Wissenschaften, Philosophisch-historische Klasse,* 1931/32, No. 3.

Carsten, F. L., "The Great Elector and the Foundation of the Hohenzollern Despotism," *English Historical Review,* LXV (1950), 175–202.

Czygan, Paul, *Zur Geschichte der Tagesliteratur während der Freiheitskriege* (3 vols. in 2, Leipzig, 1911).

Dehio, L., "Wittgenstein und das letzte Jahrzehnt Friedrich Wilhelms III.," *Forschungen zur brandenburgischen und preussischen Geschichte,* XXXV (1923), 213–240.

Delbrück, Hans, "Friedrich Wilhelm III. und Hardenberg auf dem Wiener Kongress," *Historische Zeitschrift,* LXIII (1889), 242–265.

Dönniges, [Wilhelm,] *Die Land-Kultur-Gesetzgebung Preussens, etc.* (3 vols. and index volume, Berlin, 1843–49).

Engelbrecht, H. C., *Johann Gottlieb Fichte: A Study of His Political Writings with Special Reference to His Nationalism* (New York and London, 1933).

Foerster, Erich, *Die Entstehung der preussischen Landeskirche unter der Regierung Friedrich Wilhelms des Dritten* (2 vols., Tübingen, 1905–7).

Ford, Guy Stanton, "Boyen's Military Law," *American Historical Review,* XX (1915), 528–538.

Franz, Eugen, *Bayerische Verfassungskämpfe: Von der Ständekammer zum Landtag* (Munich, 1926).

Görlitz, Walter, *Stein: Staatsmann und Reformator* (Frankfurt am Main, n.d. [1949]).

Goltz, Joachim Freiherr v. d., *Auswirkungen der Stein-Hardenbergschen Agrarreform im Laufe des 19. Jahrhunderts* (Berlin, n.d.).

Grabower, Rolf, *Preussens Steuern vor und nach den Befreiungskriegen* (Berlin, 1932).

Griewank, Karl, "Hardenberg und die preussische Politik 1804–1806," *Forschungen zur brandenburgischen und preussischen Geschichte,* XLVII (1935), 227–308.

——, "Preussen und die Neuordnung Deutschlands 1813–1815," *Forschungen zur brandenburgischen und preussischen Geschichte,* LII (1940), 234–279.

Hadamowsky, Franz, ed., "Beiträge zur Geschichte Preussens zur Zeit der Befreiungskriege: 'Ueber den Tugendbund' und 'Preussische Charaktere' von Karl v. Woltmann," *Forschungen zur brandenburgischen und preussischen Geschichte,* XL (1927), 88–124.

Hagen, Karl, "Ueber die öffentliche Meinung in Deutschland von den Freiheitskriegen bis zu den Karlsbader Beschlüssen," *Historisches Taschenbuch,* Neue Folge VII (1846), 599–700, VIII (1847), 493–666.

Harnack, Otto, *Wilhelm von Humboldt* (Berlin, 1913).

Hartung, Fritz, *Hardenberg und die preussische Verwaltung in Ansbach-Bayreuth von 1792 bis 1806* (Tübingen, 1906).

Hein, Max, *Geschichte der ostpreussischen Landschaft von 1788 bis 1888* (Königsberg, 1938).

Helfritz, Hans, *Geschichte der preussischen Heeresverwaltung* (Berlin, 1938).

Hintze, Otto, "Die Hohenzollern und der Adel," *Historische Zeitschrift,* 112 (1914), 494–524.

——, *Die Hohenzollern und ihr Werk: fünfhundert Jahre vaterländischer Geschichte* (Berlin, 1915).

Höhn, Reinhard, *Scharnhorsts Vermächtnis* (Bonn, 1952).

——, *Verfassungskampf und Heereseid: Der Kampf des Bürgertums um das Heer (1815–1850)* (Leipzig, 1938).

Huber, Ernst Rudolf, *Heer und Staat in der deutschen Geschichte* (2nd ed., Hamburg, 1943).

Janson, Friedrich, *Fichtes Reden an die deutsche Nation: Eine Untersuchung ihres aktuell-politischen Gehaltes* (Berlin and Leipzig, 1911).

Kamlah, Irmgard, *Karl Georg Maassen und die preussische Finanzreform von 1816–1822* (Eisleben, 1934).

Körner, Rudolf, "Die Wirkung der Reden Fichtes," *Forschungen zur brandenburgischen und preussischen Geschichte,* XL (1927), 65–87.

Körte, Wilhelm, *Albrecht Thaer: Sein Leben und sein Wirken, als Arzt und Landwirth* (Leipzig, 1839).

Lehmann, Max, "Die preussische Reform von 1808 und die französische Revolution," *Preussische Jahrbücher,* 132 (1908), 211–229.

Linke, Otto, *Friedrich Theodor von Merckel im Dienste fürs Vaterland* (2 vols., Breslau, 1907–10).

——, "Zur Reise des Königs Friedrich Wilhelms III. nach Schlesien 1810," *Zeitschrift* des Vereins für Geschichte und Altertum Schlesiens, XXXIX (1905), 108–132.

List, Albrecht, *Der Kampf um's gute alte Recht (1815–1819) nach seiner ideen- und parteigeschichtlichen Seite* (Tübingen, 1912).

Lobanov-Rostovsky, Andrei A., *Russia and Europe 1789–1825* (Durham, N.C., 1942).

Mannheim, Karl, *Essays on Sociology and Social Psychology* (London, 1953).

Marcu, Valeriu, *Das grosse Kommando Scharnhorsts: Die Geburt einer Militärmacht in Europa* (Leipzig, 1928).

Meier, Ernst von, *Französische Einflüsse auf die Staats- und Rechtsentwicklung Preussens im XIX. Jahrhundert* (2 vols., Leipzig, 1907–8).

Mommsen, Wilhelm, *Stein, Ranke, Bismarck: Ein Beitrag zur politischen und sozialen Bewegung des 19. Jahrhunderts* (Munich, 1954).

Müller, Karl Alexander von, *Görres in Strassburg 1819/20: Eine Episode aus dem Beginn der Demagogenverfolgungen* (Stuttgart, Berlin, and Leipzig, 1926).

Müsebeck, Ernst, "Fragmentarische Aufzeichnungen Altensteins über die auswärtige Politik Preussens vom 28./29. Dezember 1805," *Forschungen zur brandenburgischen und preussischen Geschichte,* XXVIII (1915), 139–173.

——, "Freiwillige Gaben und Opfer des preussischen Volkes in den Jahren 1813–1815," *Mitteilungen* der K. Preussischen Archivverwaltung, No. 23 (Leipzig, 1913).

——, *Schleiermacher in der Geschichte der Staatsidee und des Nationalbewusstseins* (Berlin, 1927).

——, "Siegmund Peter Martin und Hans Rudolph von Plehwe, zwei Vetreter des deutschen Einheitsgedankens von 1806–1820," *Quellen und Darstellungen zur Geschichte der Burschenschaft und der deutschen Einheitsbewegung,* Vol. II (Heidelberg, 1911), 75–195.

Rapp, Adolf, ed., *Grossdeutsch-kleindeutsch: Stimmen aus der Zeit von 1815 bis 1914* (Munich, 1921).

Raumer, Kurt von, "Friedrich Leopold von Schrötter und der Aufbau Neu-Ostpreussens," *Historische Zeitschrift*, 163 (1941), 282–304.

——, "Schrötter und Schön," *Altpreussische Forschungen*, XVIII (1941), 117–155.

Roebers, Jakob, *Die Einrichtung der Provinzialstände in Westfalen und die Wahlen zum ersten westfälischen Provinziallandtag* (Münster, 1914).

Rössler, Hellmuth, *Österreichs Kampf um Deutschlands Befreiung: Die deutsche Politik der nationalen Führer Österreichs 1805–1815* (2 vols., Hamburg, 1940).

Rothfels, Hans, *Carl von Clausewitz: Politik und Krieg, eine ideengeschichtliche Studie* (Berlin, 1920).

——, *Ostraum, Preussentum und Reichsgedanke* (Leipzig, 1935).

Sailer, F., *Der preussische Staatsrath und seine Reactivirung* (Berlin, 1884).

Scharff, Alexander, *Der Gedanke der preussischen Vorherrschaft in den Anfängen der deutschen Einheitsbewegung* (Bonn, 1929).

Schiemann, Theodor, *Kaiser Alexander I. und die Ergebnisse seiner Lebensarbeit* (Berlin, 1904).

Schmidt, Wilhelm Adolf, *Geschichte der deutschen Verfassungsfrage während der Befreiungskriege und des Wiener Kongresses 1812 bis 1815* (ed. Alfred Stern; Stuttgart, 1890).

Schmoller, Gustav, *Preussische Verfassungs-, Verwaltungs- und Finanzgeschichte* (Berlin, 1921).

Schwartz, Karl, *Leben des Generals Carl von Clausewitz und der Frau Marie von Clausewitz geb. Gräfin von Brühl* (2 vols., Berlin, 1878).

Seeley, J. R., *Life and Times of Stein, or Germany and Prussia in the Napoleonic Age* (3 vols., Cambridge, 1878).

Sell, Friedrich C., *Die Tragödie des deutschen Liberalismus* (Stuttgart, 1953).

Sering, Max, *Die innere Kolonisation im östlichen Deutschland* (Leipzig, 1893).

Simons, Walter, *Albrecht Thaer* (Berlin, 1929).

Spranger, Eduard, "Altensteins Denkschrift von 1807 und ihre Beziehungen zur Philosophie," *Forschungen zur brandenburgischen und preussischen Geschichte*, XVIII (1905), 471–517.

——, *Wilhelm von Humboldt und die Humanitätsidee* (2nd ed., Berlin, 1930).

——, *Wilhelm von Humboldt und die Reform des Bildungswesens* (Berlin, 1910).

Stein, Robert, *Die Umwandlung der Agrarverfassung Ostpreussens durch die Reform des neunzehnten Jahrhunderts* (Vol. I, Jena, 1916; no more published).

Stephan, Werner J., *Die Entstehung der Provinzialstände in Preussen 1823 mit besonderer Beziehung auf die Provinz Brandenburg* (Berlin, 1914).

Stölzel, Adolf, *Brandenburg-Preussens Rechtsverwaltung und Rechtsverfassung: Dargestellt im Wirken seiner Landesfürsten und obersten Justizbeamten* (2 vols., Berlin, 1888).

Straus, Hannah Alice, *The Attitude of the Congress of Vienna toward Nationalism in Germany, Italy and Poland* (New York, 1949).

Sweet, Paul R., *Friedrich von Gentz: Defender of the Old Order* (Madison, Wis., 1941).

Unger, W. v., *Blücher* (2 vols., Berlin, 1907-8).

Varnhagen von Ense, K. A., *General Graf Bülow von Dennewitz* (Vol. VIII of his *Biographische Denkmale;* 3rd ed., Leipzig, 1874).

Viereck, Peter, *Conservatism Revisited: The Revolt against Revolt 1815-1949* (New York and London, 1949).

Waliszewski, K., *La Russie il y a cent ans: Le règne d'Alexandre Ier* (3 vols., Paris, 1923-25).

Wallner, Nico, *Fichte als politischer Denker: Werden und Wesen seiner Gedanken über den Staat* (Halle, 1926).

Webster, C. K., *The Foreign Policy of Castlereagh 1812-1815: Britain and the Reconstruction of Europe* (London, 1931).

——, *The Foreign Policy of Castlereagh 1815-1822: Britain and the European Alliance* (2nd ed., London, 1934).

Winkler, Theodor, *Johann Gottfried Frey und die Entstehung der preussischen Selbstverwaltung* (Stuttgart and Berlin, 1936).

Wurzbacher, Gerhard, "Studien über den Wandel der sozialen und völkischen Struktur eines Landkreises im pommerschen-westpreussischen Grenzraum zwischen 1773 und 1937," *Zeitschrift für Ostforschung,* II (1953), 190-207.

Zierke, Fritz, *Die preussische Politik Hardenbergs in der ersten Periode seines staatsmännischen Wirkens 1770-1807: Ein Beitrag zum politischen Bilde des preussischen Staatskanzlers und zur Geschichte des preussisch-deutschen Problems im Zeitalter der französischen Revolution* (Frankfurt am Main, 1932).

Zimmermann, Alfred, *Geschichte der preussisch-deutschen Handelspolitik* (Oldenburg and Leipzig, 1892).

Index